Explore
NEW ZEALAND

Ma & Poppy

Have a safe trip
to NZ and enjoy!!

with love

Sue, Pete & Holly

Dec 2006

This edition published in 2005
New Holland Publishers (NZ) Ltd
Auckland • Sydney • London • Cape Town

www.newhollandpublishers.co.nz

218 Lake Road, Northcote, Auckland, New Zealand
14 Aquatic Drive, Frenchs Forest, NSW 2086,
    Australia
86–88 Edgware Road, London W2 2EA,
    United Kingdom
80 McKenzie Street, Cape Town 8001, South Africa

Managing editor: Matt Turner
Project manager: Dee Murch
Editor: Pat Field
Cartography: Barry Bradley, Cartographic Art
    Company
Cover design: Rachel Kirkland, The Fount
Design: Alison Dench

Colour reproduction by PICA Digital, Singapore
Printed by Craft Print Pte Ltd, Singapore

First published in 2001

ISBN: 1 86966 097 8

A catalogue record of this publication is available
from the National Library of New Zealand

10 9 8 7 6 5 4 3 2 1

Front cover: Kawarau Gorge, Central Otago
Page 1: Pioneer cottage, Taranaki
Page 3: Lake Wakatipu, Central Otago
Page 5: Moored boats, Auckland
Page 6: Marokopa Falls, Waikato
Page 7: Hoar frost, Southland
Page 10: Fox Glacier, South Westland

Explore
NEW ZEALAND

over 60 scenic driving tours

John Cobb

Cartography by Barry Bradley

NH
NEW
HOLLAND

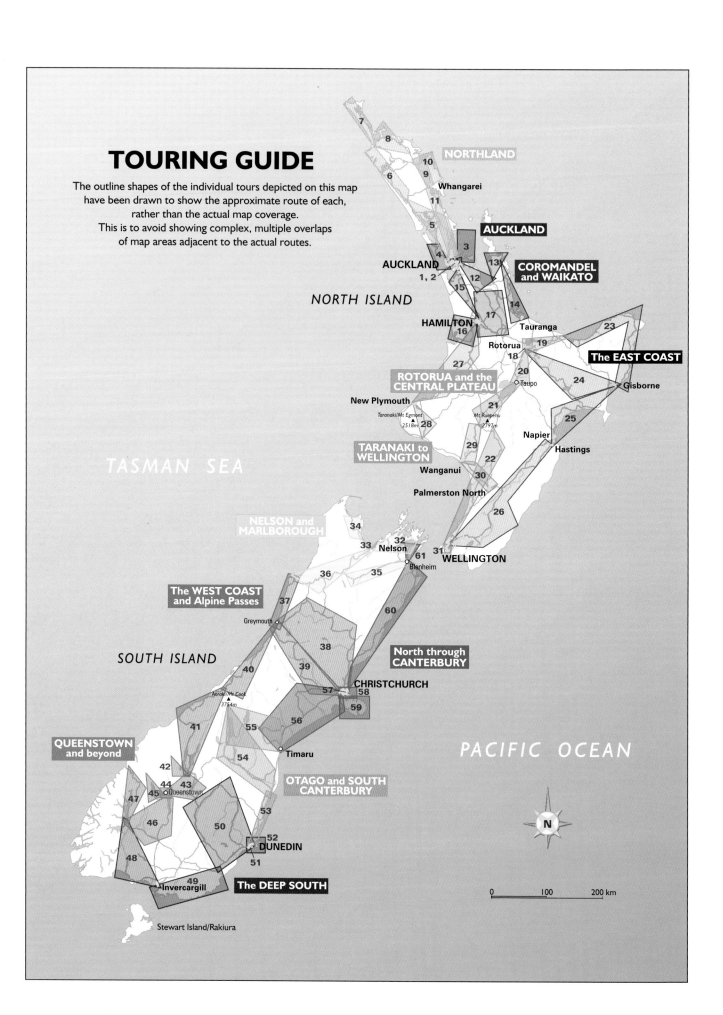

TOURING GUIDE

The outline shapes of the individual tours depicted on this map
have been drawn to show the approximate route of each,
rather than the actual map coverage.
This is to avoid showing complex, multiple overlaps
of map areas adjacent to the actual routes.

NORTHLAND

7
8
10
9
6 Whangarei
11
5
AUCKLAND
4 3
AUCKLAND 13 COROMANDEL
1, 2 12 and WAIKATO
15
NORTH ISLAND 14
17
HAMILTON 16 Tauranga 23
Rotorua 19 The EAST COAST
18
27 20
ROTORUA and the Taupo 24
CENTRAL PLATEAU Gisborne
New Plymouth 21
Taranaki/Mt Egmont 28 Mt Ruapehu 25
2518m 2797m Napier
TARANAKI to 29 Hastings
WELLINGTON 22
Wanganui 30
Palmerston North
26
TASMAN SEA

NELSON and 34
MARLBOROUGH 32
33 Nelson 31
Blenheim 61 WELLINGTON
36 35
The WEST COAST 37
and Alpine Passes 60
Greymouth
38 North through
SOUTH ISLAND 39 CANTERBURY
40 57 CHRISTCHURCH
Aoraki/Mt Cook 58
3754m 59
41 55 56
42 54 Timaru PACIFIC OCEAN
QUEENSTOWN 44 43 OTAGO and SOUTH
and beyond 45 Queenstown CANTERBURY
47 53
46 50 52
48 DUNEDIN
51
49 Invercargill The DEEP SOUTH
N
Stewart Island/Rakiura
0 100 200 km

CONTENTS

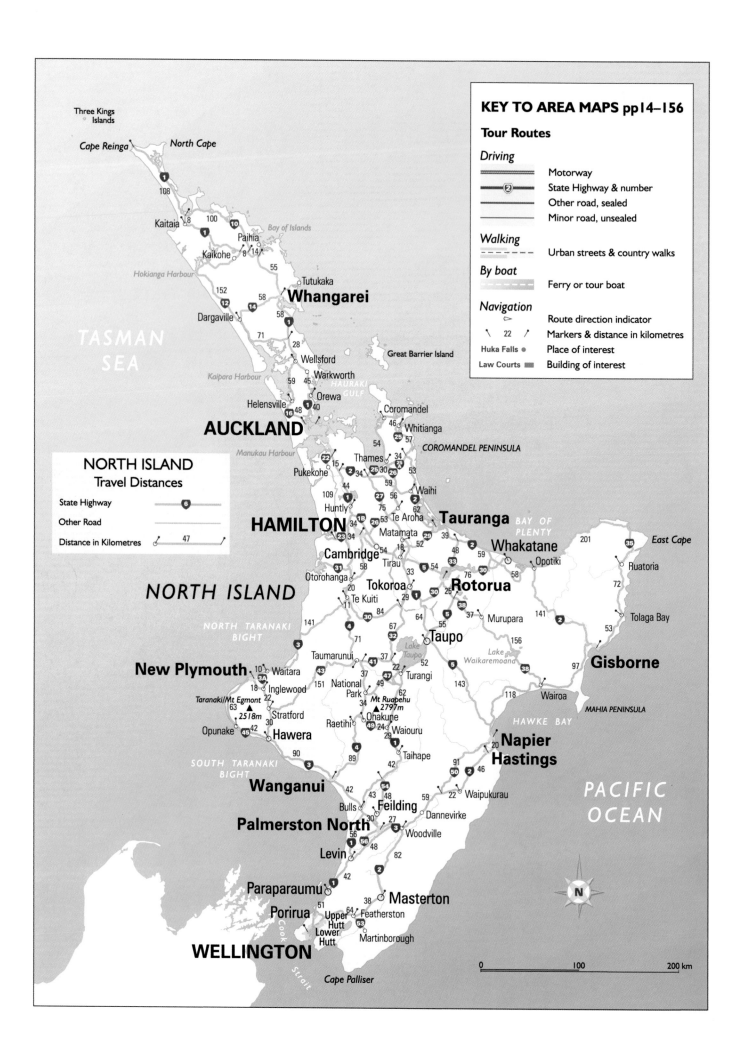

KEY TO AREA MAPS pp14–156

Tour Routes

Driving

———— Motorway
——②—— State Highway & number
———— Other road, sealed
———— Minor road, unsealed

Walking

– – – – Urban streets & country walks

By boat

≈≈≈≈ Ferry or tour boat

Navigation

⌐ Route direction indicator
↖ 22 ↗ Markers & distance in kilometres
Huka Falls ● Place of interest
Law Courts ▪ Building of interest

NORTH ISLAND
Travel Distances

State Highway ——⑥——
Other Road ————
Distance in Kilometres ↙ 47 ↗

Three Kings
Islands

Cape Reinga   North Cape

①
108
Kaitaia ⑧ 100 ⑩
Paihia
Kaikohe ⑧ ⑭
①
55
Tutukaka
152 58 **Whangarei**
⑫ ⑭
Dargaville 58
①
71 28
Wellsford
59 45 Warkworth
Helensville ⑯ 48 ① 40 Orewa

TASMAN SEA
Hokianga Harbour
Kaipara Harbour
HAURAKI GULF

Great Barrier Island

AUCKLAND

Coromandel
46 Whitianga
54 ㉕ 57
Thames 34
㉒ 15 ㉕ 30 ㉘ 53
Pukekohe ② 34 59
44 ㉗ 56 Waihi
109 ① 75 ㉖ 62
Huntly ② Te Aroha

COROMANDEL PENINSULA
Manukau Harbour

HAMILTON 34 ⑮
㉓ 34 ㉖ Matamata ㉙ 39 **Tauranga**
18 52 48 59 **Whakatane** 201
Cambridge ㉕ 54 33 ⑤ 54 ㉝ 59 ③⓪ Opotiki East Cape
Tirau 76 58 ㉟
㉛ 58 Tokoroa ⑤ **Rotorua** Ruatoria
Otorohanga 20 ㉚ ② ㉞ ㉚ ㉕ ㊳ 37 Murupara 141 72
11 Te Kuiti 84 ① 64 55 ② Tolaga Bay
141 ④ ㉚ 67 ㉜ 55 156 53
③ 71 ㉜ **Taupo** 97 **Gisborne**
Taumarunui ㊸ *Lake Taupo* ⑤ *Lake Waikaremoana*
New Plymouth 10 Waitara ㊶ 37 ㉒ 52 ㊳
③🅐 151 ㊼ ㊾ Turangi 143 118 Wairoa
18 Inglewood National 62 *MAHIA PENINSULA*
Taranaki/Mt Egmont 22 Park 34 Mt Ruapehu
63 2518m 30 Stratford Raetihi ▲2797m 20 **Napier**
Opunake ㊺ 42 **Hawera** ㊾ 24 Ohakune **Hastings**
90 89 Waiouru 91 *HAWKE BAY*
③ 42 29① Taihape ㊵ 46 *PACIFIC OCEAN*
Wanganui 42 ㊵ 54 22 Waipukurau
Bulls 48 59
Palmerston North ㉗ 27 Dannevirke
56 30 ③ Woodville
① 56 48 82
Levin ②
42
Paraparaumu ① 38 **Masterton**
Porirua 51 64 Featherston
Upper Hutt ㊾
Lower Hutt Martinborough

WELLINGTON

NORTH ISLAND
NORTH TARANAKI BIGHT
SOUTH TARANAKI BIGHT
BAY OF PLENTY

N

Cook Strait   Cape Palliser

0   100   200 km

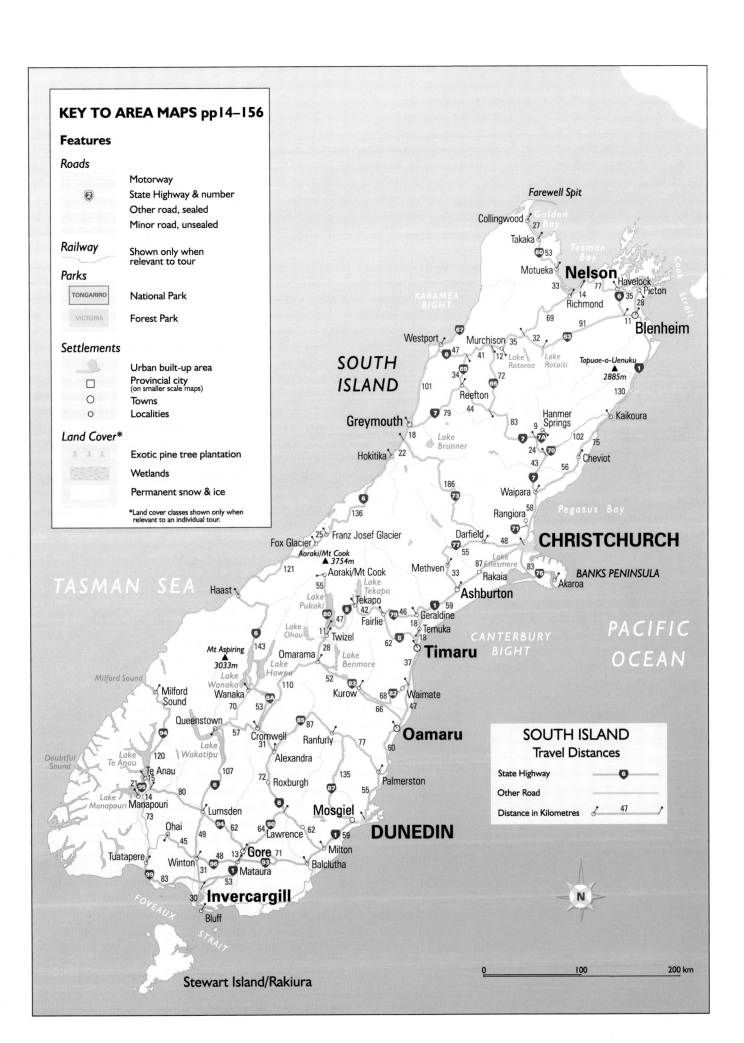

KEY TO AREA MAPS pp14–156

Features

Roads
Motorway
State Highway & number
Other road, sealed
Minor road, unsealed

Railway
Shown only when relevant to tour

Parks
TONGARIRO — National Park
VICTORIA — Forest Park

Settlements
Urban built-up area
Provincial city (on smaller scale maps)
○ Towns
○ Localities

Land Cover*
Exotic pine tree plantation
Wetlands
Permanent snow & ice

*Land cover classes shown only when relevant to an individual tour.

Farewell Spit

Collingwood
Takaka
Golden Bay
27
60 53
Tasman Bay
Motueka
Nelson
33
14
Richmond
Havelock
Picton
77
6 35
28
11
Blenheim

KARAMEA BIGHT

Westport
67
47
Murchison
35
32
69
91
63
Tapuae-o-Uenuku
2885m
1
130

SOUTH ISLAND

41
12
Lake Rotoroa
Lake Rotoiti
34
69
72
65
101
Reefton
Hanmer Springs
83
9
Kaikoura

Greymouth
7
79
44
7
24
70
102
75
Cheviot
18
56
Hokitika
22
Lake Brunner
43

186
73
Waipara
58
Rangiora
71

Pegasus Bay

Fox Glacier
25
Franz Josef Glacier
Darfield
77
48
CHRISTCHURCH
Aoraki/Mt Cook ▲ 3754m
55
87
Lake Ellesmere
83
BANKS PENINSULA
121
Aoraki/Mt Cook
Methven
33
Rakaia
75
Akaroa
Haast
55
Lake Tekapo
Lake Pukaki
Tekapo
80
8
42
79
46
Geraldine
1
59
Ashburton

TASMAN SEA

Lake Ohau
47
Fairlie
18
Temuka
11
Twizel
62
8
18
Timaru
6
28
Lake Benmore
37
CANTERBURY BIGHT

PACIFIC OCEAN

Mt Aspiring ▲ 3033m
143
Omarama
Lake Hawea
Milford Sound
Lake Wanaka
110
Wanaka
52
83
68
82
Waimate
Milford Sound
70
53
8A
Kurow
66
47
Queenstown
94
57
Cromwell
85
87
Ranfurly
77
Oamaru
Doubtful Sound
Lake Wakatipu
120
31
Alexandra
60
Lake Te Anau
107
72
Roxburgh
135
Palmerston
Te Anau
21
95
15
6
80
87
55
14
Manapouri
73
Lumsden
8
Mosgiel
Lake Manapouri
Ohai
94
62
90
62
DUNEDIN
45
49
64
Lawrence
1
59
Tuatapere
48
13
Gore
71
Milton
Winton
96
53
Balclutha
31
1
Mataura
99
83
53

Invercargill

30
Bluff

FOVEAUX STRAIT

SOUTH ISLAND
Travel Distances

State Highway	6
Other Road	
Distance in Kilometres	47

N

Stewart Island/Rakiura

0   100   200 km

INTRODUCTION

New Zealand is famous for its uncrowded roads that travel through an incredible range of scenery, most of which is packed into a geographically diverse, yet compact area so that within hours it is possible to travel from one scenic extreme to another. Consider the proximity of the upper North Island's golden sand beaches to the botanical richness of the region's dense rainforests – not much more than an hour's driving separates these two scenic wonders. And the South Island offers equally diverse possibilities, among them glaciers, mountains, fiords, and world-famous vineyards. It's even possible to avoid bad weather on many occasions, particularly in the South Island, simply by driving from one side of the mountains to the other.

Explore New Zealand has been devised to help visitors and locals make the most of their time on the road. It offers over 60 tours, making it possible to design a holiday based on the attractions that are most appealing to individual circumstances.

For travellers who have only a few days to explore New Zealand, State Highway 1 offers plenty of interesting driving options, with a wealth of scenic attractions en route. There are any number of fascinating historic buildings, especially old churches, and an intriguing array of small, often privately owned museums featuring artefacts from New Zealand's past. You'll find nine tours in this book that focus on State Highway 1 alone.

However, if time is not an issue then the country's many and varied back roads are well worth investigating, too. Some will take you through remote stretches of farmland, others along kilometre after kilometre of unspoiled coastline. In any event the choice is yours, and there are over 50 of these back country tours on the quieter highways and even, in some cases, unsealed roads.

New Zealand is a paradise for travellers of all ages and *Explore New Zealand* is the ideal companion to help you make the most of your time spent on the road.

NORTH ISLAND
AUCKLAND

1 AUCKLAND'S HERITAGE

DRIVING TOUR ■ 20 KM ■ 6 HOURS ■ NATURAL BEAUTY, GLIMPSES OF THE PAST

In a unique natural setting visitors can take in the magnificent views from two of Auckland's prominent volcanic cones, explore exotic gardens and gain an insight into the city's history in its museums and earliest homes.

The Auckland landscape is dominated by a series of volcanoes that began erupting 50,000 years ago. Polynesian settlers in the area probably witnessed the most recent eruptions, around 250 years ago, which covered their shelters on adjacent Motutapu Island with ash. By the eighteenth century the population had increased significantly, inter-tribal warfare had become widespread and many people were living in or around large defended pa sites on the volcanic cones. However, the population was depleted by warfare and epidemics to the point where, by the time the Treaty of Waitangi was signed in 1840, the area was almost deserted.

Two Europeans, John Logan Campbell and William Brown, set up camp on an island in the Waitemata Harbour after hearing rumours that land was to be purchased for the site of the new colony's capital. Governor Hobson named the settlement after Lord Auckland, Viceroy of India, and Campbell and Brown played prominent roles in the birth of the city. Auckland remained the capital until 1865, when the seat of government was moved to Wellington. Today Auckland is New Zealand's largest city, home to a third of the country's population.

Cornwall Park is a peaceful retreat from the city.

1 CORNWALL PARK
The trip begins at Cornwall Park which can be reached from central Auckland via the Southern Motorway. Heading south take the Greenlane off-ramp and turn right onto Greenlane Road West. Cross the intersection with Great South Road, continue on Green-lane Road West past Wheturangi Road to the entrance to Cornwall Park on the left, and drive into the park. When you reach the roundabout, follow the loop road through the park to the right which takes you to the visitor centre and Acacia Cottage.

The splendid park that surrounds One Tree Hill was gifted to the people of New Zealand in 1901 by Sir John Logan Campbell, affectionately known as 'the founding father of Auckland'. Campbell had the foresight to realise that the new city would need an area of parkland where its people could relax and enjoy the peaceful surroundings.

The visitor centre in Huia Lodge has a wealth of information about the park, and in the nearby Acacia Cottage you can see what living conditions were like in the early days of Auckland's settlement. Acacia Cottage was

built in 1841 by Brown and Campbell and is the oldest surviving building in Auckland.

2 ONE TREE HILL
From Acacia Cottage continue on the loop road around the base of One Tree Hill and turn left onto the 1 km road to the summit.

One Tree Hill was once a fortress for up to 4000 Maori. One of the largest earth fortifications in the world, Maungakiekie features extensive terracing, defensive ditches and food-storage pits, the locations of which can still be seen on the slopes of this volcanic cone. From the summit there are excellent views across the city and both of Auckland's harbours.

3 MT EDEN/MAUNGAWHAU
From the One Tree Hill summit return to the loop road and travel through Twin Oak Drive back to the roundabout. Return to the Cornwall Park gates, cross Greenlane Road West and continue through the northern section of the park. The drive will take you 1 km to Campbell Cresent where a statue of Sir John Logan Campbell stands near the park gates. Turn right onto Campbell Crescent, which veers to the left, and after about 200 metres turn right onto Manukau Road. Drive 0.5 km and take the third street on the left, Epsom Avenue, which becomes Stokes Road after about 1 km. Turn right from Stokes Road into Mt Eden Road, continue north to the Mt Eden summit access road on the right and drive 1 km to the summit.

This superb 196 m vantage point was used as a pa site by Maori as far back as the twelfth century, and was the starting point for Felton Mathew's original survey of Auckland city. Below lies the quarry site used to supply rock for many of the structures in Cornwall Park.

4 EDEN GARDEN
Follow the loop road down from the summit, turn right onto Mt Eden Road which veers right to become Normanby Road, then right into Clive Road and right into Mountain Road. Eden Garden is signposted to the right on Omana Avenue off Mountain Road.

In Eden Garden, tucked away on the lower slopes of the mountain, pathways lead through extensive landscaped areas of native trees interspersed with camellias, rhododendrons and azaleas.

5 HIGHWIC HOUSE
Return to Mountain Road, continue south 0.3 km, turn left into Owens Road, left into Gillies Avenue and continue for 1 km. Highwic House at 40 Gillies Avenue is signposted on the right.

Built in 1863, Highwic was the residence of Alfred Buckland, a wealthy landowner and racing enthusiast, and the building was kept in his family over successive generations. Originally a farmhouse, Highwic was extended as Buckland became wealthier and as his family became larger – he had 21 children. It is probably the best example in the country of a large Gothic-style house and is open to the public.

6 PARNELL'S HISTORIC COTTAGES
From Highwic drive north 1 km on Gillies Avenue and Crowhurst Street to the next T-junction and turn right into Khyber Pass Road. Travel 0.5 km, turn left onto Broadway, veer right into Parnell Road and take the fourth street on the right, Ayr Street. Ewelme Cottage is on the left at 14 Ayr Street.

Ewelme Cottage was built by Archdeacon Vicesimus Lush in 1864 so that his children could attend the grammar school nearby.

St Stephen's Chapel overlooking Judges Bay.

This delightful old kauri cottage displays many of its original furnishings and the interior was used in the Oscar award-winning film *The Piano*. Nearby in Ayr Street you can also visit the mid-nineteenth-century home of pioneer photographer the Rev John Kinder.

7 ST STEPHEN'S CHAPEL
From Ayr Street return to Parnell Road and continue north 0.4 km. On the right of Parnell Road just before the next major junction is the Cathedral of the Holy Trinity, alongside its predecessor, the Cathedral Church of St Mary, a magnificent wooden building erected in 1888 and moved from its original site across the road in 1982. Turn right past the cathedral into St Stephens Avenue, take the third street on the left which is Gladstone Road, then the third right, Judges Bay Road, to reach the entry to St Stephen's Chapel.

St Stephen's Chapel dates back to 1857. This tiny building features the steep-pitched shingle roof, leaded windows and external timber buttresses characteristic of the churches built under the direction of Bishop Selwyn (1809–78). You can walk down the hill from the chapel into the grounds of the Parnell Rose Gardens which border Gladstone Road.

8 AUCKLAND DOMAIN AND WAR MEMORIAL MUSEUM
From Judges Bay Road turn right back into Gladstone Road, continue 1 km down the hill, turn left onto The Strand and travel 1.5 km. At the end of The Strand turn left into Parnell Rise and continue 3 km up the hill onto Parnell Road past a fascinating array of Edwardian and Victorian homes that have been converted into shops and boutiques. Continue along Parnell Road into Broadway. The entry to the Auckland Domain is signposted to the right on Maunsell Road.

Perched on top of Domain Hill, the Auckland War Memorial Museum houses one of New Zealand's most comprehensive historical collections, featuring artefacts from around the South Pacific. The elaborately carved Maori meeting house Hotunui, built in 1878, stands near the last of the great war canoes, *Te Toki a Tapari*, which could carry up to a hundred warriors. Centennial Street is a replica of an Auckland thoroughfare in the 1860s.

Governor Grey designated the Domain land as a reserve in 1845, but it was not until the Great Industrial Exhibition of 1913 that money was raised to landscape the area. The present Tea Kiosk was built for the exhibition as an example of an ideal home, overlooking the duck ponds that were Auckland's original water supply. The Wintergardens, in two huge tropical glasshouses, were established in the 1920s.

From any angle the Auckland War Memorial Museum is imposing.

2 AUCKLAND'S WATERFRONT

FERRY/WALKING/DRIVING TOUR ■ 14 KM ■ 1 DAY ■ ON WAITEMATA HARBOUR

This trip starts with a ferry ride to historic Devonport then returns to the attractions on the bustling Auckland waterfront, followed by a drive around the city's bays and a visit to a spectacular aquarium.

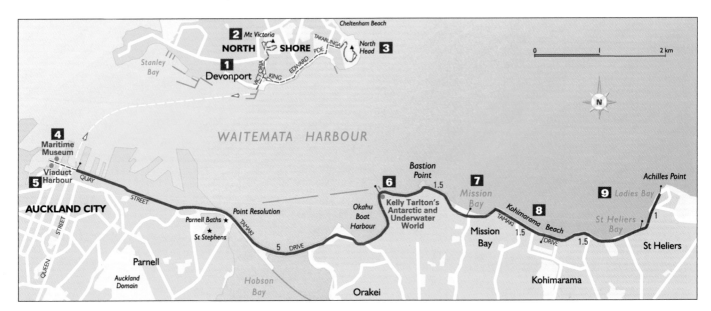

One of the most exciting waterside cities in the world, Auckland lies on a narrow volcanic isthmus between two huge natural harbours facing two oceans. With thousands of enthusiastic yachties and probably more boats per head of population than any other city in the world, it is not surprising that Auckland is known as the 'City of Sails'. In the North Shore seaside suburb of Devonport, one of the oldest parts of the city, the volcanic cones at North Head and Mt Victoria provide sweeping views across the Waitemata Harbour. City-side, a short distance from the central business district lies Tamaki Drive and the route of the famous 'Around the Bays' run which leads along a fascinating stretch of the harbour dotted with historic buildings and bordered by sandy pohutukawa-fringed beaches.

Historic guns at North Head, overlooking Cheltenham Beach.

1 DEVONPORT
The trip starts at the ferry terminus on Quay Street. Ferries to Devonport run every hour daily, and during peak times every half-hour, the trip taking about 15 minutes.

Devonport has retained an Edwardian charm with restored villas and a verandahed shopping centre. The ferry trip is the most interesting way to visit and was the main access to Devonport until the opening of the Harbour Bridge in 1959. A large part of Devonport is taken up by the Naval Dockyards, and on Spring Street you will find the Royal New Zealand Navy Museum. Brian Jackson's Museum of Automobilia, Sounds and Victoriana is located on Devonport's main street, Victoria Road.

2 MT VICTORIA
Follow Victoria Road 1 km to Kerr Street to access a walking track leading to the summit of Mt Victoria.

From the summit, which was the site of a Maori pa, there are panoramic views of the harbour and gulf. A map table at the summit identifies the offshore islands.

3 NORTH HEAD HISTORIC RESERVE
From Kerr Street walk back 1 km to the bottom of Victoria Road, turn left into King Edward Parade and walk 2 km along the waterfront, then turn left into Cheltenham Road and right into Takarunga Road to reach the entry to the North Head Historic Reserve.

The stroll along the waterfront passes many of the suburb's fine old houses and provides always-changing views of the harbour traffic and the city beyond. At North Head, walking tracks link fortifications and a complex of tunnels built during the 1880s when the colony feared a Russian invasion. Some of the tunnels are still accessible and a few old guns can still be seen, including a huge 14-tonne, 8-inch 'disappearing gun', which recoiled into a pit after firing so that it could be reloaded out of sight, avoiding return fire.

Like Mt Victoria, North Head is the site of a Maori pa and displays the prominent terraced earthworks that were part of the original fortifications. To the immediate north is the long sweep of Cheltenham Beach.

4 NATIONAL MARITIME MUSEUM
Return 3 km to Victoria Wharf and take a ferry across the harbour back to Quay Street. A few minutes' walk west of the ferry terminus is the National Maritime Museum located on Hobson Wharf.

It is easy to spend an afternoon in the Maritime Museum, which features a replica of an immigrant ship's interior complete with creaking floor joints and a swaying motion. The numerous exhibits include the world's first jet boat, invented in New Zealand in 1957, the *Taratai*, an outrigger canoe built using thousand-year-old methods for a voyage across the Pacific, and the steam launch *Puke*, on which you can take a ride. Visitors can also take a cruise out on the harbour on the restored scow *Ted Ashby*.

5 VIADUCT HARBOUR
From the Maritime Museum walk west a few minutes to the Viaduct.

The Viaduct, a great place to stroll or sit at an outdoor café watching life on the water, was purpose built for the first New Zealand defence of the America's Cup, in 2000. The story of the trophy goes back to 1851, when

Yachts moored near the Viaduct Harbour.

the *America* sailed to England to win the Round the Isle of Wight Race, the silver pitcher returning to the USA, where in 1870 the British attempted the first of a number of unsuccessful challenges to get it back. In 1995 New Zealand's *Black Magic* won all five races in San Diego, bringing the race to Auckland. The Italian yacht *Prada* challenged for the cup in 2000 but was beaten in a clean sweep by *Team New Zealand*. Swiss Syndicate *Alinghi* won the cup in 2003. While the cup is not currently held here, the legacy of this event remains.

Sunbathing near Orakei wharf. For central Aucklanders, from desk to beach is only a few minutes.

6 KELLY TARLTON'S ANTARCTIC ENCOUNTER AND UNDERWATER WORLD
From Quay Street, which leads into Tamaki Drive, drive 5 km east. Tamaki Drive spans a total 10 km length of the Waitemata Harbour's southern foreshore to St Heliers Bay. After 2.5 km you will see the saltwater Parnell Baths on the right. About 1 km further on the small Selwyn Church of St Stephen (1857) stands on the hill overlooking land-locked Judges Bay. Hobson Bay on the right has become the site of an expanding marina complex and is the home of the historic Ngapipi boatsheds with their green-painted roofs. During the summer months a Ngati Whatua waka (canoe) can often be seen on the beach at Okahu Bay. Kelly Tarlton's is located on the right side of Tamaki Drive opposite the Orakei wharf.

Established by professional diver Kelly Tarlton, this huge underground aquarium at Bastion Point features a 120 m moving walkway through an acrylic tunnel providing a fish-eye view of sharks, stingrays, moray eels and numerous species of reef fish. The 'Antarctic Encounter' starts off in a replica of the hut Scott used in his ill-fated mission to the South Pole in 1911, and visitors ride in a Snow Cat through a simulated snowstorm in an icescape complete with penguins and an attack by an orca.

7 MISSION BAY
Continue east along Tamaki Drive 1.5 km to Mission Bay.

Near Mission Bay's distinctive Trevor Moss Memorial Fountain, the stone-walled missionary college founded by Bishop Selwyn is set among a stand of Norfolk pines. The Melanesian Mission College was established in 1859 and trained missionaries until 1867 when the college was moved to Norfolk Island.

8 KOHIMARAMA
Continue east along Tamaki Drive 1.5 km to Kohimarama.

On Sunday mornings through summer the Kohimarama yacht club runs P-Class yacht races for young children from the eastern end of this long sandy beach with its rows of shady pohutukawa. Kohimarama is the finish point of Auckland's hugely popular 'Around the Bays' run, held every February, which attracts thousands of joggers from all over New Zealand and around the world.

9 LADIES BAY
Continue east 1.5 km on Tamaki Drive to St Heliers. Ladies Bay can be reached by a short walk around the rocks at low tide. A shorter but steeper access is by a flight of steps down from Cliff Road, 1 km further east from the end of Tamaki Drive.

This long white cockle-shell beach (also called Karaka Bay) has retained its seclusion despite the expansion of the city around it. A plaque on the track leading down to the beach commemorates the landing of Lt-Governor Hobson on 9 July 1840 when he arrived to collect the signatures and marks of local Maori chiefs on the Treaty of Waitangi.

It is 10 km back to central Auckland on Tamaki Drive.

SAILING ON WAITEMATA HARBOUR
The Auckland Waterfront is the base for a fleet of monohulls and catamarans which operate 'Experience Sailing' trips daily on the harbour. You can also take a day trip on the square-rigged brigantine *Soren Larsen* during summer. This handsome sailing ship, built of oak in Denmark, featured in the TV series *The Onedin Line* before circumnavigating the globe, arriving in New Zealand in 1994. Another popular cruise is on board the wooden auxiliary schooner *Te Aroha*, which sails from Marsden Wharf to the islands of the Hauraki Gulf and beyond.

3 THE ISLANDS OF THE GULF

FERRY TOURS ■ 1 DAY EACH ■ AUCKLAND'S OFFSHORE PLAYGROUND

On islands reached easily from Auckland City, visitors have the choice of exploring the lava landscape of a 'young' volcano, the exotic gardens of a colonial mansion, an open wildlife sanctuary or the villages and beaches of a laid-back holiday resort.

Part of the pleasure of visiting the inner gulf islands is the experience of getting there. As the ferry glides away from downtown Auckland, travellers gain a new perspective on the 'City of Sails'. On any day of the week boats of all shapes and sizes, bent on business and pleasure, weave and criss-cross through the water in fascinatingly colourful numbers. As the city skyline recedes and the harbour traffic thins, inner islands that were shadowy shapes viewed from the shore begin to reveal their distinctive characters.

The main part of the Hauraki Gulf lies within the natural barrier formed by the Coromandel Peninsula and Great Barrier Island. More than 50 islands make up the Hauraki Gulf Marine Park, ranging in size from not much bigger than large rocks to hundreds of square kilometres. Maori are thought to have lived on Waiheke 700 years ago, and had extensive fortified villages on many other islands. On Motutapu, adjacent to Rangitoto, archaeological evidence indicates continuous settlement for 500 years. When Europeans first established Auckland, Motutapu was a favourite destination for Sunday picnickers. Today the islands of the gulf are a Mecca for boaties, providing countless 'possies' for fishing, diving and swimming, as well as sheltered havens in the many bays and inlets.

The lighthouse on Tiritiri Matangi Island.

1 RANGITOTO

Ferry trips can be booked at the Ferry Building on Quay Street, near the bottom of Queen Street in downtown Auckland, and the ferries leave from an adjacent pier. The journey takes about 35 minutes each way. Take a picnic lunch, as no food is available on the island.

Rangitoto Island, visible from most parts of the Auckland waterfront, is the youngest volcano in the Hauraki Gulf – it blasted from the sea bed less than 700 years ago. Its 260 m summit can be reached by walking track or on a tractor-train tour and provides panoramic views of the gulf. The walk from the wharf to the summit takes an hour and passes through regenerating forest growing on the jet-black basalt rock. The island's environment is unique, with the largest pohutukawa forest in the world. Over 200 native plant and tree species grow beneath this canopy, including numerous ferns and native orchids. Side tracks lead to lava caves and, on the northern side of the island, to shipwrecks at Boulder Bay. The lava reflects heat strongly, so if you are making the trip in summer make sure you take sun protection and plenty of water to drink.

2 WAIHEKE

Ferry trips can be booked at the Ferry Building on Quay Street, near the bottom of Queen Street in downtown Auckland, and the ferries leave several times daily from an adjacent pier. The journey takes about 35 minutes each way.

Waiheke is the largest and most visited of the islands in the inner gulf. It has a permanent residential population of about 8000, many of whom commute to business in Auckland, and caters to large numbers of holidaymakers.

From Matiatia Bay, on a clear day the Auckland skyline is visible on the horizon. You can walk from the ferry wharf along the roadway to Oneroa in about 15 minutes, or take a bus. The well-marked coastal walk from Matiatia to Oneroa takes about 2 hours.

Oneroa is the main town on the island, overlooking a beautiful curving beach to the north and the sheltered bay of Blackpool to the south. As well as its idyllic location Oneroa has a charming and lively village atmosphere, excellent cafés and interesting arts and crafts. The Artworks Community Centre, on Korora Road, has a number of galleries. Whittakers Musical Museum, part of the centre, features a collection of antique instruments on which live performances are given daily. A 10-minute walk east along Oneroa beach leads to Little Oneroa, a secluded bay from where you can

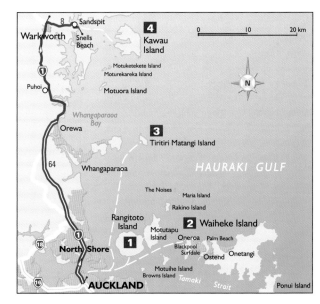

A natural rock arch carved out by the sea on the eastern shoreline of Tiritiri Matangi.

kahe. Many of these are quite tame and visitors can observe them at close hand in their natural habitat. A guided 1-hour walk is available on which you can learn about the birds and the conservation programme on this unique island. Tiritiri Matangi attracts ornithologists from all over the world and is a popular destination for school field trips.

4 KAWAU ISLAND

A ferry to Kawau departs at 10.30 am daily and at 2 pm on Saturdays and Sundays from Sandspit, about one hour's drive from central Auckland. Take SH 1 and head north 64 km to Warkworth, take the turn-off to the right signposted to Sandspit and travel east 8 km. Bookings can be made at the departure point. The ferry journey takes approximately an hour. Take a picnic lunch as no food is available on the island.

Mansion House, built on Kawau Island in 1846, was once the residence of former New Zealand Governor and Premier Sir George Grey. He transformed the old copper mine manager's house into a colonial mansion and planted extensive gardens with an array of exotic species. Grey introduced tree kangaroos, wallabies, peacocks, pheasants, quail and geese to the island, and wallabies and peacocks are still common in the grounds of Mansion House. The magnificent house has been restored and is open to visitors.

A number of tracks lead through exotic forests surrounding Mansion House including a 1-hour walk to the old copper mine on the coast. Manganese was found on Kawau Island in the 1830s and was mined by a Scottish company until a node of copper was found in 1842. The copper mine went below sea level and you can still see the chimney from the pumphouse used to stop the mine from flooding.

rejoin the main road back to the village.

The bus service on the island enables visitors to stop off at beaches and villages, or make a round trip of the island, passing numerous bays, picturesque small settlements, farms, olive groves, and the sunlit vineyards of Waiheke's renowned wineries.

The Waiheke Island Historic Village and Museum, located on the main road to Onetangi, displays a collection of farm machines, engines, cottages, furniture, historic telephones, clothing and a range of colonial domestic items. At Onetangi, a Forest and Bird reserve offers delightful walks through bush that includes large kauri. Onetangi beach is the longest on the island, a magnificent sweep of open coastline with views to the outer islands of the gulf.

3 TIRITIRI MATANGI

It is advisable to make advance bookings for the ferry trip, at the Ferry Building on Quay Street in downtown Auckland. Ferries leave on Thursdays, Saturdays, Sundays and public holidays from a pier near the Ferry Building. The journey takes about an hour and a half each way. Take a picnic lunch as no food is available on the island.

Tiritiri Matangi is a scientific reserve run as an 'open sanctuary'. The island has been replanted to restore native forest cover and features an elaborate network of walking tracks connecting a number of picturesque bays. Native birds thrive in this protected environment, including bellbirds, parakeets, little spotted kiwis, brown teal, black robins and the endangered saddlebacks and ta-

Standing at the edge of an idyllic bay, Mansion House on Kawau Island delights boatloads of visitors.

4 AUCKLAND'S WILD WEST COAST

DRIVING TOUR ■ 242 KM ■ 1 DAY ■ SURF BEACHES AND HOT POOLS

A short distance west of Auckland lie the forest-clad Waitakere Ranges, and beyond them lie exhilarating beaches where the surf pounds the rocky shore and a colony of gannets has established a rare mainland nesting site.

Black iron-sands sweep across a dramatic stretch of coastline to the west of Auckland. Framed by the rugged forest-clad Waitakere Ranges, and to the north by forest plantations and sand dunes south of the Kaipara Harbour, Auckland's west coast features a string of wild surf beaches unrivalled in character by those anywhere else in the country. Many of the distinctive landforms in the area are volcanic, and in cliff faces along the coast you can see columnar jointed lava formed when it was extruded under the sea 16 million years ago. The iron-sands are also volcanic in origin, having been swept north up the coast by strong currents from Taranaki/Mt Egmont far to the south.

1 MT ATKINSON

The trip starts at the Auckland suburb of Titirangi which is accessible off the North-western Motorway, SH 16, heading west from Auckland city centre. From SH 16 take the Great North Road exit, follow Great North Road through Avondale then turn left into Titirangi Road. From the Titirangi township travel 2 km west on Scenic Drive. An access road signposted to the right leads to the summit of Mt Atkinson.

From the top of Mt Atkinson there are good views across both the Manukau Harbour and Auckland City to the Waitemata Harbour. Most of the surrounding Waitakere Ranges have been incorporated in the 64,000 ha Auckland Centennial Park, an area of forest-clad hills only 30 minutes from Auckland and the city's main water-catchment area.

2 ARATAKI VISITOR CENTRE

Return to Scenic Drive and travel 3 km west to the Arataki Visitor Centre on the left.

With its elevated viewing platforms, audio-visual display and a range of exhibits, the Arataki Visitor Centre is the best place to get information on over 250 km of walking tracks of varying lengths through the ranges. The Arataki Nature Trail, starting next to the visitor centre, takes less than an hour and covers three loops through a part of the forest where plant and tree species are identified with labels. On this track is a 600-year-old kauri with a girth of 8 m.

3 KAURI KNOLL TRACK

From the visitor centre travel west 3 km on Scenic Drive. The Kauri Knoll Track is signposted on the right.

The Kauri Knoll Track offers a 10-minute stroll through kauri, rimu and kahikatea trees. The Waitakere Ranges were formed by a group of volcanoes that erupted beneath the sea about 20 million years ago. Although the ranges were once covered in a lush subtropical rainforest that featured numerous giant kauri, most of the big trees were logged between 1835 and 1935. Today the forest is slowly regenerating, the forest species thriving in fertile volcanic soils in an area where the rainfall is much higher than in nearby Auckland.

4 KAREKARE

Continue west on Scenic Drive for 3 km, turn left onto the road to Piha and the coast and travel for 27 km. Take the second turn-off to Karekare signposted on the left, and drive 4 km down to a car park near the beach.

The first views of the west coast that you see on this highway are of Karekare, visible across the bush-clad slopes that drop away to the left of the road. Karekare is a beach to capture the imagination with its sweeps of black sand set against lush forests covering the lava bluffs that run to the shoreline. Karekare was one of the principal locations for the award-winning film *The Piano*.

5 PIHA

Return to the Piha Road, turn left and continue for 6 km to Piha.

For years the winding gravel road out to Piha carried jolting carloads of surfers keen to reach the beach's sometimes challenging waves. Today the road is much improved, but the beach is still notorious for its rips and undertow, so visitors should always swim between the flags in the area patrolled by surf life-savers.

A walk from the end of Glen Esk Road, before you get to the beach, leads to the beautiful Kitekite Falls. From the south end of the beach you can take a short walk to a

Fine rimu in the native forest along Scenic Drive.

Piha beach is a Mecca for surfers, but on a hot summer day it's the perfect place for just splashing about.

lookout point for wide views along the coast. Rising from the middle of the bay is the 100 m Lion Rock, once the site of a Te Kawerau a Maki pa, Whakaari.

6 ROSE HELLABY HOUSE

Return on the Piha Road to Scenic Drive, turn left and drive 1 km north to Rose Hellaby House on the left.

Rose Hellaby House, one of the original guesthouses in the area, is open on weekends and its display on the area's history is one of the noisiest, most imaginative and informative museum exhibits in Auckland.

The museum concentrates on the lifestyle of the Maori and early European settlers with exhibits that include a bushman's camp, old milking machines, a kauri dam and equipment used by Maori to spear birds and trap fish.

7 MURIWAI BEACH

Continue north on Scenic Drive 23 km to Swanson. Take the Kumeu turn-off on the left and drive 20 km to Kumeu via Waitakere and then turn left onto SH 16 and drive 9 km to the Muriwai turn-off on the left. Drive west 10 km to reach Muriwai.

One of the west coast's renowned surf beaches, Muriwai is also popular for surfcasting and kite fishing and, on the sand, land yachting and various off-road sports. The beach stretches northwards all the way to the lagoon at South Head on the Kaipara Harbour.

A colony of Australasian gannets can be viewed at close range from platforms built on a series of short walks around the cliffs near Muriwai. The birds originally began nesting on an offshore island but spread to a nearby rock stack and then to cliffs on the

shoreline as the population increased. Tracks lead from the southern end of Muriwai Beach and from the car park at Maori Bay. It is also interesting to examine the twisted shapes in the huge quarried rock face behind Maori Bay. The rock is pillow lava that was formed by volcanic eruptions when the area lay below sea level.

8 HELENSVILLE

Return to SH 16, turn left and travel north 16 km to Helensville. A number of vineyards on SH 16 are open for winetasting including Coopers Creek and several smaller producers. A few kilometres before the township the highway reaches a junction, with the road to the left leading to Parakai while Helensville lies to the right.

Located near the southern end of the Kaipara, New Zealand's largest harbour, Helensville takes its name from one of the pioneering settler's wives and remains a quaint little rural town. In the early days it was linked to other centres by a perilous sea route, with many ships coming to grief on the notorious sandbar near the heads.

The Helensville and District Pioneer Museum, located behind the War Memorial Hall, features static and working displays of the early days of settlement in the area.

9 AQUATIC PARK PARAKAI SPRINGS

Return south 2 km to the junction on SH 16, take the road to Parakai and travel 4 km.

The Aquatic Park is a large complex of indoor and outdoor thermal pools of varying temperatures, and exciting waterslides. Visitors can hire swimsuits and towels.

It is 42 km back to Auckland on SH 16.

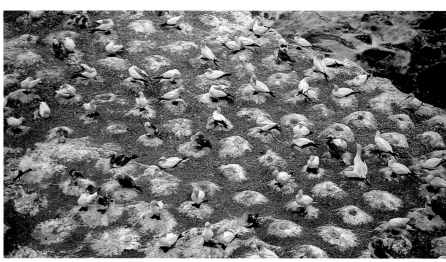

The neighbourly nests of the gannet colony on a Muriwai clifftop.

NORTH ISLAND
NORTHLAND

5 AUCKLAND TO DARGAVILLE

DRIVING TOUR ▧ 241 KM ▧ 1 DAY ▧ HISTORY IN THE COUNTRYSIDE

On the narrow strip of land north of Auckland the visitor can explore reserves and beaches on both the east and west coasts, and visit historic settlements and fascinating museums in charming rural areas.

From the long sweeping beaches and sheltered estuaries on the Hibiscus Coast north-east of Auckland to the sparkling expanse of the Kaipara Harbour and the 100 km windswept ocean beach to the north-west lies a trail of historic homes, pioneers' cottages, old townships and museums – storehouses of information that capture the history of some of Auckland's surrounding settlements. Within their walls you can find a vast range of period furnishings, memorabilia, equipment and historic photographs and are also likely to meet some interesting local people who possess a wealth of knowledge on the history of these areas.

▧ SILVERDALE
From Auckland City follow SH 1 across the Auckland Harbour Bridge 36 km north to Silverdale.

Located on the Wade River, this township was an important port for coastal shipping in the 1900s. Today, a colonial village exhibits restored farmhouses, a bushman's hut, an early church, parsonage and school.

▧ OREWA
Continue north 5 km over the hill from Silverdale to Orewa.

The first European settler arrived in Orewa in 1853, and for many years this isolated settlement was served by surf boats, which brought visitors ashore to stay at Orewa House. This three-gabled guesthouse, near the scenic reserve at the northern end of the town, was built by Major Collins de Jersey Grut who purchased the land in 1868. Today the main attraction is the long, tree-lined beach which draws thousands of campers and holidaymakers during the summer months.

▧ WENDERHOLM REGIONAL PARK
Continue north on SH 1 from Orewa for 8 km to reach the entry to Wenderholm which is signposted to the right on the hill just past the Waiwera turn-off.

Wenderholm is a regional park that combines many attractions – it has an excellent beach, an estuary, farmland, graceful groves of shady trees and some short walks that climb onto the headland to the south. The old homestead on the reserve is open to the public and dates back to the 1850s.

▧ PUHOI
4 km north of Wenderholm turn left off SH 1 and travel 1 km.

Don't miss this short detour to explore Puhoi, a small historic village that was New Zealand's first Bohemian settlement. The tiny local museum keeps irregular hours, but the 'Puhoi Pub', a two-storeyed colonial hotel, is a museum in itself and,

Locals and tourists mingle happily in the Puhoi Pub.

along with the old general store which welcomes visitors, brings to life aspects of this unique village's past. The beautiful Church of St Peter and St Paul dates back to 1881.

⑤ WARKWORTH PIONEER MUSEUM AND KAURI PARK

From Puhoi village return to SH 1 and drive north for about 12 km. Signposted on the right is the Warkworth and District Museum. Turn right into McKinney Road, at the end of this road turn right again and drive a few hundred metres to the museum.

This quaintly gabled country museum is situated in Parry Kauri Park. The McKinney kauri outside the museum is estimated to be over 800 years old.

⑥ WARKWORTH

After visiting the museum proceed 2 km via Wilson Road to reach the town of Warkworth, with an optional detour to the picturesque ruins of a cement works that operated from 1885 to 1929 on the outskirts of town.

Warkworth, built on the banks of the Mahurangi River, was once linked to Auckland by a steamship service. Today the town has become a centre for a steamship revival, and a number of enthusiasts operate restored and replica vessels out of the Mahurangi River. Warkworth was founded in 1854 and has become a flourishing centre for arts and crafts. It is a charming little town that is alive with history. The hotel on the main street opened over 130 years ago, and within walking distance in Kowhai Park you can find old lime kilns and ovens built in the 1880s.

⑦ SHEEP WORLD

From Warkworth town centre turn right onto SH 1 and travel 4 km north to Sheep World, signposted on the right.

Sheep World gives an in-depth look at the woolly animals found all over the New Zealand countryside. Visitors can feed pet lambs, see a farmer and his specially trained dogs working with sheep, watch shearers in action and try their hand at some of these skills. The processing of wool is demonstrated and a craft area displays a large variety of woollen and sheepskin products.

⑧ THE KAURI MUSEUM, MATAKOHE

Continue north 15 km on SH 1 to Wellsford via the Dome Valley. From Wellsford it is another 20 km north on SH 1 to Kaiwaka, then 8 km to the foot of the Brynderwyn Hills where SH 12 branches to the left. Follow SH 12 west 8 km to Maungaturoto and 12 km to Paparoa. Travel another 6 km from Paparoa, still on SH 12 heading west, to Matakohe. The Kauri Museum is signposted to the left off the main highway on a side road leading up onto a hillside.

The Kauri Museum at Matakohe has one of the country's most interesting collections of memorabilia, as well as the world's largest display of kauri gum. Realistic room settings full of colonial furniture and household items

A reconstruction of a typical gumdiggers' camp at The Kauri Museum, Matakohe.

portray everyday life as it was over a century ago, and the hard life of bushmen and gumdiggers is depicted with faithful recreations of their bush huts, displays of pit-sawing and fascinating photographs. The museum gives some appreciation of the scale of the devastation that took place when the great kauri forests of the north were logged in the nineteenth century.

⑨ BAYLYS BEACH

From The Kauri Museum rejoin SH 12 and drive west 16 km to Ruawai on the Wairoa River, and a further 29 km along the eastern side of the river north to Dargaville. About 2 km north of Dargaville take the road to Baylys Beach signposted on the left and drive 16 km out to the west coast.

Baylys Beach is a great place to escape at the end of the day and take a walk on the wild and windswept west coast before heading back to Dargaville. Baylys is the site of a world record haul for netting mullet, and on most days you are likely to find some of the local people down on the beach collecting shellfish. The ocean beach runs

100 km south to an old kauri lighthouse built in 1884 at Pouto Point on the Kaipara Harbour. There have been numerous shipwrecks along this stretch of coast, including a French man o'war and a Portuguese sailing ship.

⑩ DARGAVILLE

From Baylys Beach return 16 km to SH 12, then head south for 2 km to Dargaville.

Dargaville was once a thriving kauri timber port reached after a difficult journey across the treacherous Kaipara Bar and up the winding Wairoa River. The mill town was established by an Irish-Australian merchant, Joseph McMullen Dargaville, in 1872. Today the kumara (a sweet potato) is grown extensively in the area and Dargaville is known as 'the kumara capital of New Zealand'. A number of historic homes and buildings line the banks of the river, and the Dargaville Museum in Harding Park features an array of items salvaged from the many shipwrecks in the area. The building was partly constructed from bricks brought out on sailing ships from China as ballast.

Sunset at Baylys Beach.

6 AROUND THE HOKIANGA

DRIVING TOUR ▓ 219 KM ▓ 1 DAY ▓ ANCIENT FORESTS, SHELTERED HARBOURS

This trip highlights the special character of Northland's west coast. The route passes through magnificent kauri forests, then around the Hokianga Harbour, with a ferry crossing to the last stretch through farmland and out to the coast.

The northern kauri forests have a unique character. Kauri often grow in dense groves, but these forests also display great diversity, including ta-raire, tawa and a range of podocarps. The largest kauri trees are comparable in age and size to the giant sequoias of California. Many are over a thousand years old and have had their own names given to them by Maori. These magnificent trees have a special presence and viewing them is something visitors are not likely to forget.

The history of Waipoua Forest and the entire coast from Dargaville north to the Aupouri Peninsula revolves around the kauri. The straight and knot-free timber was used by Maori for canoe-building, by the British Navy for masts and spars and was pit-sawn by early settlers to build homes. After the land had been cleared, a wave of gum-diggers arrived to search for valuable kauri gum.

▓ KAI IWI LAKES
From Dargaville take SH 12 and drive north 27 km to the turn-off to Kai Iwi Lakes, turn left and continue 7 km to reach the lakes.

A popular picnic and camping spot, these three picturesque lakes cater for swimming, fishing for rainbow trout, and boating, with areas reserved for different activities.

▓ TROUNSON KAURI PARK
From the Kai Iwi Lakes return to SH 12, turn left and continue north for 4 km to Kaihu. The turn-off to Trounson is 2 km north of Kaihu township. Turn right and continue for 10 km to Trounson Kauri Park.

Trounson Kauri Park is named after James Trounson, who in 1919 gifted the original 30 ha of what is now a 500 ha park. Although smaller than Waipoua Forest, this kauri forest has its own distinctive character. A 30-minute loop walking track leads through dense stands of the brooding forest giants, even more impressive if encountered on the guided night tours.

▓ WAIPOUA FOREST LOOKOUT
Continue north from Trounson Kauri Park for 3 km to Donnellys Crossing, then 4 km north to rejoin SH 12. Continue north on SH 12 for 6 km to Waipoua Kauri Forest. Take the short unsealed side road signposted to the left of the highway just before the road descends to the river. This takes you to a forest lookout tower.

A climb to the top of the tower provides an excellent overview of the 11,000 ha Waipoua Forest. This area was set aside as a sanctuary in 1952 and preserves a segment of Northland as it was before the arrival of the axe and saw.

▓ RICKERS TRACK
Just past the bridge across the Waipoua River at the southern road entrance to the Waipoua Forest is a car park and the start of the Rickers Track.

A 10-minute walking track leads from the roadside up onto a ridgeline through stands of young kauri (rickers) growing above the Waipoua River. It is often warm and humid in these subtropical kauri rainforests. The trees release large quantities of water vapour through their leaves, creating misty clouds that rise from the forest.

▓ TE MATUA NGAHERE
From the southern road entry to Waipoua Forest drive 8 km north on SH 12 then turn left down a short unsealed road, signposted 'Kauri Walks', which leads to a car park.

From the car park a 5-minute boardwalk leads around a group of kauri trees known as the Four Sisters. A short distance further along the road is the start of a 15-minute walking track to the impressive Te Matua Ngahere (the Father of the Forest). Yakas kauri is also well worth the 30-minute walk and is accessed from the same point.

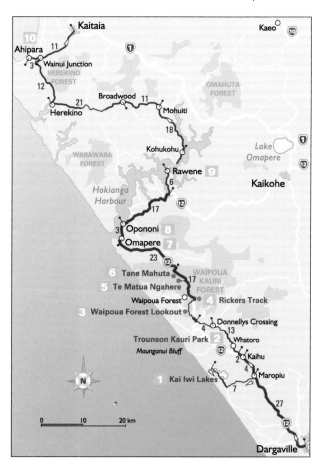

A large range of plants apart from kauri grow in the Waipoua Forest.

Tane Mahuta soars to a lofty 51.5 m above the forest floor.

The shores of the Hokianga Harbour are peaceful and unspoiled. Near the harbour entrance, huge pale sand dunes flank the serene waters.

 **TANE MAHUTA**
Return to SH 12 and drive 2 km north.

The most accessible of Waipoua's giant kauri, Tane Mahuta is signposted from a grassed clearing and picnic area in the middle of the Waipoua Forest. A 5-minute boardwalk, designed to protect the delicate feeding roots around the base of the tree, leads to the awe-inspiring 'Lord of the Forest'. Tane Mahuta, one of the largest kauri in the reserve, is close to 2000 years old.

OMAPERE
After leaving Tane Mahuta continue north on SH 12 for 23 km to the Hokianga Harbour. Before you descend the last hill to Omapere, a rest area on the left provides sweeping views across the harbour.

Omapere lies within walking distance of the Hokianga Heads, facing dramatic sand dunes on the western side of the harbour. Omapere has become a popular beach resort, but is still relatively unspoiled.

OPONONI
From Omapere drive 3 km along the southern shoreline of the Hokianga Harbour to Opononi.

Opononi was made famous by Opo, a friendly dolphin that regularly visited the beach in the mid-1950s, frolicking in the shallows with local children and the many visitors who flocked to see and swim with it. Opo is commemorated by a Russell Clark sculpture. Further along the road, at Pakenae, is a monument to Kupe, the legendary Maori voyager who is said to have departed New Zealand to return to Hawaiki from the Hokianga (great return) Harbour.

RAWENE
From Opononi head east on SH 12 for 17 km to the Rawene turn-off on the left and continue 6 km to Rawene.

Rawene Peninsula was the site of a proposed settlement in the 1820s, but when the English settlers arrived it rained so relentlessly that they refused to stay and sailed on to Sydney. Today the historic timber town is renowned for its buildings cantilevered over the waters of the Hokianga Harbour. Clendon House, built in the 1860s and maintained by the Historic Places Trust, was originally the home of the area's Resident Magistrate.

AHIPARA
A vehicular ferry crosses the harbour between Rawene and the Narrows on the northern side of the harbour, allowing travellers on SH 12 to take a direct route to Kohukohu. The car ferry operates between 7.30 am and 8 pm daily. From Kohukohu drive 18 km north to the turn-off to Broadwood on the left. Heading west, it is 11 km to Broadwood, a further 21 km to Herekino then 15 km north to the Wainui Junction where the left turn-off leads to Ahipara 3 km to the west.

It is a pleasant drive north through rolling hills and undulating farmland from the ferry landing to Ahipara at the southern end of Ninety Mile Beach. St Clement's Church at Ahipara dates back to 1872, when the kauri gum left from the forests that had been logged was attracting waves of settlers. The Gumfields Historic Reserve above Ahipara is a small area of the original gumfields that has been preserved as it was when the gumdiggers were working the land. Late in the nineteenth century most of the inhabitants of Ahipara and Kaitaia had some connection with the gumdigging industry. Many of these settlers and itinerant workers were immigrants from Bohemia and Dalmatia. The kauri gum dug from the swamps and hills was a valuable constituent of varnish and linoleum.

Leaving Ahipara, turn left at Wainui Junction and drive 14 km to reach Kaitaia.

Opo, the dolphin who loved to play with children, is immortalised in a statue at Opononi.

7 NORTH TO CAPE REINGA

DRIVING TOUR ▮▮▮ 234 KM ▮▮▮ 1 DAY ▮▮▮ EXPLORING THE AUPOURI PENINSULA

Quiet bays, fishing harbours, sculptured dunes and a vast white-sand beach stretch along the country's northernmost finger of land to the point where the Tasman Sea and Pacific Ocean meet beneath the cliffs of Cape Reinga.

People have been hard at work changing this wild and beautiful landscape for more than a thousand years. From the small groups of prehistoric Maori who travelled each year to their summer camp at Houhora below Mt Camel to the whalers, traders, missionaries and gumdiggers who came later, the land has seen its share of pioneering settlers. Signs of their endeavours remain in archaeological sites, in the defensive earthworks of the fortified pa on many headlands, the gumfields dug over by hundreds of workers when kauri gum replaced gold as New Zealand's most valuable export, and in historic buildings such as kauri-built churches.

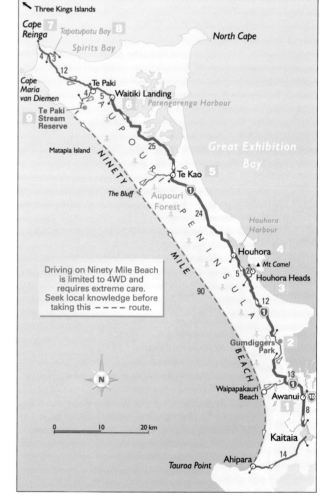

The modest wooden church of St Joseph holds memories of the days when Awanui was home to hundreds of gumdiggers.

1 AWANUI
Awanui, 8 km north of Kaitaia on SH 1, is near the intersection with SH 10.

Awanui, the gateway to the Aupouri Peninsula, is located on the banks of the Awanui River and was originally established as a port for Kaitaia to the south. Scows plied the twisting waterway to Awanui to load kauri logs and, in later years, kauri gum. A huge mass of giant kauri tree stumps, recovered from swamps where they have been submerged sometimes for thousands of years, can be seen stacked up in a yard on the side of the main road. Today this highly valued swamp kauri is used in the manufacture of furniture and ornaments. The Anglican Church of St Joseph, on the outskirts of Awanui, has been a landmark since 1887.

2 GUMDIGGERS PARK
Continue north on SH 1 for 13 km. Turn right into Heath Road to Gumdiggers Park.

Gumdiggers Park is an authentic gum digging site. These giant gumholes have been preserved from the early 1900s. The gumdiggers' village evokes the lifestyle and hardships of the times. Informative displays of the natural history of the area as well as the extensive kauri gum collection make it well worth the visit.

3 HOUHORA HEADS
Continue north along Heath Road. Turn left into Kaimaumau Road and right back onto SH 1 for 12 km. Turn right at Houhora Heads.

You can take a walk along the water's edge from the estuary towards the Houhora Heads. It takes 20 minutes to reach the main beach on the coast where you will sometimes find locals collecting scallops washed up after an easterly storm.

Along the main road is a tavern which dates back to 1902, when gumdiggers lived in the area.

Nearby is the Subritzky homestead, open

Fishing boats at the Houhora wharf.

The beam from New Zealand's northernmost lighthouse, at Cape Reinga, is visible at sea for 50 km.

by arrangement, and enterprisingly built in the 1850s by a Polish settler from materials on hand, including seashells which he crushed to make a paste to plaster the walls.

HOUHORA
Drive 5 km north to Houhora.

The wharf at Houhora is usually a colourful scene of fishing activity, especially when an incoming tide brings kingfish in search of smaller prey in the early morning. A variety of fishing boats tie up near the wharf and across the harbour lies Mt Camel, the site of some of New Zealand's oldest archaeological finds.

TE KAO
From Houhora drive 24 km north on SH 1 to Te Kao.

The distinctive twin towers of the Ratana church at Te Kao represent the sons of Wiremu Ratana, the famous Maori faith-healer and political activist who founded the church in the 1920s, and are named Alpha and Omega, after the first and last letters of the Greek alphabet. 'Kao' is a form of dried kumara once carried by travellers who used it as a convenient food on long journeys.

WAITIKI LANDING
Continue 25 km north on SH 1 to Waitiki Landing. The road climbs over hills, with expansive views across the Parengarenga Harbour.

The glistening white sands on the ocean side of the Parengarenga Harbour are home to thousands of godwits every year between February and late March as they prepare for their annual migration to Siberia and Alaska. Indigenous wading birds here include oystercatchers and wrybills. The sand, which contains one of the world's purest sources of silica, was once extracted and barged to Whangarei for use in glass-making.

Waitiki Landing is the last place to get supplies and fuel for your vehicle on the road north, and the store can provide information about tides if you are considering returning along Ninety Mile Beach (see box).

CAPE REINGA
Continue on the road north from Waitiki Landing to the lighthouse at Cape Reinga.

According to Maori legend, the great curve of Ninety Mile Beach traces the route taken by the dead on their journey to the homeland of Hawaiki. Their final departure point is said to be from the branches of an ancient pohutukawa tree at the tip of Cape Reinga (means 'place of leaping'). New Zealand's first automatic lighthouse, built in 1941, is a short walk from the car park. On a clear day you can look north-west from the lighthouse at Cape Reinga and see the shadowy forms of the Three Kings Islands. Below the cliffs, surging currents mark the often turbulent meeting point of the Tasman Sea and Pacific Ocean.

TAPOTUPOTU BAY
Heading south on the return journey, the road to Tapotupotu Bay is signposted on the left side of the road 4 km south of Cape Reinga. This unsealed side road leads down the hill for 3 km to the coast.

Driving down the narrow winding gravel road towards Tapotupotu Bay you can see dense pockets of vivid green where regenerating native forest is slowly re-establishing in the narrow gullies. Tapotupotu Bay opens up ahead as you round one of the last bends. This beautiful sheltered bay with an attractive sandy beach set between steep headlands is an inviting place to make a short stop and enjoy the scenery. Surfing here is consistently good and swimming is safe.

DRIVING NINETY MILE BEACH
More adventurous drivers with a 4WD vehicle can take the option of driving down the beach, usually on the outgoing tide. Check the tides at one of the garages or stores at Awanui or at Waitiki Landing before you set out. The best direction to make the trip the first time is south from the Te Paki Stream. The full length of the beach from the Te Paki Stream is about 90 km. Driving down the stream and along the beach is relatively easy as long as you stay on the firm wet sand and do not venture off into the softer dry sand higher up above the tide line. A sandy 4WD track at The Bluff about half-way along the beach leads back out to the main road at Te Kao, and a concrete ramp at Waipapakauri Beach offers another exit point before reaching Ahipara which is 14 km south of Kaitaia.

Another way to explore Ninety Mile Beach is on an organised tour. The round trip includes the stretch of road north along the Aupouri Peninsula to Cape Reinga as well as along the Te Paki Stream Reserve and Ninety Mile Beach. Regular bus services depart from the Bay of Islands and Kaitaia. Vehicles are available for both small or large groups.

Ninety Mile Beach is flanked to the east by the Aupouri pine forest, which limits the spread of dunes, and stretches 103 km from Cape Maria van Diemen in the north to Ahipara in the south. The Bluff is a favourite fishing spot on the beach, which hosts one of New Zealand's largest surfcasting competitions each year. Off the coast north of here is Motupia Island, a pierced rock that according to Maori mythology is the anchor stone of Maui, who fished up the North Island.

TE PAKI STREAM RESERVE
Return to SH 1 and drive 12 km south to Te Paki. Turn right and drive 4 km on a gravel road to the Te Paki Stream Reserve. From the car park at the end of the road a 4WD route, the most northerly vehicle access point to Ninety Mile Beach, follows the stream bed out to the coast.

At Te Paki Stream Reserve you can explore some of the huge windswept sand dunes behind Ninety Mile Beach. Because the coast is not visible from the road end it is tempting to walk down the stream bed to Ninety Mile Beach but you would need to allow at least an extra two hours for the return walk through soft sand.

Either return to SH 1, turn left and drive 35 km to Kaitaia, or continue south along Ninety Mile Beach (see box).

8 KAITAIA TO KERIKERI

DRIVING TOUR ▓ 178 KM ▓ 1 DAY ▓ SUN-DRENCHED BEACHES, BEAUTIFUL BAYS

At any time of year there is a summer-holiday feel to this stretch of northern coastline. On this trip the visitor can relax by the sea, visit an impressive waterfall and discover the charm of a town famed for its handcrafts.

Huge volcanic spires rise above a landscape covered in forest and farmland, with a coastline boasting a myriad of sheltered harbours and golden beaches running from Doubtless Bay to Kerikeri. It may rain occasionally, but the weather is seldom cold in this coastal environment. The area has always been a Mecca for summer holidaymakers seeking the many hideaways within the folds of its convoluted coastline, and a playground and haven for boaties of every description.

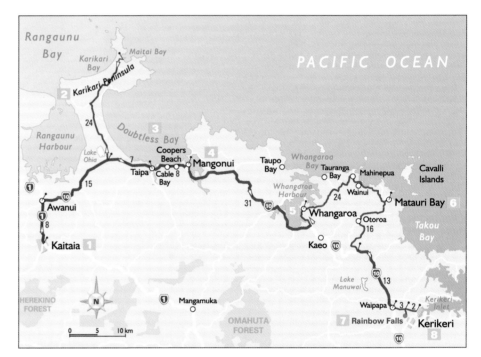

1 KAITAIA
The trip starts at Kaitaia, located on SH 1.

The European settlement of Kaitaia began with the establishment of a mission station in 1833, followed by a period of rapid growth during the 1880s and 1890s, when thousands of kauri gumdiggers came to the area. Many Dalmatian people living in the district today are descendants of these pioneering immigrants. St Savior's Anglican Church on Church Road dates from this period, having been built in 1887. Numerous historic relics can be found in the Far North Regional Museum on South Road, including an anchor lost from the ship of the French navigator Jean de Surville in Doubtless Bay in 1769. De Surville had sighted New Zealand's coast two months after Captain Cook made his first landfall, but the two sailors were unaware of each other's presence in New Zealand waters.

2 KARIKARI PENINSULA
Drive 8 km north from Kaitaia on SH 1 to Awanui then turn right onto SH 10 and continue west for 15 km. The turn-off to the

The drowned forest at Lake Ohia is 40,000 years old.

left onto the Karikari Peninsula heads north 24 km to Maitai Bay. The last kilometre of the road is unsealed.

A short detour to the left near the start of the Karikari Peninsula road leads to Lake Ohia, where a maze of stumps covering swampy ground marks the location of an ancient drowned kauri forest. The road to Maitai Bay leads to a beautiful section of coastline where you will find two idyllic horseshoe-shaped coves separated by a small headland.

3 DOUBTLESS BAY
Return to SH 10, turn left and drive about 7 km to reach Taipa.

Taipa, Cable Bay and Coopers Beach form a string of popular holiday beaches in Doubtless Bay. This pohutukawa-lined stretch of coastline features good swimming spots on golden-sand beaches that are within easy reach of the road, as well as sheltered places to stop for a picnic.

4 MANGONUI
From Taipa it is 8 km on SH 10 to the Mangonui turn-off. Turn left and drive

2 km around the coast to Mangonui township.

Although the main road now bypasses this quaint little town, it is a fascinating place to stop for a break and a walk past the picturesque buildings that line the main road on the edge of the harbour. Kauri logs felled in the forests around Mangonui were once floated to the township to be milled, but it was as a base for up to 30 whaling ships that the township was originally founded in the early nineteenth century.

Now a centre for big-game fishing, Mangonui is famous for its historic buildings. The old courthouse (1892) on the main street has been restored and is one of a number of charming buildings that capture the spirit of the past. The local tavern features mounted marlin adorning the walls and you can enjoy fresh-caught fish and chips on the waterfront and watch the fishing boats come in.
Continue round the waterfront to rejoin SH 10 a short distance south-east of the township.

5 WHANGAROA
Heading south-east from Mangonui on SH 10, it is 31 km to Whangaroa Harbour. The road crosses the southern end of the harbour via a causeway, and the turn-off to Whangaroa is on the left across the bridge at the end of the causeway. A winding sealed road continues around the edge of

Whangaroa Harbour is almost landlocked, with an irregular shoreline that provides deep bays within its coastline. The view from St Pauls Rock captures the wild beauty of this isolated waterway.

Sunlight on the 27 m Rainbow Falls sometimes produces a spectrum of colour.

the harbour for the last few kilometres to Whangaroa.

Set among forest-clad hills where the cores of ancient volcanoes rise above the trees, the sheltered bays of the Whangaroa Harbour make a pleasant diversion from SH 10. Now a tranquil deep-sea fishing base, the Whangaroa Harbour was the scene of a massacre in 1809 when the *Boyd* arrived to pick up kauri spars for delivery on her return trip to England. Local Maori killed several crew members who had gone ashore, then dressed in the sailors' clothing, boarded the ship after dark and attacked the remaining crew. A barrel of gunpowder exploded and the ship was burnt to the waterline. Relics from the *Boyd* are on view in Whangaroa's Shipwreck museum.

From the road behind the southern end of the harbour you can get excellent views across the harbour, and even better ones if you do a half-hour climb on a well-marked track to the summit (230 m) of St Pauls Rock, one of a series of small peaks known as the 'Twelve Apostles'.

6 MATAURI BAY

From Whangaroa head east for 24 km to Matauri Bay via Wainui.

From the slopes of an old headland pa site above Matauri Bay you can look across to the Cavalli Islands and their renowned deep-sea fishing grounds. It takes about 20 minutes to walk up onto the headland. Samuel Marsden, who first preached in the Bay of Islands on Christmas Day in 1814, is commemorated in a historic church on this magnificent stretch of coastline.

7 RAINBOW FALLS

From Matauri Bay, head south on the sealed road for 16 km back to SH 10 via Otoroa. Turn left onto SH 10 and drive south-east for 13 km to Waipapa. Turn left and drive east towards the coast for 3 km to the Rainbow Falls. The turn-off to the falls is on the right side of the road.

The Rainbow Falls, only a few minutes' drive from the centre of Kerikeri, plummet over the edge of a huge lava bluff. They can be viewed from a platform near the car park,

or you can take the walking track to the base of the falls and beyond.

8 KERIKERI

Continue east from the Rainbow Falls for 2 km to the Old Stone Store and Kerikeri township.

Kerikeri was the site of the country's second mission station, established in 1819. Kerikeri Mission Station (1821) and Kerikeri Stone Store (1832) stand side by side on the Kerikeri Inlet. On the other side of the road is Rewa's Village, a reconstruction of a Maori settlement (kainga). Across the water lies the site of a fortified pa used by Hongi Hika, the Nga Puhi chief who led war parties as far south as Cook Strait. The earthworks and other features of the fortified site are still clearly visible.

Kerikeri is renowned for its citrus and subtropical fruit orchards. It is also well known for handcrafts and cottage industries with many studios and potteries tucked in among the gardens and tall trees that give the town a unique character.

Kemp House, overlooking the Kerikeri Inlet, is believed to be the oldest wooden building in New Zealand.

9 THE BAY OF ISLANDS

DRIVING TOUR ▓ 127 KM ▓ 1 DAY ▓ HISTORY BY THE SEA

The Bay of Islands was the setting for a significant part of New Zealand history. The tour provides a fascinating insight into those early days combined with an exploration of the extraordinarily beautiful natural environment.

Captain Cook sailed the Endeavour *into the Bay of Islands in 1769 and made contact with the Maori living there. Whalers and missionaries followed, the Maori prospering from the trade that developed. With the Europeans, however, came muskets, and the Northland tribes were quick to exploit their new-found advantage, waging a devastating war on their ancient tribal enemies.*

Increasing British influence led in February 1840 to the signing of the Treaty of Waitangi, which vested sovereignty of New Zealand in Queen Victoria. Signed by the British and a number of Maori chiefs, the treaty was a paternalistic gesture aimed partly at protecting the interests of local Maori who were often exploited by visiting British seafarers. The imposition of customs taxes, however, deterred visits by whaling ships and had a disastrous effect on trade for the local Maori. Hone Heke led a rebellion and sacked Kororareka (Russell) in 1845, leading to the abandonment of the town while the fighting escalated to become the 'War in the North'.

Today the Bay of Islands Historic and Maritime Park preserves many of the scenic and historic features in this magnificent stretch of over 800 km of coastline, including 40 reserves and 150 islands.

1 PAIHIA

The site of a church missionary station founded by Henry Williams in 1825, Paihia has developed into a thriving resort town packed with diverse tourist attractions and cafés.

Tour operators offer a range of experiences in the Bay of Islands. From the Paihia wharf you can organise trips on water taxis or catch the ferry across the harbour to visit Russell. You can also take the celebrated Cream Trip, which visits many of the islands in the area,

or the famous Hole in the Rock trip, which heads out through the Bay of Islands to Cape Brett, including an exhilarating detour through a natural rock arch.

2 WAITANGI
Waitangi is signposted off SH 11, 2 km north of Paihia.

Assembled on site from timber that was pre-cut in Sydney, the Georgian-style home of James Busby, appointed British Resident in 1833, was to become the stage for the signing of the Treaty of Waitangi and thus one of New Zealand's most famous historic buildings. Eventually purchased by Lord Bledisloe in 1932 and presented to the nation, along with 400 ha of land, the Treaty House and surrounding area is now a historic reserve.

The interior of the Treaty House has been restored to its former glory, and cut-away sections reveal views of its construction. It is set in expansive grounds and linked to other attractions by a network of well-marked paths. An audio-visual display can be viewed in the magnificently carved meeting house, which together with *Ngatoki-matawhaorua*, a 37 m kauri waka (canoe), was built as part of the Maori contribution to the 1940 centenary of the Treaty. The meeting house incorporates carvings from tribes throughout the country.

3 HARURU FALLS
From Waitangi head back south across the bridge, turn right onto SH 11 and travel west 3 km to the Haruru Falls.

Ngatokimatawhaorua, at Waitangi Treaty Grounds.

The horseshoe-shaped Haruru Falls are clearly visible from the road, but for a closer look drive across the bridge to a small car park from where you can take a walking track that provides good views from above the falls. Haruru means 'loud noise' and Maori legend tells of a taniwha (water monster) that lives in the lagoon below the falls. The track continues around the promontory to an interesting boardwalk through a mangrove swamp. This easy walk takes 20 minutes each way.

4 OPUA
From the Haruru Falls return to Paihia and drive a further 4 km south on SH 1 to reach Opua.

Located at the head of the Kawakawa River on the Waikare Inlet, Opua was originally a commercial wharf for dairy and other products; now it is a sought-after haven for sailing, diving and fishing (including game fishing).

At this small port you can board a passenger and vehicular ferry that crosses to and from Okiato. This eliminates the need to make a 42 km journey to Russell on winding gravel roads around the southern end of the harbour.

RUSSELL

From Opua take the car ferry across the Waikare Inlet to Okiato and drive 14 km north-west from the ferry wharf on a sealed road to Russell.

Russell is a busy tourist town and a centre for big-game fishing boats operating in the Bay of Islands, but its peaceful atmosphere was not always so. Originally named Kororareka, Russell was known as the 'Hell Hole of the Pacific' at a time when drunken whalers ran wild in the town during the early 1800s. The original Russell, sited at Okiato near the ferry landing, was briefly New Zealand's capital following the signing of the Treaty of Waitangi in 1840, but was abandoned when buildings were burnt down during the northern wars.

The present-day Russell is a picturesque town with numerous historic buildings. On the waterfront – The Strand – is the Duke of Marlborough Hotel, which holds the country's oldest liquor licence, and the police station, originally the customs house (1870). At the southern end of the town is Pompallier Mission, an elegant rammed-earth building that housed a Roman Catholic mission printery. Christ Church (1836), on Baker Street, is the oldest surviving church in the country and displays bullet holes dating from the troubled years of the 1840s. The flagpole on Flagstaff Hill is the fifth erected on the site, as the four earlier flagstaffs were cut down by the Nga Puhi chief Hone Heke. The Russell Museum houses an impressive scale model of Captain Cook's *Endeavour*.

KAWAKAWA

From Russell return 14 km to the car ferry crossing and Opua then travel south 16 km on SH 11 to Kawakawa.

The public toilets on Giles Street are well worth the visit. They were created in 1997 by Austrian architect and artist Friedrich Hundertwasser. Kawakawa was his home-from-Europe for many years, and this building the only one he completed in the Southern Hemisphere. The ceramic columns supporting the entrance are fashioned from old bits of terracotta, glazed plant pots and brick. Light is shed through wall panels made of bottles.

KAWITI CAVES

Head south on SH 1 to the turn-off to the left at Waiomio, 4 km from Kawakawa, and drive approximately a kilometre to the caves.

The Kawiti glow-worm caves feature pure white limestone formations that developed over thousands of years. The caves are lit up by a galaxy of glow-worms.

RUAPEKAPEKA PA

From Kawiti Caves return to SH 1 and continue south for 13 km to Towai where you will find a side road signposted to Ruapekapeka on the left. The road is unsealed and leads 6 km up into the hills to the Ruapekapeka Historic Reserve.

Ruapekapeka (the bat's nest), built in 1845 by Te Ruki Kawhiti, was a masterpiece of

The Strand on Russell's waterfront, lined with colonial buildings, seems a world away from the more modern Paihia.

design and engineering. The gun-fighter pa was an adaptation of earlier defences that were no longer suitable for warfare following the introduction of muskets and cannon. Ruapekapeka featured trench systems, designed to withstand bombardment, well before such defences were used in the First World War and withstood a siege by over 1600 British troops for more than a month. The pa was finally taken when Tamati Waka Nene and his men, allies of the British, infiltrated the defences on a Sunday while the inhabitants were engaged in prayer behind the pa. This surprise attack ended the 'War in the North'.

WARO RESERVE

From the Ruapekapeka Historic Reserve return 6 km to SH 1 at Towai and continue south for 16 km to Waro where you will find the Waro Reserve signposted on the left side of the road near the turn-off to Hikurangi.

Waro Reserve offers a rare opportunity to examine weathered limestone rock formations that are millions of years old. The rock was formed from corals and other organisms originally laid down on the sea bed. As the sedimentary rock formed thick layers, the lower strata compressed to form limestone that was eventually uplifted above sea level. Forest covered the limestone, and natural acids, created by rainwater filtering down through the leaves carpeting the forest floor, gradually dissolved the rock, creating the beautiful fluted patterns that can be seen today.

The city of Whangarei is another 22 km south on SH 1.

The intriguingly beautiful limestone rock formations at Waro Reserve.

10 COAST ROAD FROM RUSSELL

DRIVING TOUR ▬ 180 KM ▬ 1 DAY ▬ EXPLORING THE COAST ON THE BACKROADS

Bays, beaches, harbours, islands in a glittering sea... the coast road from Russell takes you through a beautiful and remote region. Numerous side trips from the main sealed route let you explore the diverse coastal scenery.

From the kauri forests and secluded harbours of the Bay of Islands south along the spectacular volcanic coastline to Whangarei, the coast road from Russell covers some of the North Island's most interesting and diverse scenery. Never far from the sea, this route will take you out onto rugged backroads to remote unspoiled beaches set in a dramatic volcanic landscape. Off the coast lie the lava domes of the Poor Knights Islands, with their impressive rock arches carved out by an unrelenting sea. These are wild and wonderful places in a magnificent stretch of beautiful coastline.

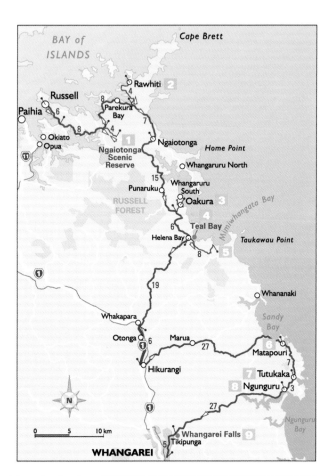

1 NGAIOTONGA SCENIC RESERVE

From Russell head east 6 km on the main road and turn off to the left to take the coastal route south. Continue for 8 km to the next major road junction and head east for 4 km on the unsealed road over the hills through the Ngaiotonga Scenic Reserve. The Twin Bole Kauri Walk is marked on the right side of the road on the way to the top of the Ngaiotonga Saddle.

Ngaiotonga is the largest reserve in the Bay of Islands Historic and Maritime Park. Its famous and unusual giant double-trunked kauri, reached on a 10-minute walking track, bears scars from the days when it was bled for gum which had many uses including setting false teeth and as an ingredient in varnish. In 1905 a government regulation put an end to Kauri gum bleeding.

2 RAWHITI

Return 4 km to the last road junction and head north towards Parekura Bay. It is an 8 km drive on unsealed road to the Rawhiti turn-off on the left side of the road, and a further 4 km out onto the Rawhiti Peninsula.

Rawhiti is in the heart of the Bay of Islands. From the road you can see the marae, the focal point for this small Maori community. Down at the beach there are often snorkellers or people diving for scallops. A 10-minute climb up onto the headlands will reward you with superb views across the channel to Urupukapuka Island.

3 OAKURA

From the Rawhiti Peninsula drive 4 km back to the coast road, and along a beautiful stretch of coastline to Ngaiotonga. Continue for 15 km via Punaruku on the road to Oakura which is signposted on the left.

Though well off the beaten track the beauty of Oakura has made it a popular holiday destination, especially for campers and boaties. The almost 1 kilometre long, east-facing beach, near the entrance to Whangaruru Harbour, is sheltered from ocean swells by several outlying islands which makes for safe swimming for all ages.

4 TEAL BAY

From Oakura rejoin the main road south and continue 6 km to the Helena Bay turn-off, turn left and continue 1 km over the hill to Teal Bay.

Teal Bay is a delightful beach to visit before you head back inland to SH 1. The promontory across the estuary at the southern end of the beach is an old Maori pa site with its terraces, defensive ditch and kumara pits still clearly visible.

The twin-trunked kauri in Ngaiotonga Reserve.

THE POOR KNIGHTS

A number of companies run dive charters from Tutukaka out to the Poor Knights Islands, 24 km off the coast. An underwater haven for subtropical marine life, the Poor Knights are fed by warm currents and provide a habitat for an incredible variety of species that would not normally be found this far south.

The submarine lava cliffs, caves and extensive reef systems are rich with multi-hued sponges, invertebrates and spectacular shoals of fish. The luxuriant marine life is protected by legislation passed in 1981 that made the islands part of a marine reserve, preserving one of the best subtropical diving locations in the world.

Recently surveyed Riko Riko cave was found to be the largest sea cave in the world.

MIMIWHANGATA BAY

From Teal Bay continue on the winding 8 km gravel road along the ridgelines to reach Mimiwhangata. Because this is a farm park, most of the access roads have gates that you will have to open then close behind you as you drive through to the beach.

Administered by DOC, Mimiwhangata features a number of marked walks and a small camping area. In 1984 the waters around Mimiwhangata were designated a marine park to preserve the colourful sponges and hydroid trees, the beautiful reef fish and other forms of marine life. The diving is excellent in this protected environment, where the only fishing permitted is for pelagic species like kahawai and kingfish, which range the coastline in large schools.

MATAPOURI

From Mimiwhangata return 8 km to the sealed road and continue 19 km south-west to Whakapara and SH 1. Continue south on SH 1 for 6 km to the next turn-off, sign-posted to Matapouri on the left. This is a 27 km drive to the coast.

Matapouri is one of a string of attractive bays along this coast. Sandy Bay and Whale Bay (known by locals as Snail Bay) are prime surfing locations and feature many excellect walking tracks.

TUTUKAKA

Continue south from Matapouri for 7 km to Tutukaka.

The home of the Whangarei Deep Sea Anglers' Club (the largest aquatic social club of its kind in the Southern Hemisphere), Tutukaka is set in a beautiful harbour. Towards the end of the day, while seated on the deck at the clubhouse, you can often see game fish, including sharks and marlin, being weighed in at the marina.

The yacht club based here launched the challenge for the America's Cup in 1995, which was won by *Black Magic*.

NGUNGURU

Ngunguru is 3 km south-west of Tutukaka on the main road.

Sheltered behind a large sandy peninsula, Ngunguru is a haven for boaties. Its pohutu-kawa-shaded domain and safe beach make it an inviting place to swim or picnic.

WHANGAREI FALLS

From Ngunguru head south-west for 27 km to the Whangarei Falls which are signposted at Tikipunga.

A short walking track leads to the top of the spectacular Whangarei Falls which plummet 25 m over a lava bluff. For a better look at the interesting columnar jointed lava rock formation, follow the track down to the base of the falls. The walk takes 10 minutes and will give you a close view of these impressive lava cliffs which were formed from volcanic eruptions when the area lay beneath the sea bed.

It is 5 km from the falls to Whangarei city centre.

In the waters at remote Mimiwhangata, protected as a marine park, colourful fishes and plants can be seen by boat, diving or snorkelling.

Crashing to a deep pool below, Whangarei Falls are dramatised by their rocky backdrop.

11 EAST COAST FROM WHANGAREI

DRIVING TOUR ▓ 247 KM ▓ 1 DAY ▓ EXPLORING OCEAN BEACHES

Much of the main highway south to Auckland can be bypassed on a relaxed coastal route. A chain of wide, dazzling white-sand beaches borders fishing villages, marine reserves and historic settlements.

Sharp, shadowy peaks stand like sentinels above Whangarei looking out across a landscape that at one time was part of the ocean floor. According to Maori legend, the volcanic peaks of Mt Manaia to the east of the city are people turned to stone. These spires that dominate the landscape are the remnants of ancient volcanoes that have eroded to reveal their central lava cores, creating dramatic natural rock sculptures that stand silhouetted against the sky. Off the coast lie more impressive peaks, the rugged pinnacles of the Hen and Chickens group, named by Captain Cook in 1770. To the south stretch the beautiful white sand beaches that run from Ruakaka to Waipu Cove and from the Mangawhai Heads to Pakiri.

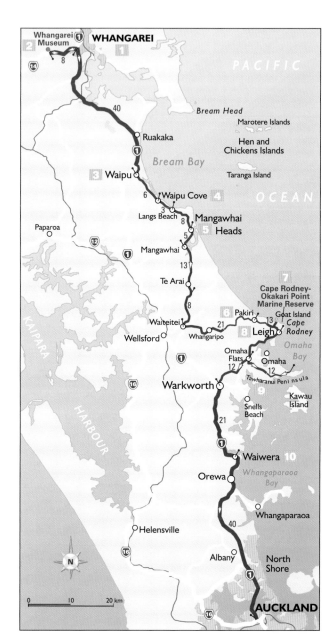

1 WHANGAREI

Framed by the five jagged peaks of Mt Manaia, Whangarei has retained its rural character and boasts a number of attractive parks and gardens, including the colourful flowerbeds of Cafler Park, located on First Avenue on the banks of a small stream flowing through the city centre. The nearby Margie Maddren Fernery and Snow Conservatory features over 80 varieties of New Zealand native ferns. The Clapham Clock Museum, on the quayside in the picturesque Whangarei Town Basin, has the largest collection of clocks, time-pieces and music boxes in the Southern Hemisphere and is open daily.

An excellent place to get a view of the city is the summit of Mt Parahaki which can be reached either by walking track or road. The mountain was the largest fortified pa site in the country at one time and today many of the excavation features are still visible, identified by explanatory signs. There are more bush walks at the A. H. Reed Memorial Kauri Park on Whareora Road, and at Onerahi, the Waimahanga Walkway follows an old railway line, crossing a timber truss bridge and passing mangrove swamps along the harbour. The complete walk takes about 2 hours.

The Clapham Clock Museum at Whangarei.

2 WHANGAREI MUSEUM

Whangarei Museum and Heritage Park is 8 km west of the city on SH 14, on the right.

The Whangarei Museum features the Clarke Pioneer Homestead, a range of vintage machinery, and Maori artefacts including superb feather cloaks and a rare burial chest. In the museum park a vintage locomotive runs during the summer months, and you can also visit an old mercury mine.

3 WAIPU

From Whangarei Museum return east 4 km toward the city on SH 14 and turn right onto SH 1. Head south for 40 km and take the turn-off to the left to Waipu. On the long stretch from Ruakaka the road is never far from the beach and provides glorious ocean views.

Located on the Waipu River 2 km inland from the coast and Bream Bay, the town was founded in 1853 by 120 Scottish Highlanders who were moved out of their homes during the 'Clearances'. After unhappy attempts at settling in Nova Scotia and then Australia, they eventually established themselves in Waipu. In the main street a small museum called the Waipu Heritage Centre contains relics from the early days of settlement, and the nearby church features stained-glass windows commemorating the Rev Norman McLeod, who led the doughty immigrants.

The estuary near the mouth of the Waipu River is the home of a number of shore birds including the variable oystercatcher, the fairy tern and rare New Zealand dotterel.

4 WAIPU COVE

From Waipu township it is 6 km heading east to Waipu Cove and a further 3 km to Langs Beach.

This idyllic stretch of coastline with long white-sand beaches presents views across Bream Bay to the volcanic spires of the Hen

Pristine sand and sea at Mangawhai Heads.

Mathesons Bay, just south of Leigh, is a tucked-away beach that is a real 'find'.

and Chickens group of islands. The small village beachside setting of Waipu Cove and the more architecturally styled development at Langs Beach are dominated by the expanse of the Pacific Ocean.

⑤ MANGAWHAI HEADS
From Langs Beach it is 8 km heading south-east along the coast to Mangawhai Heads.

With its distinctive white crystalline sands, Mangawhai Heads is a popular family holiday resort and often provides good surfing. The boat-building industry thrived here in the 1870s when large quantities of kauri timber and kauri gum were shipped out of Manga-whai Harbour. The bar claimed a paddle steamer in 1893.

⑥ PAKIRI
Continue south from Mangawhai Heads for 5 km to Mangawhai. From here it is 13 km south via Te Arai to the next major road junction. Turn left and continue south 8 km on a gravel road to Waiteitei. Turn left here and head east 21 km to Pakiri. The road is sealed 8 km from Waiteitei to just past Whangaripo but continues unsealed to Pakiri. The turn-off to the beach is sign-posted to the left.

Pakiri is a beautiful sweeping white-sand beach with views across the gulf to Little Barrier Island. As well as surfing, horseriding is a popular pastime here. Horses can be hired from a business in Rahuikiri Road, offering rides from one hour to longer treks.

⑦ CAPE RODNEY–OKAKARI POINT MARINE RESERVE
From Pakiri it is 10 km over the next hill heading east to Goat Island and the Cape Rodney–Okakari Point Marine Reserve which is signposted to the left.

Usually referred to as Goat Island, the marine reserve at Cape Rodney is also used by Auckland University for research undertaken by their marine laboratory. Marine life is protected within the reserve, which is a quite magical place for both snorkelling and diving. Many of the fish are fairly tame and very inquisitive. You can also take a trip in a glass-bottomed boat all year round, weather permitting.

⑧ LEIGH
From Goat Island it is 3 km heading south to Leigh and another 1 km to Mathesons Bay.

Nestled on a small inlet, this quiet fishing village is located just north of Mathesons Bay, a sheltered and secluded beach often overlooked by holidaymakers. Leigh is a good place to watch boating activity and enjoy a takeaway picnic of freshly caught fish and chips.

⑨ TAWHARANUI PENINSULA
From Leigh head south-west towards Wark-worth. The turn-off to Tawharanui and Omaha is signposted on the left side of the road 11 km from Mathe-sons Bay at Omaha Flats. It is 12 km to the Tawhara-nui Peninsula and the entry to the regional park at Jones Bay.

A marine reserve surrounds a major portion of the Tawharanui Peninsula, with its sheltered coves and vast ocean beaches. A popular camping ground over the summer months, Tawharanui Farm Park has some of the best surf on the east coast. To the north-west lies Omaha Beach, a housing subdivision that made headlines when shifting sand dunes reclaimed a number of homes shortly after its development. Tawharanui has a number of walking trails and some especially beautiful beaches and bays on the northern side of the peninsula. It is a great place for body surfing and boogie boarding.

⑩ WAIWERA
From Tawharanui return to the main road and continue west 12 km to Warkworth. Head south from Warkworth 20 km on SH 1 to Waiwera which is signposted on the left.

Located on a small estuary and tucked in below the shelter of a pohutukawa-clad hillside, Waiwera has a small sandy beach and an extensive complex of thermal pools, private spa pools and waterslides that attract large numbers of visitors throughout the year. It is open in the evening and is the perfect place to stop for a snack and a relaxing soak towards the end of the day (you can even hire a swimsuit).
From Waiwera it is 40 km south to Auckland city on SH 1.

Visitors can see schools of many kinds of fish up close at Cape Rodney marine reserve.

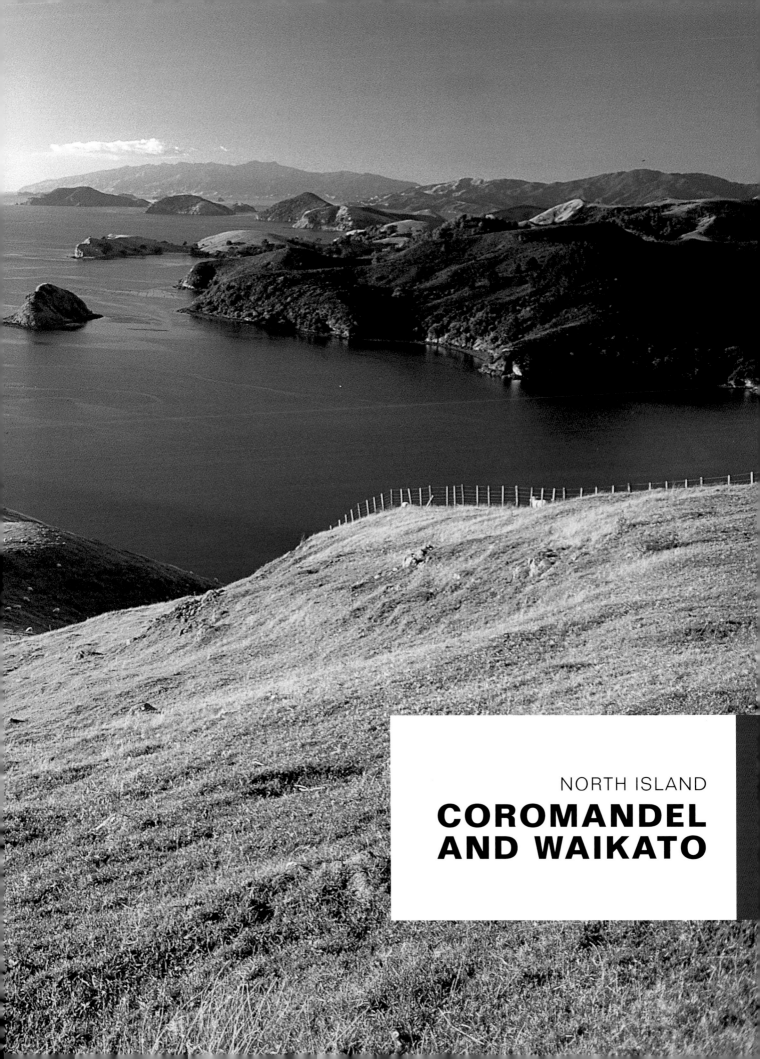

NORTH ISLAND
COROMANDEL AND WAIKATO

12 AROUND THE FIRTH OF THAMES

DRIVING TOUR ■ 135 KM ■ 5 HOURS ■ BIRDS AND AN OLD GOLD TOWN

There is something for everyone on this trip, including historic homesteads, botanical gardens, vintage planes, wildlife reserves, and hot mineral pools on the way to Thames, an old goldmining town at the base of the Coromandel Peninsula.

The Firth of Thames and the Hauraki Plains occupy a sunken block of the earth's crust bordered by two parallel fault lines about 220 km long. On the Coromandel side of the fault line the ranges are slowly being uplifted, while the trough that forms the Firth of Thames fills with sediment as fast as it sinks. This process has been taking place over millions of years and has determined the characteristics of the Hauraki Gulf.

Travellers can explore the eastern coastline of the gulf from Auckland all the way to Thames on a scenic coastal highway that runs from the Regional Botanic Gardens on Auckland's Southern Motorway out through the countryside to the western shores of the Firth of Thames, where thousands of migratory birds are the main occupants of the landscape.

1 AUCKLAND REGIONAL BOTANIC GARDENS

From central Auckland take the Southern Motorway and drive 24 km south to the Manurewa off-ramp. Turn left into Hill Road, and enter the Auckland Regional Botanic Gardens down the first driveway on the left.

The 40 ha Regional Botanic Gardens were established to create a park-like setting for both native and exotic species. Auckland's largest flower show is hosted in November each year on an adjacent site. Nearby, bush-walks run from the Botanic Gardens through the 122 ha Totara Park Reserve, which also has swimming pools, tennis courts and barbecue areas.

2 ARDMORE WARBIRDS

Continue on Hill Road 1 km and turn right down Stratford Road, continue straight ahead via the roundabout at the base of the hill on Alfriston Road and drive 3 km to the next roundabout. Turn right into Mill Road and drive 2 km, then turn left into Airfield Road at the next roundabout and drive 1 km to the Ardmore Aerodrome entrance which is on the right.

The airfield took its name from the neighbouring farm of pioneer settler John Henry Burnside and was originally an RNZAF pilot-

A Warbirds Douglas DC3 Dakota at Ardmore Airfield.

training school. Many Second World War-era buildings survive here. As well as being an important airfield for small commercial airlines and private operators, Ardmore hosts a number of classic 'warbird' aircraft, including a Catalina, DC3 and a number of Harvards. The societies that own these aircraft offer attractively priced flights to the public.

3 CLEVEDON

Continue along Airfield Road 1 km, turn right into Mullins Road and drive 1.5 km to the Papakura-Clevedon main highway. Turn left and drive 7 km to Clevedon. After 1 km you will pass St James Church (1893) on the right, one of the distinctive churches built under the direction of Bishop Selwyn. Many of the surrounding graves are older than the church which replaced the original one built in 1861 and destroyed by fire.

This worker's cottage was the original building on the McNichol property.

A small rural township with a strong sense of identity, Clevedon dates back to the 1850s when the first land titles were granted to a number of Scottish farmers and sawmillers. On North Road at the northern end of the Clevedon Township, All Souls' Church dates back to 1861 and was opened by Bishop Selwyn. The church features vertical kauri weatherboards, shingle roofing and a distinctive belfry. Soldiers were stationed here in 1863 while building the nearby Galloway Redoubt during the Waikato War. The old wooden post office in Clevedon dates back to 1909.

4 MCNICHOL HOMESTEAD

At the intersection in the middle of the Clevedon Township turn right onto Kawakawa Road and travel 1 km to McNichol Road on the right and the McNichol Homestead.

The Clevedon Historical Society maintains

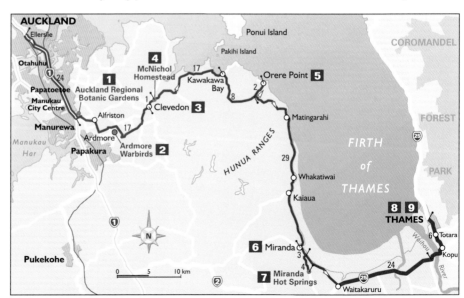

These oystercatchers are one of several bird species that call the mudflats around Miranda home. Some of the birds that share their feeding grounds are migrants escaping the Arctic winter.

the McNichol homestead (1878), a two-storeyed kauri building which is now a museum covering the pioneering days in the Clevedon area. Duncan and Marion McNichol sailed up the Wairoa River in 1852 to become the first European settlers in the Clevedon area and built the homestead on their farm to accommodate their nine children. In those days the river provided the fastest route to Auckland.

5 ORERE POINT
From the McNichol Homestead continue east 17 km on Kawakawa Road. You will pass the Clevedon Polo grounds on the left-hand side of the road. At Kawakawa Bay the road turns right and heads inland over the hill. Drive 8 km to the Orere Point turn-off on the left. A 2 km side road winds its way down to Orere Point on the coast.

A pleasant place to stop for a short break, Orere Point is an unusual beach made up of smooth round stones set below a line of cliffs bordering a small estuary.

6 MIRANDA
Return to the main road and travel 20 km east to Kaiaua where the store proudly proclaims itself to be New Zealand's best fish and chip shop. Continue east along the coast for another 9 km to Miranda.

The vast mudflats on the western shores of the Firth of Thames are a rich feeding ground for wading birds such as the pied oystercatcher, wrybill, banded dotterel and pied stilt, which come to feed on crustacea and aquatic worms.

During the Arctic winter, thousands of birds migrate from their ice-bound Northern Hemisphere homes to the warmer climes of New Zealand, including the bar-tailed godwit, the lesser knot, curlew, sandpiper, turnstone and red-necked stint. Many of these migrants gather at the mudflats of Miranda before making their return flight, and the wildlife reserve is a popular and easily accessible destination for birdwatchers. The Miranda Naturalists Trust has established a bird-watching hide on the shell-bank which is open for use by the public. The best viewing time is an hour or two before high tide when the birds move off the mudflats closer to the shore.

7 MIRANDA HOT SPRINGS
The hot springs are signposted from the coast road. Turn right 3 km south-east of Miranda and travel 4 km inland.

Here you will find the largest thermal pool in the Southern Hemisphere as well as smaller pools and spas. The complex is open daily.

8 THAMES
From the Miranda Hot Springs return to the coast road and continue south-east 6 km to Waitakaruru. Turn left onto SH 25 and continue east 18 km to the Waihou River, crossing the river on the long one-way bridge. Turn left at the next intersection and travel north 6 km to Thames.

This peaceful town once resounded to the thunder of 693 stamper batteries pounding quartz rock for the extraction of gold. The town began life as two separate settlements: Shortland, a small port on the Waihou River, and Grahamstown further north. The towns grew together and amalgamated in 1873, taking the name given to the area by Captain Cook when he visited in 1769 and compared the Waihou to London's famous river.

Gold was discovered in the area in 1867, and over the next few years additional fields were discovered at Coromandel, Kuaotunu and Karangahake. By the 1880s, logging was established in the nearby Kauaeranga Valley and north at Coroglen and Tairua.

The gold rush and the kauri timber trade briefly made Thames one of the biggest towns in New Zealand. Among the survivors of the town's original 80 hotels are the imposing Brian Boru and the elaborately verandahed Lady Bowen, which was fabricated on Auckland's North Shore and shipped to Thames in 1868.

The Hauraki Prospectors' Association operates a restored stamper battery on the Golden Crown mine site, and you can take a guided tour into an old mine tunnel and see the huge steam-operated pump that was built to remove water from the Queen of Beauty goldmine.

9 THE SCHOOL OF MINES
Corner of Brown and Cochran Streets.

The Thames School of Mines and Mineralogical Museum, which features a stamper battery, laboratory, furnace, assay room, lecture rooms and mineral collection, was built in 1886 and is crammed full of relics. The museum also includes New Zealand's first jailhouse.

The streets of Thames are lined with character-filled buildings like the Brian Boru Hotel.

13 COROMANDEL PENINSULA

DRIVING TOUR ■ 157 KM ■ 1 DAY ■ SPECTACULAR VIEWS AND TRANQUIL TOWNS

The Coromandel Peninsula, with its dramatic scenery and unrivalled beaches, has attracted to its small population many energetic individuals who have combined arts and crafts and alternative lifestyles with a keen desire to preserve this unique corner of New Zealand.

The mountain backbone of the peninsula is made up of rugged volcanic peaks and steep gorges shrouded in forest. The beautiful landscape and unspoiled beaches attract throngs of visitors over summer, but the further north one travels the more the crowds dwindle, and a sense of remoteness prevails.

A few remnants of kauri forest managed to survive heavy logging in the early nineteenth century followed by the devastation caused by thousands of miners who flooded into the area after the first gold strikes were made. Now the majestic kauri is slowly regenerating on the peninsula and the conservation-minded residents are fiercely protective of the natural environment yet also proud of the hard-working traditions and the historic relics left from the days of the pioneering settlers.

Beyond Manaia Harbour lie many small islands, with Great Barrier in the distance.

1 THE SQUARE KAURI

From Thames head north on SH 25 for 19 km along the coast via Whakatete, Ngarimu Bay, Thornton Bay and Te Puru to Tapu. At Tapu turn right and drive inland 7 km towards the hills to the east, past the Rapaura Water-gardens (worth a visit if you have time). The Square Kauri is signposted on the right.

The remarkable 1200-year-old Square Kauri stands majestically above the road on Tapu Hill. A short but steep track leads to a boardwalk around the base of the tree, with fine views back across the Firth of Thames.

2 MANAIA HARBOUR

Return to SH 25 and continue north for 25 km via Te Mata to Manaia.

On this road heading north on the western side of the Coromandel Peninsula you will have spectacular views from up on the hills before you make the descent to the small settlement of Manaia. From a lookout point at Manaia you can gaze across the harbour and out to the islands off the coast.

3 WAIAU KAURI GROVE

Continue on SH 25 for 7 km to the Route 309 turn-off to Whitianga, on the right side of the road. Follow Route 309, a stretch of winding gravel road that crosses the peninsula, for 5 km to the Waiau Kauri Grove on the left side of the road.

A short walking track off Route 309 leads into the Waiau Kauri Grove, with boardwalks around splendid stands of kauri overlooking a small forest stream.

4 COROMANDEL

Return to SH 25 and continue north 4 km to the Coromandel township.

The town was named after HMS *Coromandel*, which visited the harbour in 1820

Magnificent kauri in Waiau Kauri Grove.

The unspoiled beauty of New Chums Beach, reached by a short walk around the headland from Whangapoua, is one of the Coromandel's hidden treasures.

to pick up a load of kauri spars. The timber trade was well established by the 1830s, but it was the gold rush of the 1850s that left its mark on the town's history. Charles Ring made the first gold strike in 1852, but fever was short-lived as it was found that the gold had to be dug out of rock with picks and shovels. The search for easier-won alluvial gold continued until 1869, when a large strike was made on Tokatea Hill and the town boomed.

Today Coromandel is a tranquil, sprawling little seaside town with some charming old buildings that reflect its prosperity during the goldmining era. The Coromandel Mining and Historic Museum can be visited on Rings Road, along with the Coromandel Stamper Battery, used to crush gold-bearing ore.

5 DRIVING CREEK RAILWAY
Travel 3 km north of Coromandel to the Driving Creek Railway.

When Barry Brickell set up his pottery at Driving Creek in 1974, he built a railway to carry clay down from the hills, as well as wood to fuel his kilns. The scenic 5 km line through the bush features two spirals, four high trestle bridges and two tunnels, and the train makes the 1-hour return trip loaded with tourists as well as raw materials. The Driving Creek Railway operates daily at 10.15 am and 2 pm with additional trips in summer.

6 WHANGAPOUA
Return to Coromandel township and continue east on SH 25 for 13 km Te Rerenga. Turn left and drive 4 km to Whangapoua Beach.

A sweeping sandy surf beach fronts the expansive Whangapoua Harbour, which once served as a timber port. A 2-hour round-trip walk around the point through pohutukawa and nikau palms takes you to Wainuiototo Bay (New Chums Beach), one of the finest yet least-known beaches in the country. There, jointed columns of lava rock framed by crystal white sands and the green of the forest stretch to the shoreline.

7 OPITO
Return to Te Rerenga on SH 25 and continue east 16 km on the sealed road to the beach in the old goldmining area of Kuaotunu where the main road branches off south to Whitianga. The road is sealed to this point.

Turn left at the junction and follow the 9 km unsealed road to the east over the Black Jack Hill to make the winding descent to Otama and Opito Bay.

Opito is an idyllic beach resort with views across to the Mercury Islands, five of which are nature reserves harbouring a diverse collection of rare insects and lizards. The coastline between Otama and Opito Bay is among the most beautiful locations on the Coromandel Peninsula. You can walk along the beach onto the old Maori pa site on the headlands for views along the coast which feature the distinctive weather-sculptured rock formations found along this east coast of the peninsula.

On many Coromandel beaches gemstones such as beach agates, reddish-coloured cornelian and the opaque quartz known as jasper can be found.

8 WHITIANGA
Return to Kuaotunu and follow SH 25 which winds south 17 km over the hills to Whitianga via Buffalo Beach, named after the ship Buffalo, which was wrecked here in 1840.

Captain James Cook anchored the *Endeavour* in Mercury Bay in 1769, claiming possession of New Zealand in the name of King George III. The main purpose of his journey was to observe the transit of the planet Mercury; a cairn on Shakespeare Cliff commemorates his visit. Whitianga was a centre for the timber trade in the 1830s, with numerous ships sailing to Mercury Bay to take on kauri spars: more than 150 million metres of timber was exported from Whitianga over a period of 60 years.

Today, tourism and fishing are the area's major attractions. A ferry takes pedestrians from the town wharf across to an old stone wharf built in 1837 on the Cooks Beach side of the harbour. Whitianga is a big-game fishing base for marlin, mako and thresher sharks. The jaws of a 1350 kg white pointer caught in 1959 hang in the Whitianga Museum which is housed in an old dairy factory on the Esplanade.

Historic Whitianga in Mercury Bay offers plenty of fascinating sightseeing, by ferry, car, on foot or in horse-drawn style.

14 DOWN THE COAST TO TAURANGA

DRIVING TOUR ■ 240 KM ■ 1 DAY ■ SENSATIONAL SURFING AND CAFÉ CULTURE

This stretch of coastline boasts some of New Zealand's most famous beaches, where hot water bubbles from the sand, people come from all over the world to surf, and the variety of seascapes is awe-inspiring.

Mercury Bay was named by Captain Cook in 1769 when he visited the bay to observe the transit of the planet Mercury. The region was well populated by Maori, who called the area Te-Whitianga-a-Kupe (the crossing point of Kupe), referring to the landing made here by the great Polynesian explorer Kupe more than 1000 years ago. Moa, now-extinct huge flightless birds, were abundant on the Coromandel Peninsula, and evidence from archaeological sites indicates that moa-hunters once lived in the area.

The absence of a sand bar made Mercury Bay one of the most accessible anchorages on the coast, and Whitianga developed into a thriving timber port. The history of the region is embedded in the old buildings and towns on the coast, the gold mines at Waihi and the colonial settlement at Tauranga that has become the economic hub of the Bay of Plenty with its thriving port and city.

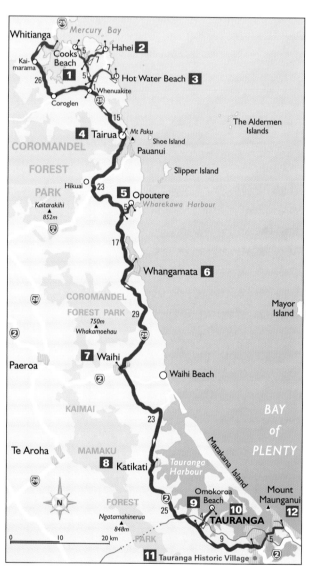

Headstones tell poignant stories in the settlers' graveyard above Cooks Beach.

1 COOKS BEACH

From Whitianga head south-west on SH 25 for 7 km to Kaimarama then continue south for 11 km to Coroglen. This tiny town once had a 10,000-tonne export trade in kauri gum. Originally known as Gum-town, it was renamed Coroglen, after a successful race-horse, in 1922. Continue east on SH 25 for 8 km to Whenuakite and take the turn-off to the left signposted to Hot Water Beach, Hahei and Cooks Beach. Drive east 1 km to the Cooks Beach turn-off on the left and continue 5 km to the next intersection with the Hahei Road, turn left and drive 5 km to Cooks Beach.

This is a glorious stretch of coastline that no visitor should miss. At Cooks Beach you

can drive up onto Shakespeare Cliff, where a short track leads to a lookout point across Mercury Bay, before continuing to the Ferry Landing, said to be New Zealand's oldest wharf. On the hillside above the landing is an old cemetery with headstones dating back to the early days of the settlement.

2 HAHEI

Return 5 km to the Hahei turn-off and turn left to Hahei 7 km to the east.

The white-sand beach at Hahei is one of the best on the Coromandel Peninsula. On the northern side of this small beach resort a road climbs onto the headland, providing views across Mercury Bay. Protected as part of a marine park, the waters off the bay and

its outlying islands are excellent for diving and snorkelling.

3 HOT WATER BEACH

Drive 7 km back to the Hahei turn-off and turn left. Continue 5 km to the Cooks Beach turn-off and turn left onto the road sign-posted to Hot Water Beach. It is a 7 km drive to the coast and the last stretch of road is unsealed, but don't let that stop you from visiting this unique beach.

This spot takes its name from the hot water that seeps through the sand near a pro-minent rock outcrop. At low tide each day, visitors to the beach can dig mineral bathing pools in the sand. Even after the tide has covered the site, you can feel the hot water

At Hot Water Beach you can dig your own thermal pool in the sand.

Tauranga Historic Village.

developments, including the invention of the cyanide extraction process, enabled the area to produce over £1 million worth of bullion. Up to 1400 tonnes of gold- and silver-bearing ore were crushed daily, and the Martha Mine (1881–1953) became the most productive in the country. The concrete shell of a pumphouse at the mine remains as a monument to Waihi's golden past.

The legacy of the gold era remains in the town's classic hotels and in the Waihi Arts Centre and Museum on Kenny Street, which features a number of working exhibits. The Goldfields Steam Train Society operates trains daily on a restored 8 km stretch of line between Waihi and Waikino. Waikino is the site of the Victoria and Albert Battery, the second-largest stamping battery in the world. It was here that 1500 men worked the 20 stampers that crushed the ore from the Martha Mine in Waihi.

when you dig your toes into the sand. At the southern end of the beach huge agaves grow.

4 TAIRUA
Return 8 km to SH 25, turn left and head south 15 km to Tairua.

With its harbour and excellent ocean beach framed by the twin volcanic peaks of Mt Paku, Tairua is a popular tourist resort. In the nineteenth century it was a centre for the timber trade. Earthworks are visible on the slopes of a pa site on Mt Paku, and the walk to the 178 m summit offers fine views across the harbour towards Pauanui, a luxuriously developed resort and marina.

5 OPOUTERE
Continue south 23 km on SH 25 via Hikuai to the Opoutere turn-off. Turn left and head east 5 km to Opoutere on the coast.

From this beautiful beach on the Wharekawa Harbour you can take a 15-minute walk to the Wharekawa Wildlife Refuge, a breeding ground for the endangered New Zealand dotterel and the variable oystercatcher.

6 WHANGAMATA
Return to SH 25, turn left and continue south 17 km to Whangamata.

Whangamata is famous for its 4 km stretch of surf beach, with an excellent break near the bar. Non-surfing visitors can enjoy its interesting shopping centre and cafés.

7 WAIHI
Drive 29 km south from Whangamata to Waihi on SH 25. Waihi Beach, a popular holiday and surfing location, is 11 km east of Waihi township.

The discovery of gold near Waihi in the 1870s attracted miners from California and New South Wales, with production reaching its peak in the early 1900s. Technological

8 KATIKATI
From Waihi township drive south on SH 2 for 23 km to Katikati. The road passes through the Athenree Gorge and provides views of Bowentown and the prominent terraced slopes of Te Kura a Mai, an ancient Maori pa site overlooking Matakana Island.

Founded by Irish settlers in 1875, Katikati has become a horticultural centre supporting kiwifruit and citrus orchards. The town is gradually becoming an open-air art gallery, with many of its buildings adorned with murals. The Morton Estate winery, 8 km south of the town, is open for tours and winetasting.

9 OMOKOROA BEACH
From Katikati head south on SH 2 for 25 km to the Omokoroa Beach turn-off, turn left and continue 4 km to Omokoroa Beach.

Located on a promontory that protrudes into Tauranga Harbour, Omokoroa has a regular ferry service across to Matakana Island. Covered mainly in pine forest and with a 24 km stretch of pristine beach, this island is a popular location for surfing and windsurfing.

10 TAURANGA
Return to SH 2 and continue south for 9 km to Tauranga.

European traders came

to Tauranga in the early 1830s, and by 1835 a mission station had been established. The Elms on Mission Street, once the residence of Archdeacon Alfred Brown, preserves period furnishings. Brown's missionary work was disrupted in 1864 when government troops suffered heavy casualties in a clash with Maori at Gate Pa on the outskirts of Tauranga.

St George's Church (1900) stands on the battle site, which is now a reserve. In the centre of Tauranga you will find a military cemetery and the earthworks of the Monmouth Redoubt, with some of its guns still in position on the parapets.

11 TAURANGA HISTORIC VILLAGE
Located on Seventeenth Avenue.

This fascinating museum captures the spirit of a New Zealand town at the turn of the century. Exhibits include a number of colonial buildings, an 1877 steam locomotive, an old tugboat, farming equipment and other vintage vehicles.

12 MOUNT MAUNGANUI
5 km from Tauranga, accessible via the Waikareo Expressway across the harbour bridge, or across a causeway on the southern end of the harbour.

With an excellent surf beach that stretches south to Papamoa, Mount Maunganui is a popular holiday resort on a long peninsula reaching out into Tauranga Harbour. The mount itself is a 232 m volcanic cone, the summit of which can be reached in an hour on a well-graded track that runs from Adams Avenue on the western side of the peninsula. An easier track runs around the base of the mount. Also on Adams Avenue is a complex of heated saltwater pools.

The glorious sweeping beach at 'the Mount'.

15 SOUTH TO HAMILTON

DRIVING TOUR ■ 168 KM ■ 5 HOURS ■ MILITARY HISTORY AND MAORI HERITAGE

The area south of Auckland is steeped in history, much of it relating to nineteeth-century military activity in the area when the strong and proud Waikato Maori resisted encroaching British settlement.

When Auckland was in the throes of becoming established in the mid-1800s, settlements to the south were created as a defensive barrier against the threat of hostile Waikato Maori tribes. Former Imperial soldiers were recruited and brought to Auckland, where they were granted land in return for undertaking military duties. These 'Fencible' settlements included Onehunga, Otahuhu, Panmure and Howick, where the soldiers divided their time between growing crops to sell in the city and preparing to defend it from attack. The history of the area is proudly preserved, with many restored historic buildings, museums and landmarks.

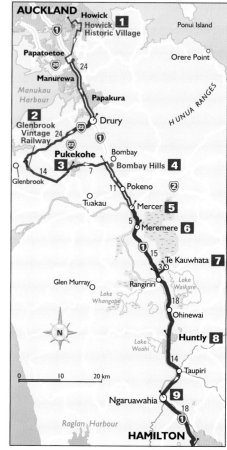

1 HOWICK HISTORIC VILLAGE

Head south from central Auckland on SH 1, take the South Eastern Highway off-ramp and follow South Eastern Highway over the Waipuna Bridge for about 3 km. Turn left into Ti Rakau Drive, then right at the next traffic lights into Pakuranga Road and travel 3 km. The Howick Historic Village in Bells Road is signposted on the right.

During the early days of Auckland's development Howick was a small Fencible settlement at the end of a long ride by horse and cart on dirt roads. The town was populated by pensioned-off British soldiers and their families who had been shipped out to New Zealand to form a defence force while also farming smallholdings. The Fencibles were promised four-roomed cottages, to be ready for them on arrival, but instead the 804 new arrivals were crammed into two long sheds that had been hastily built in four days. Most of the soldiers preferred to live in thatched raupo (reed) huts while their wooden cottages were being built.

Howick Historic Village has a number of original buildings from the era, including New Zealand's oldest courthouse and schoolhouse, 14 Fencible cottages, and a two-storeyed officer's home, all of which have been faithfully restored. On the third Sunday of each month fully costumed historical interpreters play the roles of Fencible women, soldiers and settlers.

2 GLENBROOK VINTAGE RAILWAY

Continue east on Pakuranga Road 1 km, turn right into Aviemore Drive and travel south for 2 km. Turn left at the roundabout into Cascades Road, then right at the next roundabout into Botany Road, drive 2 km south into Te Irirangi Drive and continue 7 km to Great South Road. Turn left and drive 1 km to the southern motorway on-ramp signposted on the left. Drive south on SH 1 for 9 km to Drury and turn right onto SH 22 heading west 7 km to the next major intersection. Take the Waiuku turn-off to the right onto Glenbrook Road and travel 8 km to

Patumahoe then continue 6 km towards Waiuku. The Glenbrook turn-off is signposted to the left and it is another 3 km to the Glenbrook Vintage Railway.

On Sundays and public holidays, steam enthusiasts can ride on 70-year-old carriages hauled by one of the pre-1914 locomotives along the 12 km line at Glenbrook. The rides depart from a restored station and return after visiting workshops where a number of locomotives are under restoration.

Directly adjacent to the railway is Ray Skinner's petting zoo with a range of animals, including deer, goats, Arabian horses and a llama, many of which can be hand-fed.

3 PUKEKOHE

From the Glenbrook Railway continue south 2 km, turn right onto Waiuku Road and drive east 12 km to Pukekohe.

The name Pukekohe means 'hill of kaikohe', the trees which once covered the

A sleek locomotive chuffs up the line at the Glenbrook Vintage Railway.

The coal-fired Huntly Power Station generates electricity that is fed into the national grid.

distinctive hill in the centre of this market-gardening area. The Pioneer Memorial Cottage in Roulston Park was built in 1859. The Presbyterian church on the road to Bombay dates back to 1862 and bears bullet holes from a skirmish when it was used as a garrison by 17 settlers who managed to fight off a war party of 200 Maori.

4 BOMBAY HILLS
From Pukekohe take Pukekohe East Road and travel 7 km to the Bombay Hills to rejoin SH 1 heading south.

The distinctive rich red soils in this area are covered by extensive market gardens. The original settlement, known as Williamsons Clearing, was located on a military road cut through puriri forest between Drury and Pokeno, and was the scene of the opening skirmish in the Waikato War in 1862. The township was renamed Bombay after the ship that brought settlers to the area in 1863.

5 MERCER
Head south on SH 1 for 11 km to Mercer. The motorway bypasses the small township of Pokeno, the site of the first military headquarters developed during the Waikato campaign.

Just behind the group of shops at Mercer on the right off SH 1, near a small bridge over the Waikato River, stands a gun turret from the gunboat *Pioneer*, mounted as a memorial to those lost in Waikato battles.

6 MEREMERE
Continue south 5 km on SH 1 to Meremere.

The Waikato War began in earnest when British troops crossed the Mangatawhiri River in July 1863, the first major engagement taking place at Meremere. A Maori force held up the British from fortified positions for almost three months but was forced to retreat when numerous troops from armed steamers landed further upriver. Today the focal point of the area is the Champion Dragway, one of the main venues for drag racing in New Zealand.

7 TE KAUWHATA
Continue south 15 km on SH 1 and take the turn-off on the left to Te Kauwhata. It is 3 km to the township heading east.

Te Kauwhata is the home of the Rangiriri Battle Site Heritage Centre, dedicated to the history of the Waikato War. You can explore the old cemetery, battleground and the redoubt where a small group of Maori warriors made a stand against 1500 British troops in 1863. A vineyard near the town offers tours and winetasting.

8 HUNTLY
From Te Kauwhata return to SH 1 and continue 18 km south to Huntly. The main highway passes the old white hotel on the left at Rangiriri which has been a landmark on the main road south for years and is a focal point for the local community.

Huntly is a coal-mining town and the location of the Huntly Power Station, which operates a 2-hour guided tour for groups by appointment. The Waikato Coalfields Museum is open daily at Harlock Place, while 2 km south of town is a native bush trail, the Hakarimata Walkway.

9 NGARUAWAHIA
Continue 14 km south from Huntly on SH 1 to Ngaruawahia. Approximately 3 km past Huntly is Mt Taupiri, the sacred mountain of a number of Waikato tribes. The crest of a spur on the side of the mountain is the burial place of Maori kings and Tainui chiefs.

The home of the Maori Queen, Te Arikinui Dame Te Atairangikaahu, Ngaruwahia is also the location of the impressive Turangawaewae Marae, which includes a number of historic buildings and canoes important to the river tribes. The marae is not open to the public but can be viewed from River Road, to the left off the main highway.
It is 18 km south on SH 1 to Hamilton.

WAIKATO RIVER

The Waikato is the longest river in New Zealand, flowing 425 km from the icy slopes of Mt Ruapehu on the volcanic plateau, passing through forest and steamy thermal areas, thundering down waterfalls, then making a more placid journey through farmland on its way west to the Tasman Sea.

For Maori the Waikato was a well-used travel route for small hunting canoes and large war canoes. During the nineteenth-century wars British gunboats and troop carriers steamed up the waterway and its banks became the scene of some of the fiercest battles.

One of Hamilton's arched bridges spanning the Waikato River.

16 HAMILTON AND ITS WEST COAST

DRIVING TOUR ■ 223 KM ■ 1 DAY ■ SURF BEACHES AND WATERFALLS

Hamilton city, on the mighty Waikato River, offers a range of cultural and historic sightseeing and is also within easy reach of famous surfing beaches, hot springs and one of the best zoos in the country.

The Maori had thousands of hectares of land in the Waikato region under cultivation in pre-European times. Missionaries arrived in the 1830s, introducing European farming methods, and by the 1840s Waikato Maori were trading produce with settlers in Auckland. In the 1860s the 'King Movement' grew from the desire to have a Maori leader who would have a status equivalent to the British Crown when dealing with land-hungry Europeans. The British sent a fleet of gunboats up the Waikato River in 1863 to put down what they regarded as the threat posed by the King Movement. The Waikato War lasted until 1864, when the Maori were forced to retreat south into what is now known as the King Country.

The town of Hamilton was founded immediately after the campaign, with soldiers settled on plots of confiscated land and redoubts constructed at East and West Hamilton. Today the Waikato is one of the world's richest dairy-farming areas and Hamilton is New Zealand's fifth-largest city.

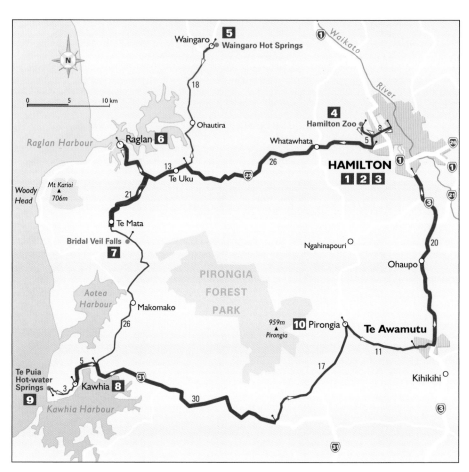

1 HAMILTON

The Waikato Militia were the early occupants of the town that sprang up on the site of an abandoned Maori village and took its name from Captain John Hamilton, RN, the commander of HMS *Esk* who was killed in the fighting at Gate Pa on the outskirts of Tauranga. The site where the first settlers landed is marked on the riverbank, and the old paddle-steamer that carried them has been recovered from the river for restoration. The *Rangiriri* was built in Sydney, shipped to New Zealand in sections and assembled at Port Waikato.

Hamilton Gardens on Cobham Drive cover 58 ha, including English, Chinese and Japanese theme gardens. The Waikato Museum of Art and History on the corner of Victoria and Grantham Streets features a range of exhibits including *Te Winika*, a waka more than 150 years old which was used on the Waikato River before the arrival of Europeans. The museum also holds an impressive collection of Maori wood-carvings, many of which were recovered from swamps in the area.

2 HAMILTON'S HISTORIC HOMES

Hamilton has a number of well-preserved colonial buildings. Beale House (1872) was the home of a prominent Hamilton doctor, and the homestead on the Rukuhia Estate also dates back to 1872. An old stone house on Hood Street was built in 1878, and Hockin House (1893) is now the premises of the Waikato Historic Society. A number of interesting commercial buildings from the 1870s and 1880s can be seen on Victoria Street, including the 1878 Bank of New Zealand. The Woodlands Estate manager's house at Gordonton, 18 km north-east of Hamilton, was once the headquarters of the Waikato Land Association, the organisation responsible for developing the surrounding swamplands. An illustrated guide to these and other historic buildings is available from the Hamilton Visitor Centre on the corner of Anglesea and Bryce Streets.

3 MV *WAIPA DELTA*

This vessel, which came into service in 1877, now takes visitors on cruises on the Waikato River from Hamilton's Memorial Park. The river, with its classic bridges and picturesque tree-lined banks, passes through the centre of the city and was the main transport link for Hamilton until the railway was established in 1878.

4 HAMILTON ZOO

From Hamilton central, head west 8 km via Forest Lake Road, which becomes Ellicott Road, turn right into Newcastle Road and continue straight ahead on Brymer Road to reach the Hamilton Zoo.

This excellent zoo emphasises strong conservation themes, with New Zealand's largest walk-through aviary, a Waikato wetlands area and a rainforest exhibit.

5 WAINGARO HOT SPRINGS

From the zoo return via Brymer and Newcastle Roads to the next T-junction, turn right and drive west on SH 23 towards Raglan for 26 km. Take the turn to the right signposted to the Waingaro Hot Springs. This road heads north 12 km to Ohautira and continues a further 6 km north to Waingaro.

A welcome stopping place for weary travellers, there are three thermal mineral pools, private spa pools and giant waterslides at Waingaro.

6 RAGLAN

Return south 18 km to SH 23, turn right and drive west 13 km to Raglan.

Raglan beach is world famous for its left-hand surf break, reputed to be the longest in the world. The 1966 film *Endless Summer* was filmed at Manu Bay, where the swell from the Tasman Sea meets the coastline at an angle, creating long uniform waves that can produce incredible surfboard rides lasting up to 10 minutes.

7 BRIDAL VEIL FALLS

Return east 7 km towards Te Uku, take the turn-off right to Te Mata and drive south 14 km to the Bridal Veil Falls.

A 20-minute walk descends to the base of the Bridal Veil Falls, which plummet over a 50 m cliff formed from an enormous slab of columnar basalt.

8 KAWHIA

Continue south for 26 km on an unsealed road via Makomako to rejoin SH 31 just east of Kawhia. Turn right and drive 5 km on SH 31 to Kawhia.

The countryside here is dotted with pa sites, and the history of Kawhia is intertwined with famous names from Maori history, including Pourewa, a Ngati Mahanga chief, the warrior Te Rauparaha, who was born at Kawhia in 1820, and King Tawhiao, whose final battle with settlers took place here. Kawhia is said to have been the final destination of the *Tainui* canoe, which brought Waikato ancestors from Hawaiki in the great migration. The canoe's resting place is the site of the Maketu Marae, and an ancient

Mt Karioi dominates the skyline west of Raglan.

pohutukawa tree is revered as its mooring place.

9 TE PUIA HOT-WATER SPRINGS

Drive 3 km west from Kawhia township to the ocean beach.

With a bit of luck or local knowledge you will find Te Puia hot-water springs on the beach 2 hours either side of low tide. The beach has a very gentle slope and the tide goes out a long way past the springs, so you can build elaborate hot pools and relax in them for a few hours before the sea overwhelms your work.

10 PIRONGIA

Return to Kawhia, head east on SH 31 and drive 30 km across the hills to the Pirongia turn-off. Turn left and head north-east 17 km

to Pirongia. You will get some of the best views of the Kawhia Harbour as you drive out over the hills.

Pirongia was originally a military settlement, founded in 1864. Just north of the township, at Matakitaki, a plaque on the roadside marks the scene of a battle between the musket-armed Nga Puhi and the traditionally armed Waikato tribes, who were decimated by their opponents in 1822. Pirongia was garrisoned by the Armed Constabulary during the Te Kooti campaigns. Among the historic buildings in the township is the public library, built as a schoolroom in 1864 and taken over by the local Mechanics Institute in 1871.

From Pirongia head east 11 km to Te Awamutu, then take SH 3 and travel north for 20 km back to Hamilton.

Bridal Veil Falls.

Sheep patiently await shearing on a farm near Kawhia.

17 THE HAURAKI PLAINS

DRIVING TOUR ■ 249 KM ■ 1 DAY ■ QUAINT MUSEUMS, HOT POOLS, GEMSTONES

Once covered in extensive stands of kahikatea, New Zealand's tallest-growing tree, the Hauraki Plains are criss-crossed by scenic highways and back roads which lead to historic towns and intriguing little museums run by local enthusiasts.

In the nineteenth century much of the low-lying Hauraki Plains was a swampy wilderness, choked with fern and scrub, where soldiers turned farmers struggled on muddy smallholdings to win a living. Then the ambitious Josiah Firth acquired huge tracts of land and began to transform the district. He cleared the scrub, drained the swamps, built windmills to lift water from the boggiest areas, freed the Waihou River of snags, and pushed through roads. At a time when farming relied largely on labour he used an impressive array of machinery on his land. The sodden plains began to turn green.

Today the Hauraki Plains are a richly productive area with prosperous picture-book farms, one of the country's most concentrated populations of sleek dairy cows, luxuriant orchards, and pleasant rural towns.

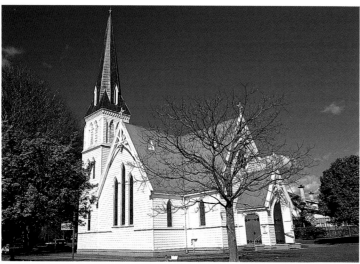
St Andrew's Church, Cambridge.

1 CAMBRIDGE
From Hamilton, head south-east on SH 1 for 24 km to Cambridge.

Cambridge was founded as a military settlement in 1864 on the banks of the Waikato River at the furthest navigable point for the British gunboats in operation on the river. During the Waikato Land Wars the Cambridge Redoubt was manned by 1000 British troops, many of whom stayed in the area at the end of the fighting after they were granted land that laid the framework for the developing town.

With its village green (Victoria Square) and tree-lined streets, Cambridge remains very English in its appearance. Among the notable buildings on the main road are the old brick water tower, two hotels, a courthouse, post office and town hall as well as the elegant wooden St Andrew's Church which dates back to 1881.

2 KARAPIRO
Continue south-east from Cambridge 6 km on SH 1 to Karapiro. On the right there is a car park and viewing area across the lake and dam as well as access to the dam and power station.

Regarded as one of the finest rowing venues in the world, Lake Karapiro is also used for sailing, water skiing and powerboat racing. The lake is 8 sq km in area and was formed by the construction of the Karapiro Dam. You can walk across the dam and visit the powerhouse which was completed in 1947. The powerhouse has three turbines together generating 90,000 kW.

3 MATAMATA
Continue south-east on SH 1 for 14 km from Lake Karapiro to the intersection with SH 29, turn left and travel north-east 13 km to the next major junction. Turn left onto SH 27 and travel 10 km north to Matamata.

Matamata was the name of a Maori pa near Waharoa. Europeans arrived in the area around 1830 to trade for flax, and in 1833 a mission station was opened. This was abandoned when war broke out, but by 1865 a settler, Josiah Firth, had formed a good relationship with the Maori chief Wiremu Tamihana. Firth's land purchases grew to 22,000 ha by 1884 and his estate laid the foundations for the town, which was sub-divided by the Crown in 1904. Tours operate to a local farm, transformed into 'Hobbiton' for the *Lord of the Rings* film trilogy.

4 FIRTH TOWER
Driving north into Matamata on SH 27, turn right at the roundabout on the edge of the town and head south-east down the main street. Turn left and take the road signposted to the Okauia Hot Pools and drive north-east

Josiah Firth's grand ideas included a defensive tower on his land.

3 km to the Firth Tower which is on the right.

Built by Josiah Firth, the Auckland entrepreneur who founded Matamata, the Firth Tower was erected in 1881 at a time when Maori and Europeans were working together to drain the swampland that restricted farm development on the Hauraki Plains. Other nearby restored historic buildings include a schoolhouse built in 1893, a church, gaol, post office, worker's cottage and machinery barn. The area is now a historical reserve and the buildings house displays that trace the history of Matamata.

5 OPAL HOT SPRINGS
Take the turn to the right immediately after the Firth Tower and head east 4 km to the Opal Hot Springs.

This complex of thermal baths and hot springs is based around the historic Ramaroa Pool, renowned for its curative properties.

6 WAIRERE FALLS
Continue north on Old Te Aroha Road for 3 km, turn right into Goodwins Road and drive 1 km to the Wairere Falls Track.

The spectacular 150 m Wairere Falls are visible from many points on the Hauraki Plains especially after heavy rainfall. For a closer look at this impressive two-tiered waterfall you can venture 30 minutes from the road end on a well-formed track that climbs through forest to a lookout near the base of the falls. The track continues to the top of the falls for views across the plains.

7 TE AROHA
Return to Old Te Aroha Road and continue north for 6 km to Gordon, then keep heading north for another 20 km on this scenic backroad to Te Aroha. Although narrow, the road is in good condition and carries little traffic, passing through lush green farmland beneath the towering volcanic ramparts of the forest-clad Kaimai Range.

Te Aroha was founded in 1880 and developed by the government as a tourist resort because of its thermal springs. In the Domain on Whitaker Street a number of buildings and small kiosks survive from this era. The original bath house (1898) houses a museum which has exhibits on mining and the agricultural development of the area. The Hot Soda Water Baths are also in the Domain. The Mokena geyser is claimed to be the only hot soda-water geyser in the world and is usually active every half hour, spurting to 3.5 m.

In St Mark's Church on Kenrick Street is the oldest organ in the country, a 1712 Renatus Harris instrument made in England by John Snelzer and shipped to New Zealand in 1927.

8 PAEROA
From Te Aroha take SH 26 and head north for 21 km to Paeroa.

This town's name is immortalised in the famous New Zealand beverage Lemon and Paeroa, and a huge replica bottle of the soft drink stands proudly on the main street. On the Ohinemuri and Waihou Rivers, Paeroa was a busy port servicing the nearby goldfields. An old depot of the Northern Steamship Company to the north-west of the town on the left side of the road has been converted into a maritime museum, while nearby a stone memorial commemorates the first European settlement of the district.

9 WILDERNESS GEMS
From Paeroa take SH 2, drive 24 km north-west towards Ngatea and turn right into River Road just before the township.

Wilderness Gems exhibits a huge and fascinating array of gemstones, from the original uncut rocks to finely crafted jewellery, including New Zealand jade.

10 MORRINSVILLE
Continue west on SH 2 for 11 km then turn left onto SH 27 and head south for 49 km to the junction with SH 26. Turn right onto SH 26 and drive south-west 8 km to Morrinsville.

East of Hamilton, lowland plains stretch towards the Piako and Waihou Rivers. Maori in this area had affiliations with Waikato tribes and supported the King Movement. At Rukumoana Pa, near Morrinsville, a marble statue of Mahuta, the third Maori King, stands next to the meeting house. In Morrinsville township a museum on the corner of Lorne and Anderson Streets displays items relating to the Maori and European history of the district, including a large Maori canoe. An 1870s cottage that was moved from its original farm location has been restored and is part of the museum.

From Morrinsville it is 32 km south-west on SH 26 to return to Hamilton.

The Karapiro Dam was built in 1947 to harness the Waikato River. The opening of the dam's spillway gates gives a thrilling impression of the power of this mighty resource.

ROTORUA AND THE CENTRAL PLATEAU

18 IN AND AROUND ROTORUA

DRIVING TOUR ■ 55 KM ■ 5 HOURS ■ MAORI CRAFT, MAZES AND FARM SHOWS

There is so much to do and see in Rotorua that it can be hard to choose. This trip packs into a few hours an excitingly diverse range of some of the area's most fascinating sights and experiences.

In an area steeped in Maori legend and history, it is not surprising that Rotorua has its own Romeo and Juliet story. Hinemoa, a girl of high birth, loved Tutanekai who lived on Mokoia Island, but was forbidden by her family to marry him. Every evening she sat forlornly on a rock on the edge of the lake listening to the sound of his flute lilting across the water until one night she decided to join him. With the aid of floating gourds she swam all the way to the island and was reunited with her lover. In the face of such passion their families relented and the couple lived happily.

Maori legends also tell of the coming of the people from the Arawa, one of the canoes said to have brought the first settlers from the Hawaiki homeland many centuries ago. The Arawa tohunga (priest) Ngatoroirangi is credited with introducing volcanic activity to the region by praying to the gods to keep him warm in the new land.

Rotorua is one of the best-known thermal areas in the world. It was developed as a spa in the early 1900s and has retained many of the old buildings from the period which, combined with more modern attractions, make this one of the main tourism centres in the North Island.

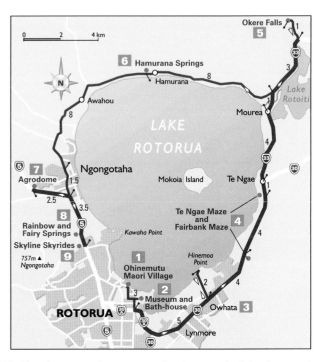

1 OHINEMUTU MAORI VILLAGE
The trip starts on Lake Road at the Ohinemutu Village on Rotorua's lakefront.

Some of the finest examples of nineteenth-century Maori wood-carving can be found in the Ohinemutu Maori Village. This was the original Maori settlement in the Rotorua district. Its Tudor-style St Faith's Church was built in 1910 and has a traditional Maori interior featuring carvings and tukutuku woven panels. A bust of Queen Victoria, outside the church, was given to Te Arawa in recognition of their services to the Crown during the wars of the 1860s. Tamatekapua, built in 1878, is the meeting house of Ngati Whakaue, a subtribe of Te Arawa. Some of its carvings are older than the meeting house itself, dating back to 1800.

2 MUSEUM AND BATH-HOUSE
Continue east along Lake Road into Tutanekai Street and take the third street on the right, which is Arawa Street. Continue east across Fenton Street. The entrance to the Government Gardens and Bath-house is straight ahead. It is 2 km from the Ohinemutu Maori Village.

The original Tudor-style bath-house was built in 1906–07 as part of a government plan to develop Rotorua as a spa. Featuring classical marble statues in its foyer, the building was equipped with up-to-date balneological equipment, massage rooms and thermal pools, and operated until the 1920s, much of it recently restored. The building also houses a museum with exhibits tracing the history of the Te Arawa Maori, the development of Rotorua as a spa town and the effects of the Tarawera eruption of 1886. You can walk through the nearby Government Gardens on the lakeshore and visit the Orchid Gardens which feature displays of ferns and a variety of exotic plants as well as orchids. Also within walking distance are the Polynesian Pools with hot springs and mineral pools, and the recently reopened Blue Baths.

3 OWHATA
Return down Arawa Street and turn first left into Fenton Street, continuing south to take the fifth turn on the left into Amohau Street. Continue east on Amohau Street, which becomes Te Ngae Road, head east out of Rotorua on SH 30 for 5 km to Owhata Road on the left and travel 2 km to Hinemoa Point.

Here, on the southern shoreline of Lake Rotorua, is Hinemoa Rock on which the legendary maiden sat while listening to the music of her lover Tutanekai drifting across the water from Mokoia Island. At Owhata you will also find an interesting Maori meeting house and a quaint little church.

4 TE NGAE 3-D MAZE
Return to SH 30 and continue north-east to Te Ngae. Te Ngae 3-D Maze is 7 km from Owhata.

There were once two mazes on the outskirts of Rotorua, but since the Fairbank Maze closed down, only the Te Ngae Maze remains. Its layout changes regularly and it is open seven days a week.

Fine Maori carving at Ohinemutu village.

The formal Government Gardens are an appropriate setting for Rotorua's grandly styled bath-house.

5 OKERE FALLS

Continue north-east 2 km on SH 30 to the next major junction, take SH 33 and drive north 4 km to Mourea near the shoreline of Lake Rotoiti, 270 m above sea level and 70 m deep, which is renowned for its trout fishing. Continue north 3 km on SH 33 to the Okere Falls, signposted on the left, 1 km down a side road.

A 10-minute track winds through native podocarp forest to a steep flight of stone steps, cut into the rock face of a cliff, leading to Hinemoa's Caves which were used as a refuge during the days of inter-tribal warfare. The caves overlook the Trout Pool, an excellent fly fishing spot, while the track continues to the site of an old hydro station (1910) above the Okere Falls on the Kaituna River. This stretch of the river is frequently used for exciting rafting trips, including a 7 m plunge over the falls.

6 HAMURANA SPRINGS

Return south 2 km on SH 33 towards Mourea and turn right onto Hamurana Road around the northern shoreline of Lake Rotorua. Drive west 6 km to the Hamurana Springs.

From the road, a bridge crosses the Hamurana Springs and leads to a group of imposing Californian redwoods planted in the 1920s. Hamurana Springs, welling up from a cavernous hollow in solid rock, have provided a constant flow of pure water for centuries. Coins thrown into the water rise and settle on small ledges surrounding the spring.

In the nearby park you will find the remains of two Maori villages which hosted a visit by Governor Grey in 1849.

7 THE AGRODOME

Continue south-west on Hamurana Road for 6 km to the township of Ngongotaha, where pottery and copper jewellery are among local crafts on sale. Past Ngongotaha turn right onto SH 5 to visit the Agrodome which is signposted on the right, 3 km north-east.

This showcase of New Zealand agriculture features demonstrations of sheep-shearing, performing rams, working sheepdogs, a farmyard nursery and a dairy display. You can also take a giant 'swoop', bungy jump, go jet-sprinting, off-road boarding or zorbing, hit the driving range or go clay pigeon shooting.

8 RAINBOW AND FAIRY SPRINGS

Return south-east on SH 5 towards Rotorua 7 km to the Rainbow and Fairy Springs on the right.

Located in a luxuriant native forest setting, the springs are famous for their crystal-clear pools and streams stocked with large rainbow and brown trout. Over 24 million litres of water per day rise up through the black obsidian and white pumice sands of the Fairy Springs. Known as Te Puna a Tuhoe – the spring of Tuhoe, a Maori chief – this is said to be the home of the patupaiarehe, the ancient fairy folk of Maori legend.

At Rainbow Springs kiwi can be seen in a nocturnal aviary, as well as deer and wild pigs in enclosures. Across the road at Rainbow Farm shows include World of Bees, explaining the lifestyle of bees and honey gathering, and a farm show, featuring demonstrations of sheep shearing, sheepdog work and milking cows. You can also bottle-feed baby lambs, ride a bull and try churning cream and butter using traditional hand methods.

9 SKYLINE SKYRIDES

Right next to Rainbow and Fairy Springs is the Skyline Skyrides gondola which will take you 900 m up onto the slopes of Mt Ngongotaha for panoramic views across the lake and city.

If you are feeling adventurous you can descend by luge, a wheeled toboggan sliding on a choice of concrete tracks that wind their way back to the base of the mountain, or (at weekends) by mountain bike.

Live sheep-shearing at the Agrodome shows visitors how it's done. Here raw wool is ready for sorting.

19 ROTORUA LAKES AND HOT SPOTS

DRIVING TOUR ■ 146 KM ■ 1 DAY ■ COOL CRYSTALLINE WATER, BUBBLING MUD

Between Rotorua and the coast at Whakatane is a string of extraordinarily beautiful lakes whose tranquillity contrasts sharply with the rumbling, boiling and erupting of the area's underworld.

The first Maori settlers are thought to have arrived in this area in the fourteenth century, descendants of navigators who sailed to the Bay of Plenty from Hawaiki in the *Arawa* canoe from which they took their tribal name. For hundreds of years warfare between the increasing numbers of subtribes was a way of life and in the mid-nineteenth century the Arawa supported government troops against Waikato tribes. The fighting was virtually over by the 1870s and tourists began to arrive to view the natural wonders and bathe in the hot mineral waters. The forces that created this unique landscape are still at work and can be experienced first-hand.

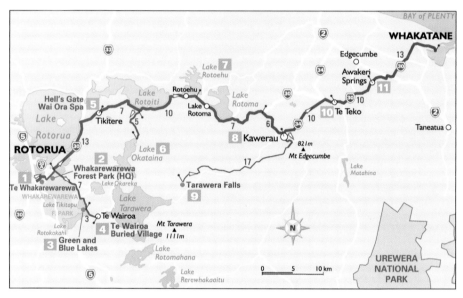

1 TE WHAKAREWAREWA AND TE PUIA

Te Whakarewarewa and Te Puia can be reached in a few minutes from Rotorua heading south via SH 5. Take the SH 30 turn-off to the left and follow Hemo Road 1 km north-east to the Te Whakarewarewa Thermal Area on the right.

One of Rotorua's main attractions, 'Whaka' is an extensive thermal area with silica terraces, mud pools and the famous geyser Pohutu, which erupts every hour. The park also features a replica of a pre-European fortified Maori village. At Te Puia (a short

walk from 'Whaka') visitors can watch – or even dabble – in Maori crafts such as weaving, carving and sculpture. Midday and evening performances allow the visitor an insight into Maori culture.

2 WHAKAREWAREWA FOREST PARK (REDWOOD FOREST)

Continue north-east on Hemo Road 1 km, turn right into Sala Street following SH 30 for 2 km to Long Mile Road on the right. Continue past the Forest Research Institute on the left, to the Whakarewarewa State Forest Visitor Centre signposted to the right.

The forest visitor centre provides maps of the trails and information about this interesting area of forest which was originally planted in 1901 with 170 exotic tree species as an experiment to determine which would be suitable for New Zealand plantations. The Californian Coastal Redwoods have thrived and become a major attraction. Waitawa Walk (1 hr return) is a relaxing and educational walk with a nature trail where many trees and plants are identified. The mountain biking trails here were designed by Fred Christansen, and are some of the country's finest.

3 GREEN AND BLUE LAKES

Continue on Long Mile Road east 2 km to the T-junction, turn right onto Tarawera Road and drive south-east 7 km to the viewing area between the Green and Blue Lakes.

Under the right lighting conditions you can see the remarkable difference in colour between these lakes, which are separated by a narrow isthmus. The Blue Lake (Tikitapu) is a venue for kayaking and water-skiing. The Green Lake (Rotokakahi) which is tapu (sacred) has a walking track along its northern shoreline.

4 TE WAIROA BURIED VILLAGE

Continue south-east 3 km beyond the Blue and Green Lakes along Tarawera Road to Lake Tarawera and the Te Wairoa Buried Village.

At the time of the Tarawera eruption in 1886, Te Wairoa was a staging point for visitors crossing Lake Tarawera to get to Lake Rotomahana to see the famous Pink and White Terraces which were rated as one of the wonders of the world. These silica formations were destroyed in the eruption, which buried three villages and killed over 150 people. From the 1930s this village has been enjoying the process of excavation, restoration and preservation – making it one of the oldest tourist attractions in New Zealand. A number of these buildings and historic items are on display in the village.

A 20-minute walking track leads down through the forest to the 30-metre Te Wairoa Falls overlooking the bush-clad Waitoharuru Valley below.

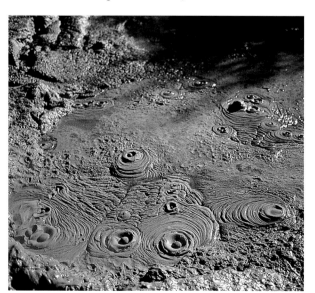

Boiling mud pools at Te Whakarewarewa.

The Devil's Cauldron seethes and steams at Hell's Gate, one of the most active thermal areas.

5 HELL'S GATE WAI ORA SPA
Return 12 km north-west on the Tarawera Road past the Green and Blue Lakes to SH 30, turn right and drive 13 km north-east to Tikitere on the left.

With impressive sulphurous vents, boiling waters and bubbling mud pools Hell's Gate is one of the more active of the thermal parks. When George Bernard Shaw visited in 1934 he said, 'I wish I had never seen the place, it reminds me too vividly of the fate theologians have promised me.' The park also features a hot waterfall, therapeutic mud baths and the petrified remains of an old forest.

6 LAKE OKATAINA
Continue east 7 km on SH 30 to the southern shoreline of Lake Rotoiti and turn right at the turn-off to Lake Okataina. Travel south 5 km to the lake.

Encircled by bush-clad hills, Okataina is the most picturesque lake in the Rotorua district. It was raised 12 m by the Tarawera eruption, which hid all traces of its former flourishing Maori settlement. The road to the lake passes through luxuriant native forest with towering tree ferns and overhanging kotukutuku (native fuchsia). Okataina is popular for trout fishing and swimming, with safe sandy beaches.

7 LAKE ROTOEHU
Return to SH 30, turn right and continue east 7 km along the southern shoreline of Lake Rotoiti. The road enters the forest between Lake Rotoiti and Lake Rotoehu. The start of Hongi's Track is signposted on the left. Lake Rotoehu is 3 km further east on SH 30.

In 1832 a musket-armed Nga Puhi war party led by Hongi Hika landed in the Bay of Plenty and made their way inland, paddling where possible and dragging their canoes between waterways on their way to attack Te Arawa on Mokoia Island. Hongi's Track, between Rotoehu and Rotoiti, was one of the portages used in this campaign. Today it is a splendid 1.5 km walk through unspoiled forest.

8 KAWERAU
Continue east on SH 30 over the hills 7 km to the Kawerau turn-off. Turn right and drive 6 km on SH 34 to Kawerau.

Kawerau, derived from the Maori words 'kawe' (to carry) and 'rau' (leaves) is situated beneath the 820 m summit of Mt Edgecumbe. With the construction of the massive Tasman pulp and paper mill in 1953, Kawerau became the hub of the timber industry in the eastern Bay of Plenty. A 90-minute guided tour through the mill is available.

To the south of the town lie some of the most extensive pine forest plantations in the world, Matahina and Kaingaroa. Nearby Lake Pupuwharau is popular for water-skiing, and the Tarawera River provides good trout fishing.

The Tarawera River erupts from underground at the spectacular Tarawera Falls.

9 TARAWERA FALLS
The visitor centre on Plunket Street in the centre of Kawerau provides directions and maps for the forestry roads. The forestry access road leading to the Tarawera Falls crosses the river directly below Mt Edgecumbe and follows a well-marked route 17 km out through the forest to the Tarawera Falls Track. Keep your lights on when you are driving through the forest and look out for logging trucks.

Most visitors come to Kawerau to see the spectacular Tarawera Falls, located in the pine forests west of the town. The falls surge out of deep tunnels in the lava rock and can be reached on a pleasant 20-minute river-bank walk through native bush. The track continues up to the top of the falls, where a bridge crosses the river and leads to the shoreline of Lake Tarawera.

10 TE TEKO
Return 17 km to Kawerau and drive north-east on SH 34 for 8 km, turn right onto SH 30 and travel east 2 km to Te Teko.

Ruataupere, the important meeting house of the Ngati Awa people on the Kokohinau Marae, was built by Te Kooti and his followers in 1882 as a gesture of gratitude to the people who had supported him in his conflict with the government. It features painted carvings that were carefully renovated in 1927.

11 AWAKERI SPRINGS
From Te Teko drive north-east 10 km on SH 30.

The soda thermal pools at the Awakeri Springs, in a peaceful bush setting where birds far outnumber people, are a relaxing place to stop at the end of the day before continuing to the coast.

It is another 13 km north-east on SH 30 to Whakatane.

Lake Okataina's sandy shoreline and clear waters invite picnickers and swimmers.

20 ROTORUA TO TAUPO

DRIVING TOUR ■ 118 KM ■ 5 HOURS ■ IN THE HEART OF THE GEOTHERMAL AREA

The fierce volcanic eruption that reshaped much of this area in the late nineteenth century was devastating at the time, but its legacy is a unique landscape of impressive and often unexpected beauty.

Some of the more spectacular geothermal fields are situated south of Rotorua at Waiotapu and Waimangu, formed by the eruption of Mt Tarawera on 10 June 1886. On this day earthquakes preceded a series of explosions that tore a huge cratered rift, almost 19 km long, across the top of the mountain, and the resulting cloud of ash could be seen from Gisborne, 140 km away. An even higher column of steam erupted from the Lake Rotomahana basin and the surrounding land was smothered with mud. The eruption ended almost as quickly as it had begun, leaving nine deep craters in the mountain and a layer of black basalt scoria and ash spread over most of the Bay of Plenty and south to Hawke's Bay.

Many of the natural features seen today are the result of the Tarawera eruption and provide a fascinating glimpse of the intriguing volcanic landscape that stretches south to Wairakei, Taupo and beyond into the mountains of the central North Island's volcanic plateau.

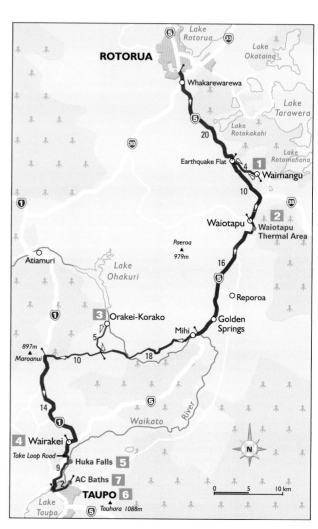

1 WAIMANGU
From Rotorua head south out of the city on SH 5 for 20 km, take the turn-off to Waimangu on the left and travel 4 km east.

The Waimangu volcanic valley was formed by the Tarawera eruption. An easy walk descends to the steaming blue Waimangu Cauldron, a huge spring known as the Frying Pan Lake, and fascinating sinter terraces. A short climb leads to the Inferno and Echo Craters. Many of the plants growing in the thermal area have had to adapt significantly to this unique environment. The track continues to Lake Rotomahana, where you can take a half-hour boat trip out to steaming cliffs and the former site of the famous Pink and White Terraces, destroyed in the 1886 eruption.

The walk downhill to the lake shore takes about 2 hours, but a free shuttle is available to take visitors back to the road.

2 WAIOTAPU
Return to SH 5 and drive for 5 km heading south-east, veering right at the junction with SH 38 and continuing south-west a further 5 km to the Waiotapu turn-off on the left. It is 1 km to the Waiotapu thermal area from the turn-off.

The terrace formations, craters and mud pools of the dramatic Waiotapu thermal area can be explored on a number of tracks. The Champagne Pool is a huge hot spring fed with water rising from a depth of 400 m. Lady Knox Geyser bursts into life daily at precisely 10.15 am. This regularity is achieved by an attendant temporarily blocking the vent and adding soap powder, which decreases the surface viscosity of the water and causes an almost immediate eruption.

3 ORAKEI KORAKO
Return to SH 5 and continue south-west 16 km to Mihi. The turn-off to Orakei Korako is to the right. Drive west 18 km to the next turn-off, turn right and drive north 5 km to the thermal area on the right.

The Champagne Pool, Waiotapu, bubbles from great depths.

Following the destruction of the Pink and White Terraces, the formations at the 'hidden valley' of Orakei Korako became the best surviving example of this colourful geothermal phenomenon. A short boat ride across Lake Ohakuri provides access to a series of tracks and boardwalks that lead through the thermal area and to Ruatapu Cave with its sacred pool.

4 WAIRAKEI
Head south 5 km from Orakei Korako back to the Mihi Road, turn right and head west 10 km. Turn left onto SH 1 and drive south 14 km to Wairakei.

Geothermal steam is used to make electricity at Wairakei, and the huge pipes that are part of the power project can be seen from the road. A few kilometres further south along the highway is the Wairakei International Golf Course on the right-hand side

Massive pipes at Wairakei conduct steam from natural underground cauldrons to generate power.

of the road. Signposted off Karapiti Road are the Craters of the Moon where an elaborate system of boardwalks and walkways, administered by DOC, leads around steam vents and mud pools.

5 HUKA FALLS
Continue south on SH 1 for 3 km and turn left onto Huka Falls Road which runs adjacent to SH 1 as you drive towards Taupo. This 4 km loop road provides access to the falls, to the jet boat and steamer operating below the falls and to a number of other attractions before rejoining SH 1.

The Waikato River ploughs through a narrow gap in the volcanic rock 4 km north of its source, Lake Taupo. Walking tracks lead from the parking area to a bridge across the point where the river surges through a narrow chasm towards the falls, while a short distance further on you can view the falls from wooden platforms. The control gates open daily at 10 am, midday, 2 pm and, in summer, at 4 pm.

Downstream from Huka Falls is the base for the jet boats and a steamboat, *African Queen*, that ply upriver to the base of the falls. Built in 1908 and originally named *Waireka*, the steamer once operated on the Whanganui River.

6 TAUPO
Continue south on SH 1 for 2 km to Taupo.

Taupo is one of the main centres on the volcanic plateau. It is famous for trout fishing and offers a variety of chartered boat trips out on the lake, as well as scenic flights. The settlement dates back to 1869, when a military outpost was established on the eastern bank of the Waikato River near its outfall from the lake. A redoubt was built and mounted constabulary remained until 1885, after the defeat of Te Kooti.

The Taupo Regional Museum and Art Gallery, on Story Place, displays photos and mementos from the colonial days as well as Maori carvings and a moa skeleton.

Among the many cruise vessels on the lake are the *Barbary*, a yacht once owned by Errol Flynn, the ketch *Spirit of Musick*, the *Ernest Kemp*, a replica of a 1920s steam ferry, and the modern *Cruise Cat*.

7 AC BATHS
The AC Baths are 2 km east from central Taupo, at the top of Spa Road.

The AC Baths feature a large heated pool, a waterslide and private mineral pools. Opposite, you will find Dinosaur Valley, where giant concrete dinosaurs are set among hissing steam vents.

LAKE TAUPO

Lake Taupo is the largest lake in New Zealand, over 40 km long and 30 km wide, with a depth of over 150 m. A great many rivers feed the lake and the Waikato River carries its water hundreds of kilometres to the sea.

The serene surface of the lake, with its peaceful bays and picturesque outlook to the snow-capped mountains in the south, belies its tumultuous beginnings.

This huge body of water fills a crater that was formed over 1800 years ago in what may have been the most violent series of eruptions in recorded history. Enormous volumes of ash and pumice (a super-heated volcanic rock) were thrown skywards, producing spectacular sunsets around the globe that were recorded by the ancient Romans as well as in China.

The full force of the Waikato River, the only outlet for Lake Taupo, is channelled through a narrow chasm and over the Huka Falls.

21 THE VOLCANIC PLATEAU

DRIVING TOUR ■ 200 KM ■ 1 DAY ■ AMONG THE MOUNTAINS

The harshness and dramatic impact of this region is softened by features such as small, tucked-away lakes, ancient forest and sparkling trout-filled streams, and enlivened by the bustle of modern ski resorts.

Rising majestically above the North Island's volcanic plateau are Ruapehu, Ngauruhoe and Tongariro, three active volcanoes that have emerged on a huge rift between two of the continually moving continental plates that make up the earth's crust. This fault line runs across the North Island and out to White Island, another active volcano off the coast of the Bay of Plenty. The blast and debris from the eruption that created Lake Taupo nearly 2000 years ago flattened forests for hundreds of miles, but in the lee of Mt Ruapehu a tiny pocket of forest survived that today provides a glimpse back in time to the ancient forests that once covered this region.

1 TURANGI

From Taupo head south-west along the eastern shoreline of Lake Taupo 49 km on SH 1 to Turangi. The road passes a number of attractive bays as well as the Waitahanui, Tauranga Taupo, Waimarino and Waiotaka Rivers, all of which are renowned for their trout fishing.

Turangi became the construction centre for the Tongariro power project in 1965 and has since developed into a thriving commercial and tourism centre at the southern end of Lake Taupo. The nearby Tongariro River is also a popular destination for fishing, kayaking and white water rafting.

2 TONGARIRO NATIONAL TROUT CENTRE

3 km south of Turangi on SH 1.

These park-like grounds are situated on the banks of the Tongariro River, with displays and information on trout-spawning activity. The Waihukahuka Stream, which runs through the park, has an underwater viewing chamber to enable visitors to get a close up look at wild trout in their natural habitat. These trout would have swum here from Lake Taupo.

3 TOKAANU

From the Trout Centre, drive 2 km west on SH 41 to Tokaanu. The hot pools are on Mangaroa Street.

Signs of thermal activity are often visible in the hills near Tokaanu, where steam rises from numerous hotspots in the bush. Near the shores of the lake, Tokaanu Thermal Park has private and public thermal pools, and huge trout swim in cool stream waters. A short boardwalk leads around bubbling springs and mud pools. An historic jetty on the shoreline is a reminder of the steamship service that operated to Taupo.

4 LAKE ROTOPOUNAMU

Drive east 2 km on SH 41. Turn right onto

SH 47. This is a beautiful drive over the hills and through the forest covering the slopes of Mt Pihanga with views across Lake Taupo. 6 km from the turn-off as the road descends towards Lake Rotoaira after crossing the saddle is the start of the Lake Rotopounamu Track on the left.

Lake Rotopounamu, which is surrounded by forest, is tucked away in a sheltered location below Mt Pihanga. It takes 20 minutes to walk to the lake on a well-formed track that continues in a loop around the shoreline. The full track takes up to 2 hours to walk, but you can explore part of the way, past sandy beaches and bird-filled bush.

5 OPATAKA PA

Continue south-west 2 km down the hill from the saddle and turn left onto a short access road that leads to the edge of Lake Rotoaira.

This important archaeological site on the shores of the lake has revealed three distinct periods of occupation. Small shelters protect parts of excavations undertaken at the pa site on the lakeside.

6 TE PORERE REDOUBT

Continue south-west 14 km on SH 47 to the Te Porere Redoubt Track, signposted on the right. To the south, Mt Tongariro rises above the landscape and on the upper slopes you will be able to see steam rising from an active thermal area, the Ketetahi Valley, with its boiling mud, fumaroles, geysers and hot springs.

The earthworks of the Te Porere Redoubt are a 10-minute walk from the road. The scene of the last battle (1869) in the New Zealand Wars, the redoubt was built by Te Kooti and his followers after they had been driven from the East Cape by government forces. Although the redoubt was overwhelmed and Te Kooti was wounded, he escaped and lived in the King Country until he was pardoned in 1883.

Sparkling, secluded Lake Rotopounamu.

The mountain road to the Top of the Bruce and the Whakapapa Skifield climbs the boulder-strewn slopes of Mt Ruapehu. In the clear mountain air the volcanic peak seems almost within touching distance.

7 THE CHATEAU

Continue south-west on SH 47 for 15 km and turn left onto SH 48 to reach the Chateau which is 7 km south. There are magnificent views across the tussock-clad landscape towards the Mangatepopo Valley, Mt Tongariro and Mt Ngauruhoe. Like Ruapehu's, the 2290 m conical summit of Ngauruhoe still belches steam and occasionally ash. The darker jet black lava flows on its slopes are the product of its more recent eruptions.

Built in 1929, the imposing Grand Chateau catered for tourists to Mt Ruapehu during the early days of its development as a ski resort. In the early 1900s tourists travelled by steamer from Wellington to Wanganui, then continued by river boat to Pipiriki and by stagecoach to Raetihi, Waiouru and the Desert Road track to the Waihohonu Hut on the east of the mountain.

The western side of the mountain was not developed until after the completion of the Main Trunk Railway line in 1908. Whakapapa village was built and a narrow winding road was cut across the western flanks of the mountain. The first trip from Wellington to Auckland by car was made in 1912, and following this the mountain received increasing numbers of visitors. Tourist huts were erected during the 1920s, and in 1938 the first ski tow was set up on the mountain.

Today the Whakapapa village and the Chateau are a popular tourist destination all year round.

8 TOP OF THE BRUCE

Continuing through the village, the mountain road to the 'Top of the Bruce' and the Whakapapa skifields is an excellent 7 km scenic drive in any season.

A number of good walks start from the road to the Top of the Bruce. In the summer you can ride the ski lifts onto the upper slopes of the mountain to enjoy the breathtaking views. From the top lift the acidic (and sometimes boiling) crater lake near the summit of Mt Ruapehu (2769 m) can be reached after a climb of about 2 hours. DOC rangers run a summer holiday programme, including guided walks and climbs, from the visitor centre at Whakapapa village.

9 OHAKUNE

Return to SH 47 and turn left, heading west 9 km to the National Park township, then turn left onto SH 4 and drive south 13 km to the Makatote Viaduct. This 262 m long, 78 m high viaduct is one of the engineering masterpieces created to span rivers flowing from Ruapehu that are crossed by the Main Trunk Railway. Nearby is a monument commemorating the completion of the line in 1908. Continue south for 13 km on SH 4 and turn left onto SH 49. Drive 9 km southeast to Ohakune.

Ohakune, the major service centre for the skifields on the southern side of Mt Ruapehu, is crammed with motels, ski shops and restaurants. Opposite the DOC Headquarters on Mangawhero Terrace you can explore an ancient forest that survived the cataclysmic Taupo eruptions on this sheltered southern side of the mountain. The Mangawhero Forest Walk takes about 30 minutes and follows the Mangawhero Stream in a loop through the forest.

10 THE MOUNTAIN ROAD

From Ohakune township take the Ohakune Mountain Road and travel 17 km.

This drive up to Turoa skifield is interesting in both summer and winter. As the road climbs the slopes of the mountain the vegetation becomes smaller. The small stunted kaikawaka (mountain cedar) that border the road on one stretch may be hundreds of years old but have grown only a few metres high in this harsh alpine environment. *Return 17 km to Ohakune.*

The Grand Chateau has offered generations of tourists accommodation in a magnificent setting.

22 ON THE MAIN TRUNK LINE

DRIVING TOUR ■ 294 KM ■ 1 DAY ■ TRAINS, PLANES, TRAMS AND VINTAGE CARS

Many motorists drive the main highway from Waiouru to Wellington without stopping, but for those with an interest in the history of transport or military technology the route offers a trail of fascinating discoveries.

State Highway 1 from Auckland to Wellington is often referred to as the 'main trunk line', after the Main Trunk Railway which played an important part in the development of the North Island. In many of the towns along the route the skills of the surveyors, engineers and workmen who completed the railway in 1908 are commemorated in small museums, and rows of the workers' original cottages, built to a uniform design, give a special character to many main streets.

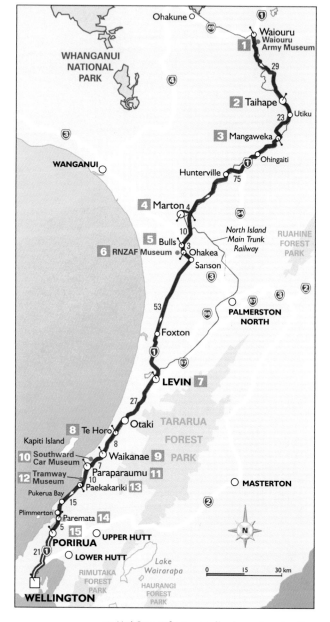

Near Mangaweka the Rangitikei River snakes below steep cliffs.

1 WAIOURU ARMY MUSEUM
The trip starts at Waiouru. The museum is situated at the southern end of the Desert Road on SH 1.

The Queen Elizabeth II Army Memorial Museum, close to the Waiouru army base, exhibits a wide range of military memorabilia, weapons, medals, paintings, models and films. Outside the museum are a number of retired armoured fighting vehicles including a Centurion tank.

The army makes use of the Rangipo Desert for manoeuvres.

2 TAIHAPE
From Waiouru head south on SH 1 for 29 km to Taihape.

Taihape has had a long and close association with the railway and generations of New Zealanders fondly remember the railway station's cheery cafeteria which stayed open to serve refreshments at ungodly hours to travellers on the overnight express.

The distinctive houses on the side of the town's main street were built for railway workers in 1904 when the Main Trunk Railway line reached Taihape. The Taihape Museum

on Hui Street features displays showing the development of the railway, as well as the forest clearance and sawmilling that preceded the main European settlement of the area.

3 MANGAWEKA
Continue south-west on SH 1 for 23 km to Mangaweka.

There are three old churches on the main highway through Mangaweka but the main landmark is a 1940s vintage DC3 airliner, containing a café, perched on the side of the road. The Rangitikei River has become popular for jet boating, white-water rafting, and an 80 m bungy jump from a bridge.

4 MARTON
Continue south-west 75 km on SH 1 then turn off right to Marton, 4 km to the north-west.

Once a watering-place for farmers driving stock, Marton was formed when four early settlers subdivided their holdings into house lots. The town grew quickly after 1885 when the building of the railway began.

The Church of St Stephen on Maunder Street is one of the town's oldest surviving buildings, dating back to 1871 when construction of the church began on the site of a redoubt. The old bank and tavern on Broadway have been preserved as part of the historic commercial precinct while the brick courthouse built in 1897 is an excellent example of Victorian architecture. You can visit the Captain Cook Pioneer Cottage on Wellington Road, which is furnished with colonial period household items.

5 BULLS
Return to SH 1 and continue 10 km south-west to Bulls.

This small farming community located at the junction of SH 1 and SH 3 has made the most of its curious name by incorporating 'bull' in the name of almost every shop in the town. The police station is 'Const-a-bull', the pharmacy 'Indispens-a-bull' and the public toilets 'Relieve-a-bull'.

6 OHAKEA RNZAF MUSEUM
Drive south 3 km from Bulls on SH 1 to Ohakea Airbase on the right.

The RNZAF Museum features a number of flight simulators and covers the history of the base, its personnel and its aircraft since its establishment during the Second World War.

7 LEVIN
Travel 4 km south-east from Ohakea on SH 1 to Sanson, turn right and continue south on SH 1 for 31 km to Foxton. It is another 18 km south to Levin, still on SH 1.

Levin is a pleasant rural township located in the heart of the Horowhenua region and was founded as a railway town in the 1880s.

8 TE HORO
Continue south-west 27 km on SH 1 to Te Horo.

The Hyde Park Museum at Te Horo features

Velvet-upholstered horseless buggies and 'convertibles' with roofs seemingly based on umbrella design are part of an astounding collection at the Southward Car Museum.

an incredible collection of Kiwiana, including a complete grocery store stocked with over 3000 items still bearing their 1937 price tags.

9 WAIKANAE
Travel south 8 km on SH 1 to Waikanae.

Located on the north bank of the Waikanae River, which flows from the Tararua Range, this is a popular retirement town with a beach settlement 5 km away. Nga Manu Sanctuary, off Te Moana Road signposted from the highway, comprises 15 ha of swampland and scrub. This is the home of mute swans, pied stilts, ducks, parakeets and kea. You can see kiwi, morepork and tuatara in a nocturnal house and explore the area on a number of bush walks.

10 SOUTHWARD CAR MUSEUM
From Waikanae drive 6 km south on SH 1 and turn right into a side road signposted to the Southward Car Museum.

The largest and most varied collection of cars in the Southern Hemisphere includes an original De Lorean, the car made famous in the movie *Back to the Future*, as well as relics from the Second World War such as the amphibious Schwimmwagen and the Kettenkrad, a tracked motorcycle. The museum also houses Marlene Dietrich's Rolls-Royce, a gull-winged Mercedes Benz and an 1895 Benz 'horseless carriage'.

11 PARAPARAUMU
Travel a further 1 km south on SH 1 to Paraparaumu.

The town of Paraparaumu grew around a railway station, with a beach settlement springing up 4 km away on the coast. Offshore lies Kapiti Island, once the stronghold of the Maori chief Te Rauparaha, and later the site of whaling stations. Kapiti was made

a nature reserve in 1897 and protects a number of rare and endangered species.

12 TRAMWAY MUSEUM
Drive south 6 km to Mckay's Crossing, just off SH 1.

The Tramway Museum in Queen Elizabeth Park operates the wooden trams that ran in Wellington until 1964. A 2 km section of track is used to provide rides down to the beach.

13 PAEKAKARIKI
Continue south 4 km on SH 1 to Paekakariki.

Restored steam locomotives are on display near the busy train station beside the main highway.

14 PAREMATA
Drive south on SH 1 for 15 km to Paremata.

On the southern entrance to the Pauatahanui arm of the Porirua Harbour, Paremata was the site of barracks built in 1846 to quarter British troops protecting Wellington from Maori attack. However, the buildings soon collapsed as a result of shoddy materials and a series of earthquakes.

15 PORIRUA
Drive south 5 km on SH 1 to the Porirua turn-off.

Porirua Harbour attracted whalers and sealers as far back as the 1830s and became the site of a military outpost during the mid-1840s. Today, this well-protected Y-shaped harbour is home to a number of yachting and boating clubs.

Porirua Museum on Te Hiko Street features exhibits from the township's colourful past. You can also visit the museum at the Police College on the hillside just north of the city. *It is another 21 km to Wellington heading south on SH 1.*

An RNZAF Skyhawk at the Ohakea Airbase.

NORTH ISLAND
THE EAST COAST

23 AROUND EAST CAPE

DRIVING TOUR ■ 368 KM ■ 1 DAY ■ BEWITCHING BEACHES AND LAZY TOWNS

This is a very full day's journey, but the highway is good all the way and travellers can choose to bypass some stops, sightseeing from the car, to spend more time at the places they simply can't resist.

The easternmost extremity of the North Island is bounded by a steep coastline rising from a rocky shoreline to the north-west and long flat beaches set between headlands to the east. The heart of East Cape is dominated by the rugged expanse of the Raukumara Range, part of an almost continuous chain of mountains stretching northwards all the way from Wellington. The main river in the region is the Motu, which traces its course from the hill country down through forests and steep-sided gorges in some of the most rugged and trackless parts of the land.

Between Opotiki and the East Cape the beaches are alive with people in summer, but in winter this is still a wonderful trip to make on a fine day long after the crowds have departed.

1 WHAKATANE

Located at the mouth of the Whakatane River, which forms a sizeable harbour, this town is the main centre on the Rangitaiki Plains, bordering the Bay of Plenty. On a clear day from up on the hill above the town you can see the steaming volcanic cone of White Island off the coastline.

On a cliff south-east of the town, on the highest point of the headland, is Toi's pa, claimed to be the oldest in New Zealand. Toi is said to have been in search of his grandson Whatonga when he decided to settle here in 1150, and it was to be another 200 years before a later chief, Hoaki, decided to return to the homeland of Hawaiki. His journey led to the great fleet of canoes –*Te Arawa*, *Tainui*, *Mataatua* and *Aotea* – making their legendary voyage to Aotearoa.

On the harbour front stands a statue of Wairaka, daughter of Turoa, captain of the *Mataatua*. A replica of the *Mataatua* can be seen at Pohaturoa Rock, near the Strand and Commerce Street, close to a sacred archway.

Walking tracks run around archaeological sites on the Kohi Point Walkway. The Whakatane Museum and Gallery, on Boon Street, holds a wealth of historical information on the early settlement of the area as well as an exhibit on White Island.

Whakatane is a departure point for boat trips to White Island, an active volcano in the Bay of Plenty, and site of an ill-fated sulphur-mining venture.

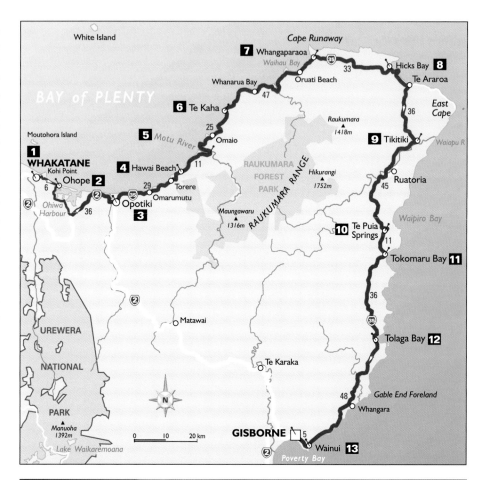

On the coast near Opotiki.

The tiny Anglican church beside the sea at Raukokore, on the way to Whangaparaoa.

2 OHOPE

From Whakatane drive east 6 km over the hill to Ohope.

Ohope lies at the western end of a long sandy peninsula stretching across the Ohiwa Harbour. This is a popular beach resort with safe swimming and good fishing.

3 OPOTIKI

Drive south 16 km from Ohope along the Ohiwa Harbour to SH 2. Turn left and follow SH 2 for 20 km north-east to Opotiki.

Opotiki is the gateway to the East Cape. The Historical and Agricultural Society Museum is located on Church Street, along with St Stephen's Church, built by the Rev. Carl Volkner who was killed outside the church in a Hauhau attack in 1865.

4 HAWAI BEACH

From Opotiki take SH 35 and drive east for 12 km to Omarumutu where the War Memorial Hall contains excellent examples of Maori carving. Continue east 12 km to Torere, with its steeply shelving pebble beach, then a further 5 km north-east to Hawai Beach.

Hawai Beach is an interesting place to make a quick stop and explore the coast on a shore that is literally covered with driftwood. Most of the timber has come from inland forests and been washed down the many rivers along the coast.

5 MOTU RIVER

From Hawai Beach the road winds its way up onto the Maraenui Hill to a lookout point before descending to the Motu River, 11 km east of Hawai Beach on SH 35.

Koromiko, hebes and native orchids carpet the banks of the river, which runs through magnificent virgin forests from high in the hill country near Matawai and is covered by a special conservation order.

6 TE KAHA

Drive 25 km from the Motu River bridge north-east on SH 35 to Te Kaha.

Te Kaha means 'to stand firm', a name referring to the many sieges by invading tribes that were withstood by the local defenders. Today you will find the remains of an old redoubt and a beautifully carved meeting house at Te Kaha Tukaki. This was one of the old whaling settlements on the coast and an area of early missionary activity.

7 WHANGAPARAOA

Continue on SH 35 for 47 km.

This stretch of the journey takes in some of the most beautiful coastline in the area. The highway passes a series of picturesque bays, including Whanarua Bay, which has perhaps the best beach on the East Cape. A distinctive Anglican church at Raukokore nestles among Norfolk pines on a promontory west of Orete Point. Waihau Bay has a general store and a post office that was established in the 1870s.

As you near Cape Runaway you pass Oruati Beach, which is sandy and good for swimming. At Whangaparaoa there is a restored pa site and meeting house. The cape itself is not accessible by road.

8 HICKS BAY

From Whangaparaoa continue on SH 35 for 33 km east to Hicks Bay.

Named after one of Captain Cook's crew members on the *Endeavour*, the magnificent Hicks Bay was the home of Tuwhakairiora, a famous Ngati Porou fighting chief.

9 TIKITIKI

Continue south-east 12 km from Hicks Bay over a hill and down across Tokata Flats to Te Araroa, where a 600-year-old pohutukawa tree, Te Waha o Rerekohu, stands in the school grounds. From here, SH 35 cuts inland from East Cape, which is the first mainland area in the world to see the sunrise. Continue south on SH 35 for 24 km through farmland to Tikitiki.

A distinctive landmark at Tikitiki is an Anglican church that incorporates Maori architectural design. The flat hilltop above the town was an ancient pa site occupied in pre-European times and later fortified with trenches during the New Zealand Wars.

10 TE PUIA SPRINGS

Drive south on SH 35 for 45 km to Te Puia Springs.

Sir Apirana Ngata, a prominent Maori politician from 1905 to 1943, and Lieutenant Te Moana-nui-a-Kiwi Ngarimu, post-humous Victoria Cross winner, were both raised in this district. At the small, attractive settlement of Te Puia Springs is the historic Te Puia Hotel, with thermal pools nearby.

11 TOKOMARU BAY

Continue south on SH 35 for 11 km to Tokomaru Bay.

A picturesque town with rugged cliffs at the southern end of the bay and an excellent beach, Tokomaru Bay is a centre for crayfishing and arts and crafts. Pakirikiri Marae features a large carved meeting house, opened in 1934.

12 TOLAGA BAY

Drive south 36 km on SH 35 which heads inland to emerge on the coast at Tolaga Bay.

A huge old wharf that stretches 660 m out to sea is one of the first things you will see as you arrive at Tolaga Bay. The town has a colonial-style hotel and the streets are named after members of Captain Cook's *Endeavour* crew.

13 WAINUI

SH 35 leads inland again from Tolaga Bay for 26 km south to Whangara, a small settlement that is the setting for Witi Ihimaera's novel The Whale Rider. *Continue south-west 22 km on SH 35 to Wainui Bay.*

Although Wainui Bay is only a short way from Gisborne, this beautiful surf beach has retained a sense of peace and tranquillity usually enjoyed in more remote locations. *Gisborne is another 5 km north-west on SH 35.*

The Tolaga Bay Wharf, the longest in the Southern Hemisphere, once hummed with coastal shipping activity.

24 TE UREWERA

DRIVING TOUR ■ 318 KM ■ 1 DAY ■ DEEP FOREST, HIDDEN LAKES, WATERFALLS

The drive itself through this magnificent wilderness is an unforgettable experience. Exploring deeper into the forest on the numerous easy walking tracks will reveal enchanting beech-fringed lakes, ancient caves and superb views.

The most striking feature of Te Urewera is its forests, huge tracts of native bush that stretch away as far as the eye can see, broken only by the shimmering waters of lakes. Many of the ancient trees that stand in these forests might have seen the coming of the first Maori – the Tuhoe, 'Children of the Mist', said to be descended from the marriage of the 'Maid of the Mist' Hine-Pukohu-Rangi to the mountain Maungapohatu. Standing in the swirling mists that cover the ranges and creep into the valleys, the forest giants saw tribal wars rage for hundreds of years, then the arrival of missionaries and other Pakeha and the conflict that followed.

Today the forests are silent except for the call of native pigeons, the sound of the occasional car winding its way along the road above Lake Waikaremoana and the murmur of trampers on the renowned 'Around the Lake' track.

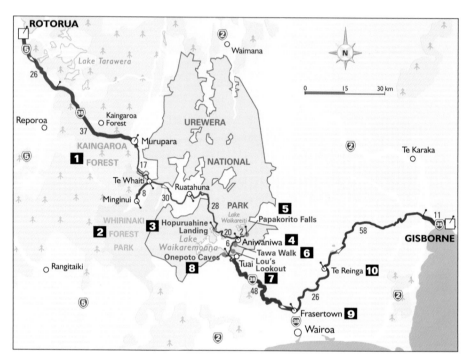

1 KAINGAROA FOREST

From Rotorua head south-east on SH 5 for 26 km, then turn left onto SH 38 and drive south-east through the Kaingaroa Forest 37 km to Murupara.

Kaingaroa Forest, the world's largest pine plantation, was created as part of an employment project during the years of economic depression in the 1930s.

2 WHIRINAKI FOREST PARK

From Murupara the road continues for another 17 km to Te Whaiti before beginning the climb into the hills of the Ikawhenua Range and onto the winding gravel road through Urewera National Park. 1 km past Te Whaiti turn right onto a side road that leads 8 km to a DOC field centre in the small sawmilling township of Minginui. A drive through the pine forests that surround the town leads to Whirinaki Forest Park.

This beautiful area of native bush has a number of excellent walks and scenic drives. Longer tracks lead to the rapids and waterfalls on the Whirinaki River as well as the Arahaki Lagoon, but for the day visitor the best option is to take a drive through these magnificent forests on the old logging roads. A signposted 30-minute loop walking track leads through tall, dense stands of podocarps including rimu, totara and kahikatea. These trees produce fleshy seeds that are eaten and spread by birds like the kereru, New Zealand's colourful pigeon. As a result, podocarps are usually spread randomly through forests, except in areas where the bush was devastated by natural events such as volcanic eruptions. In these locations podocarps form the distinctive dense forests that are typical in this park.

3 HOPURUAHINE LANDING

Return to SH 38, turn right and continue south-east 30 km on the winding gravel road to Ruatahuna. Drive another 28 km east across the Taupeupe Saddle to the Hopuruahine Landing on the shores of Lake Waikaremoana. A short access road leads to the right down to the lake.

Hopuruahine Landing, one of the starting points for the well-known tramping track around Lake Waikaremoana, is a pleasant place to relax by the lakeside before the road starts to climb high above the water to Aniwaniwa.

Timber is an important regional industry.

Te Urewera rainforest.

A huge rockfall more than 2000 years ago created a natural dam at the head of a valley which filled up with water to become Lake Waikaremoana.

4 ANIWANIWA

The 20 km section of unsealed road from Hopuruahine Landing south-east on SH 38 passes some of the most scenic locations in the Urewera National Park. The road climbs above the lake shore, passing the impressive Mokau Falls clearly visible on the right as you drive, before descending towards the DOC visitor centre and park headquarters at Aniwaniwa.

Te Urewera receives high rainfall which maintains the luxuriant forests. These can be explored on a number of short walks near the visitor centre. A 30-minute loop track leads down along the Aniwaniwa Stream on the right side of the road from the visitor centre to a series of waterfalls dropping down towards Lake Waikaremoana. If you have an hour, a beautiful forest walk leads from the left side of the road to Lake Waikareiti. Surrounded by beech forest, the lake was formed millions of years ago when huge sedimentary blocks were tilted and uplifted to form a series of basins.

5 PAPAKORITO FALLS

From Aniwaniwa drive east on SH 38 for 2 km and turn left into Old Gisborne Road. The track to the falls is signposted left, 3 km from the main road.

Lake Waikareiti is 300 m higher than Waikaremoana and its overflow runs along the Aniwaniwa Stream and over the Papakorito Falls before flowing into Lake Waikaremoana. A 5-minute walk leads to these impressive falls which cascade over a huge uplifted block of sedimentary rock that rears from the valley floor.

6 TAWA WALK

Return to SH 38, turn left and drive south 2 km to Waikaremoana. On the left of the road 1 km south of Waikaremoana is the start of the Ngamoko Track and the short Tawa Walk.

The Tawa Walk is an easy half-hour loop through impressive stands of tawa with their brilliant green foliage filtering the light as it penetrates the forest canopy. The track joins the Ngamoko Track to return to the road but before you head back you can follow the main track for another 5 minutes to a giant 800-year-old rata tree.

7 LOU'S LOOKOUT

Drive south 3 km to Rosie Bay. Lou's Track is signposted on the left of the road.

The Panekiri Bluff, an enormous block of sedimentary rock that was uplifted to a height of 1200 m, is clearly visible from most parts of the road around Lake Waikaremoana, but far more impressive views can be obtained by taking a 30-minute track to Lou's Lookout. Lou's Track is a well-graded walk up through the forest onto a series of rocky bluffs above the road, to a lookout platform with superb views of the bluff and across the expanse of the lake.

8 ONEPOTO CAVES

Drive 1 km south on SH 38 and turn off right onto Onepoto Road for a short distance to reach the track to the caves.

Nearly 3000 years ago many of the rivers of Te Urewera flowed into a large basin, exiting through a narrow gorge between the Ngamoko Range and the Panekiri Bluff. The river gradually cut deeper into the gorge and undermined the base of the ranges on either side until a huge rockfall sealed the gorge, forming the natural dam that created Lake Waikaremoana.

Drowned forests still stand on the bed of the lake, and at the park headquarters you can see the preserved stump of a totara that was 500 years old when it was covered by the rising waters of the lake over 2000 years ago. The 20-minute Onepoto Track leads to a series of small caverns formed by the landslide that created the lake. Moa bones have been found in the caves which are dry and can easily be explored with a torch.

9 FRASERTOWN

From Onepoto return to SH 38 and sealed roads for the drive 48 km south-east to Frasertown.

Frasertown was originally founded as an outpost for the armed constabulary and was named after a commander in the Hauhau–Te Kooti rebellion.

10 TE REINGA

From Frasertown turn left onto SH 36 and drive north-east 26 km to Te Reinga.

The name Te Reinga means 'place of the departed spirit' and refers to a Maori legend which tells of a maiden who committed suicide at the site of the spectacular Te Reinga waterfall, below the confluence of the Hangaroa and Ruakituri Rivers, after her loved one was killed by a rival.

It is 58 km north-east on SH 38 to SH 2, and another 11 km on SH 2 south-east to Gisborne.

The Waikaretaheke River follows SH 38 from Lake Waikaremoana to Wairoa on the coast.

25 GISBORNE AND HAWKE'S BAY

DRIVING TOUR ■ 255 KM ■ 1 DAY ■ BIRDS, ART DECO AND DINOSAUR FOSSILS

The cities on this stretch of the east coast are perfect holiday destinations, offering historical and art museums, Maori culture, unique architecture, winetasting, diverse amusements and entertainments, all in a setting of spectacular natural beauty.

A memorial on the beach at the foot of Gisborne's Kaiti Hill marks the spot where Captain James Cook and members of his crew from the Endeavour *first set foot in New Zealand, on 9 October 1769. At the southern end of Poverty Bay are the white cliffs of Young Nicks Head, the headland named after a lad in Cook's crew, Nicholas Young, who made the first sighting of land and earned himself a gallon of rum and a place in history books.*

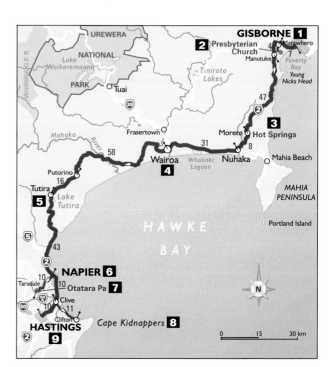

◼ GISBORNE

A city of bridges, Gisborne is criss-crossed by three rivers and boasts a number of fine parks and recreational facilities. The city was originally laid out in 1870 and named Turanga, later taking the name of the Colonial Secretary Sir William Gisborne to avoid being confused with Tauranga.

Among a number of historic buildings in the city is Wyllie Cottage (1872), located next to the Gisborne Museum and Arts Centre on Stout Street. The small maritime museum on the riverbank is part of the complex. It incorporates parts of the *Star of Canada*, a 12,000-tonne ship that was wrecked on the Gisborne reef in 1912. Its bridge and the captain's cabin were salvaged and built into a house that was later moved and restored to become part of the museum. The East Coast Museum of Transport and Technology is open daily near the A&P Showgrounds in Makaraka, while Te Poho-o-Rawiri meeting house can be found at the base of Kaiti Hill.

One of the largest in the country, this meeting house has elaborately carved bargeboards and is most interesting to visit.

◻ MATAWHERO PRESBYTERIAN CHURCH

Drive west 7 km from Gisborne on SH 2 to the Matawhero turn-off on the left. It is 1 km to Matawhero.

At Matawhero you will find the oldest church in Poverty Bay. Built originally as a storehouse in 1862, it became an Anglican then a Presbyterian church, and was spared destruction during a rebel Maori raid in 1868. When the Treaty of Waitangi was signed in 1840 many chiefs from the East Coast did not acknowledge its authority and numerous battles took place during the 1860s, with government troops taking control in 1866. A number of rebellious Maori, together with the chief Te Kooti, were exiled to the Chatham Islands and Europeans began to settle the area, bringing with them flocks of sheep. Te Kooti escaped and with 200 warriors attacked the settlement at Matawhero, killing 33 Europeans and 37 Maori.

◼ MORERE HOT SPRINGS

Return to SH 2, turn left and drive west 4 km to Manutuke then south on SH 2 for 47 km to Morere.

Statue of Captain Cook, Kaiti Hill, Gisborne.

Huge cliffs loom above the beach leading to Cape Kidnappers.

The 200 ha reserve protects a small part of the forest that once cloaked much of the East Coast and provides a lush setting for a complex of hot pools where you can soak and listen to the many birds.

4 WAIROA

Continue south on SH 2 for 8 km to Nuhaka then west 31 km to Wairoa.

Lines of Phoenix palms border the Wairoa River and the Marine Parade, with its historic lighthouse relocated from the Mahia Peninsula. Takitimu meeting house is a memorial to Sir James Carroll, the first Maori to serve as a minister of the Crown. Whakaki Lagoon, to the east of Wairoa, is an important wetland area and a good place for birdwatching.

5 LAKE TUTIRA

Travel south-west from Wairoa 37 km on SH 2 to the Rabbit Bridge and then 3 km to the scenic Mohaka Viaduct. Continue south-west 18 km to Putorino and another 16 km south-west to Lake Tutira, where the car park is on the left off the highway.

Lake Tutira is a wildlife reserve set in pleasant farmland where many bird species are protected. There are walking tracks around the lake, some very long, but visitors can explore for a short distance and return.

6 NAPIER

From Lake Tutira continue south 20 km on SH 2 to Napier.

Named after the British General Sir Charles Napier, the city developed from a whaling and trading station established in the 1840s. It was rebuilt almost entirely after the 1931 earthquake which devasted most of the buildings, and is probably a unique example of an entire city that has been built in a single coherent architectural style. Art deco was at the height of its popularity in the 1930s, and Napier possesses one of the most significant collections of these buildings in the world. An Art Deco weekend is held in February.

A stroll along Napier's Marine Parade will take you to many of the city's attractions including performing seals and dolphins at Marineland, the Hawke's Bay Aquarium, Centennial Gardens, an illuminated fountain and a bronze statue of Pania of the Reef. The Stables Museum examines the 1931 earthquake, which measured 7.9 on the Richter scale, raised an area of 40 sq km from beneath the sea and caused 256 deaths. The Hawke's Bay Art Gallery and Museum has an impressive collection of moa-hunter artefacts and dinosaur fossils, many of which were discovered by local amateur palaeontologist Joan Wiffen.

Fine views of the city and port can be enjoyed from a lookout on Bluff Hill. At the Botanical Gardens, near Hospital Hill, a huge aviary is set among the flowerbeds, shady walks and miniature waterfalls.

7 OTATARA PA

10 km from Napier city on Springfield Road, signposted from the Taradale shopping centre.

NAPIER/HASTINGS WINERIES

Visitors are welcome at all of the vineyards between Napier and Hastings. These include Te Mata Estate, which first began production in 1896, and Mission Vineyards, where Marist Brothers planted vines in 1851.

Hawke's Bay has very warm summers and a grape-growing season that extends right through to April, ideal for late-maturing varieties such as riesling and cabernet sauvignon. With a wide range of soil types in the region, including much sought-after river gravels, the district offers scope for all the classic grape varieties.

This historic reserve includes earthworks that have been enhanced by a conservation and reconstruction programme, recreating palisades and the carved ancestral figures surrounding the pa.

8 CAPE KIDNAPPERS

From Otatara Pa return to Napier and take SH 2, heading south 10 km to Clive. Turn off left to the coast road and travel 11 km to Clifton, passing through Haumoana and Te Awanga.

This is a spectacular stretch of coastline even if you only have time for a brief visit.

From the coastal settlement of Clifton you can take a walk along the beach at low tide under dramatic sheer cliffs. A few kilometres further up the beach is the world-famous Cape Kidnappers gannet colony on a plateau 120 m above the sea near the top of the peninsula. Up to 10,000 birds occupy the area in November and December each year. From October to April guided tours to the colony depart daily from Te Awanga.

9 HASTINGS

Return to SH 2, turn left and drive 10 km south-west to Hastings.

Fruit processing and winemaking are the major industries in this area and the countryside around Hastings is covered in orchards and vineyards.

Like Napier, the city suffered substantial damage in the 1931 earthquake and was rebuilt in similar style to Napier. The art deco clocktower in the paved Civic Square is an interesting example of post-quake reconstruction. Fantasyland, on Grove Road, is an exciting leisure park designed for children.

Napier boasts the most extensive collection of art deco buildings in the world. Splendid structures adorned with friezes, moulded motifs and decorative panels house many of the city's businesses.

26 THROUGH THE WAIRARAPA

DRIVING TOUR ■ 464 KM ■ 1 DAY ■ TOWNS CARVED FROM THE BUSH

This trip from Hawke's Bay to Wellington is easy driving through rolling farmland and low-key country towns, with a detour to explore one of the most remote and scenic points on the east coast.

In the early nineteenth century the plains and hill country east of the Ruahine and Tararua Ranges were covered with dense forest. The settlers who struggled to farm here cleared the bush with back-breaking effort, brought in flocks of sheep from as far away as Australia and gradually established sheep stations and dairy farms that thrived on the rich soil. Towns sprang up to service the growing farming industry.

The conditions that allowed farming to flourish also proved ideal for growing grapes, leading to the establishment of many successful wineries. As transport improved, the Wairarapa became more easily accessible from Wellington. Today the towns of the Wairarapa retain a charming rural character with flashes of sophistication that reflect their proximity to the capital and popularity as an escape for urbanites.

1 WAIPAWA

Waipawa is 36 km south-west of Hastings on SH 2.

Waipawa stands near the confluence of the Tukituki and Waipawa Rivers and was once a port for steamers carrying wool and grain to Napier. Originally named Abbotsford, it was founded as a private town by sheep-station owner F. S. Abbot. Most of the area south of Napier was taken up by sheep stations, and towns like Waipawa and Waipukurau were established to service these large estates. The towns grew as the estates were broken up into smaller farms from the late nineteenth century.

2 DANNEVIRKE

Driving out of Waipawa on SH 2 you will pass the Tukituki Wildlife Reserve which stretches upriver from the Waimarama Bridge. The peaceful backwaters and braided river channels of this reserve provide a haven for ducks, stilts, shags and pheasants. Continue 7 km south-west from Waipawa to Waipukurau on SH 2 and then travel west 21 km to Takapau. Continue south-west 12 km to Norsewood on SH 2 and a further 21 km south-west to Dannevirke.

This town was cut out of Seventy Mile Bush by Scandinavian settlers in the 1870s and has

Castle Rock offers stupendous views over the lagoon near Castlepoint out to the ocean.

become a major southern Hawke's Bay farming centre. From Norsewood and Dannevirke south into the Wairarapa many of the towns originated as bush settlements established by Scandinavian migrants. Some Scandinavian traditions are still maintained in these areas and the local museums record the special character that Danes, Swedes and Norwegians brought to the early settlements.

3 WOODVILLE

Continue south-west 26 km to Woodville on SH 2.

The township of Woodville was named because of its location between two vast areas of totara forest – Forty Mile Bush to the south and Seventy Mile Bush to the north-east. This railway junction town has retained a line of the old railway houses on Atkinson Street and has a small pioneer museum on Ormond Street.

4 PAHIATUA

Drive 16 km south to Pahiatua on SH 2.

Pahiatua was founded in 1881 in the heart of Seventy Mile Bush. Its wide main street was originally planned to carry the railway line that passes the outskirts of the town, and today the extensive centre strip is made good use of as gardens and rest areas. The Manawatu and Mangatainoka Rivers nearby are renowned for their excellent trout fishing.

5 PUKAHA MT BRUCE

Drive south-west 24 km to Eketahuna and continue south-west 10 km to Pukaha Mt Bruce located on the left side of the road on SH 2.

Huge tree-filled aviaries are home to a variety of endangered native New Zealand birds. Established in 1958 to rear the rediscovered takahe, the centre currently studies and breeds Auckland and Campbell Island teals, the New Zealand pigeon, the saddleback, stitchbird and kokako. Here you can meet a kiwi, watch the kaka being fed and walk through a 600-year-old rainforest.

6 MASTERTON

Continue south-west a further 31 km on SH 2 to Masterton.

Masterton is a busy rural town. An international sheep-shearing competition, the Golden Shears, is held here each year in the

Feeding the kaka at Pukaha Mt Bruce.

first week of March. Queen Elizabeth Park on Dixon street is a delightful complex of gardens and streams with an aviary and a deer park. Aratoi Wairarapa Museum of Art and History on Bruce Street is well worth a visit, as is the Museum of Early Childhood, on Makora Road, which has a fascinating collection of antique dolls, toys, teddy bears, games and books.

7 CASTLEPOINT

The turn-off to Castlepoint is clearly signposted just north of Masterton township. Drive east 61 km on sealed roads via Tauweru, Tinui and Whakataki, to the coast. This detour will take approximately 2 hours return.

Castlepoint is one of the most picturesque locations on this remote stretch of coastline. There are a number of walks from the end of the road. You can visit a huge limestone cave, walk to Deliverance Cove and climb the 162 m Castle Rock for impressive views along the coast, or cross the bridge on a short boardwalk to the old Castlepoint lighthouse built in 1913.

8 CARTERTON

Return 61 km to Masterton and travel 15 km south-west to Carterton on SH 2.

Originally known as Three Mile Bush, Carterton was renamed after a local member of Parliament. St Mark's Church, the public library and a cast-iron band rotunda are the few early structures that survived a fire that devastated the town in its early days. Despite this setback, Carterton grew along with the dairy industry which prospered on the rich alluvial soils.

9 GREYTOWN

Travel a further 9 km south-west on SH 2 to Greytown.

Greytown was the first settlement in the Wairarapa area, established in 1854 and named after Governor Sir George Grey, who endorsed the Small Farm Association which aimed to place labourers on their own farms. Both Greytown and Masterton were originally settled under this scheme.

The town is set among mature trees, many dating back to 1890 when Greytown introduced Arbour Day to New Zealand. Its main street is a charming and functional showcase of Victorian architecture with beautiful wooden buildings many of which house art and antiques shops as well as excellent cafés. Cobblestones Museum, on Main Street, displays farming equipment, transport and household items inside a restored 1850s cottage. On the outskirts of the town is Papawai Marae and its meeting house, Te Wai Pounamu. This was the centre of a Maori self-government initiative,

Cobblestones Museum, Greytown.

Kotahitanga, in the late 1890s. Waiohine Gorge, to the north-west of Greytown and on the fringe of the Tararua Forest Park, has fine stands of kahikatea, rimu, rata and beech.

10 FEATHERSTON

Drive south-west 14 km to Featherston on SH 2.

Originally named Burlings after an 1840s pioneer, the town was renamed in 1854 after Dr Isaac Featherston, Wellington's first provincial superintendent. During the First World War it was the site of New Zealand's largest military camp, which became a Japanese prisoners-of-war camp in the 1940s.

Historic buildings include Anzac Hall, built in 1915 as a place to entertain troops in training, the courthouse, library and two churches. The Fell Engine Museum on the main highway has the last of the locomotives that made the 1 in 5 grade climb on three rails over the Rimutaka Incline from 1890 until a tunnel was opened in 1955. The old railway line is now a walking and mountain bike trail.

11 MARTINBOROUGH

From Featherston turn left onto SH 53 and drive 18 km south-east to Martinborough.

The first flocks of sheep in New Zealand were brought from Sydney to Nelson in 1843 by Charles Bidwill. They were then transported to Wellington and driven around the rugged coast to the Wairarapa, where Bidwill leased land from the Maori for grazing. He established the country's first sheep station near Martinborough in 1844.

The town is a popular destination for day trippers from Wellington. The area around Martinborough has many wineries and is well known for its pinot noir. The town's street plan is based on the design of the Union Jack, with eight streets radiating from the central square, many named after places local runholder Sir John Martin visited overseas.

From Martinborough, return to Featherston and travel 64 km to Wellington on SH 2, including a steep and winding stretch over the Rimutaka Range soon after leaving Featherston.

27 THE KING COUNTRY

DRIVING TOUR ■ 322 KM ■ 1 DAY ■ CAVES, GLOW-WORMS AND MOA BONES

The west coast route south from Hamilton passes through a singular countryside dominated by stark limestone formations that once were part of the sea bed. Beneath this dramatic landscape hundreds of kilometres of caves form a strangely beautiful world of their own.

The rugged area south-west of the Waikato, around Otorohanga, Waitomo and extending to the coast, is known as the King Country. The Maori King Movement, which sought to unite the tribes on a national basis, developed in the Waikato in the 1850s. After the Waikato War of 1863–64, King Tawhiao, the second Maori king, and his people moved south and the region became known as the King Country, with access forbidden to Europeans until the 1880s. The arrival of the Main Trunk Railway line ended its isolation in 1908.

The area is notable for its geological features, especially the distinctive rock formations and complex cave systems formed over thousands of years as water carrying acids from decomposing plant matter dissolved its way through the limestone rock.

1 TE AWAMUTU
From Hamilton travel 30 km south on SH 3 to Te Awamutu.

For many years Te Awamutu was a frontier town, located on the northern border of land confiscated from Maori 'rebels'. The Otawhao mission was established here much earlier, in 1839, by the Rev. John Morgan who initiated the construction of St John's Church (1854), located in Arawata Street. Gravestones around the church mark the final resting place of a number of soldiers who fell in the historic battle of Orakau. The Te Awamutu and District Museum on Roche Street houses a significant collection of Maori and European artefacts including the 'Uenuku' carving, said to have been brought to New Zealand on the *Tainui* ancestral canoe.

Te Awamutu is known as the 'Rose Town', and in early summer over 2000 roses bloom in a magnificent display in the Rose Gardens at the northern end of the town.

2 KIHIKIHI
Drive 4 km south-east on SH 3 to Kihikihi.

The centre of this town features a monument to the venerated Maori warrior Rewi Maniapoto. Kihikihi was the venue of the final battles of the Waikato War. A few kilometres east of the town at Orakau, 300 Maori dug in behind hastily prepared earthworks to face over 1000 Imperial troops armed with muskets and hand grenades and supported by artillery. Rewi Maniapoto regarded the position as untenable, but his proven military judgement was overruled by a local chief. They stayed and fought a legendary defence, repelling several major attacks before retreating to what was to become known as the King Country.

3 OTOROHANGA
Drive south-west 25 km to Otorohanga on SH 3.

The Otorohanga Zoological Society gained an international reputation for successfully breeding the kiwi, New Zealand's national symbol, in captivity. In the Kiwi House and Native Bird Centre on Alex Telfer Drive you

Stalactites in Aranui Cave, Waitomo.

The Marokopa River hurtles over a precipice at the awesome Marokopa Falls.

can see kiwi under simulated nocturnal conditions. A walk-through aviary houses over 300 species of native birds, including the saddleback, kakariki, bellbird, tui and morepork.

4 WAITOMO CAVES
Drive 8 km south on SH 3 to the Waitomo turn-off. Turn right and travel west 8 km on SH 37 to the Waitomo Caves.

The Waitomo cave systems are a subterranean wonderland. The caves were discovered in 1887 and have delighted generations of tourists since. Ruakuri and Aranui Caves have impressive formations of stalagmites and stalactites, and Waitomo Cave offers a boat trip into a glow-worm grotto.

The nearby Ohaki Maori Village is a replica of a pre-European pa. From the car park, a half-hour walk climbs to a site where plaques identify many of the features of the pa as well as describing traditional plant medicines found in the forest.

5 MANGAPOHUE NATURAL BRIDGE SCENIC RESERVE
Continue west 26 km to the Mangapohue Natural Bridge Scenic Reserve. A walking track starts from the car park on the right side of the road.

A short boardwalk leads through a forest-clad gorge to an impressive natural rock arch carved out of soft limestone by the Mangapohue River. From the adjacent farm you can arrange to take a guided tour to the Marokopa Tunnel, a massive 270 m long natural rock tunnel that is up to 50 metres high.

6 PIRIPIRI CAVES
Continue west 3 km to the Piripiri Caves signposted on the right.

The caves, reached on a 30-minute walking track, have the fossilised remains of shellfish embedded in their walls, a reminder that the landscape was once submerged beneath the sea. You will need a torch if you want to explore the caves beyond the entrance.

7 MAROKOPA FALLS
Travel 2 km west to the Marokopa Falls. There is a viewing platform near the top of the falls on the left not far from the road, and a short distance further down the hill on the left a 10-minute track leads down from the road to the river below the falls.

The Marokopa Falls are among the most beautiful in the North Island. Located right on the edge of the contact zone between limestone and volcanic rock formations, these spectacular falls drop 37 m over a faultline into a deep valley cut by the Marokopa River.

8 TE KUITI
Return east 39 km to SH 3, turn right and drive south 12 km along lowland river valleys to Te Kuiti and the starting point of the hill country.

The township of Te Kuiti, heralded as the 'Shearing Capital of the World', boasts a prominent statue of a shearer. Te Kuiti was the home of King Tawhiao from 1864 to 1881. He provided sanctuary for Te Kooti and his rebel followers, who built the Te Tokanganui-a-Noho meeting house in 1878 as a sign of their gratitude. This meeting house, on the main road, possesses probably the best examples of Maori carving outside a museum anywhere in the country.

9 AWAKINO
Drive 73 km south-west on SH 3 to Awakino via Piopio and Mahoenui. The road passes through the scenic Awakino Gorge to the Tasman coast. This is limestone country, a landscape perforated by caves and potholes, many of which contain the skeletal remains of the now-extinct moa and other flightless birds.

This coastal township was a port of call for river steamers during the early days of settlement. To the south of the town are the earthworks of Maniaroa Pa, once the resting place of the anchor stone from the fabled *Tainui*. The canoe is said to have landed at Mokau to the south, and its anchor now lies on the grave of Tamati Kingi Te Wetere in the Awakino cemetery.

10 MOKAU
Drive 5 km south along the coast to Mokau.

Mokau was a busy nineteenth-century port, shipping coal and timber that had been hauled out from along the Mokau River. The Tainui Museum has a collection of photographs recording the history of the area.

11 THE THREE SISTERS
Continue south 18 km on SH 3 to Tongaporutu. An access road to the right on the southern side of the driftwood-strewn inlet leads to the coast.

A 25-minute walk leads to the Three Sisters, a series of towering coastal rock stacks. This is part of the White Cliffs Walkway which runs for nearly 10 km south along the coast to Pukearuhe.

12 MOTUNUI
From Tongaporutu drive 4 km south on SH 3 to Ahititi, continue inland on SH 3 across the forest-clad slopes of Mt Messenger and back down to the coast 32 km south-west at Urenui, a popular beach in summer. About 5 km before Urenui, near the turn-off to Pukearuhe, the White Cliffs Brewing Company offers sampling of its naturally brewed beer. From Urenui continue west 8 km to Motunui.

Motunui's huge synthetic-fuel operation was opened in 1986 as a government 'Think Big' project. It converted natural gas from the offshore Maui field to methanol, which in turn was converted to a synthetic fuel that was blended with petroleum refined from imported crude at Marsden Point. Synthetic petrol is no longer made, but Synfuel remains the largest methanol-production facility in the world. A visitor centre outside the plant has displays explaining the process.

From Motunui travel 22 km via Waitara to New Plymouth.

Weirdly formed rock stacks, known as the Three Sisters, on the Taranaki Coast.

28 TARANAKI

DRIVING TOUR ▪ 225 KM ▪ 1 DAY ▪ RAINFOREST AND DAIRYLAND

The scenic roads on this trip climb through rainforests high into the subalpine zone on Taranaki/Mt Egmont, and cross the plains through old timber towns to exotic gardens, unusual museums and a 400-year-old Maori fortress.

The mountain known as both Taranaki and Egmont is the symmetrical centrepiece of this province, and its influence spreads far and wide. Scientists believe the mountain may once have had a crater lake from which, during numerous eruptions, mudflows spread across the plains, nourishing the lush rainforests that covered the region. The earliest European settlers were largely engaged in the timber industry, then when the forests were felled, the rich volcanic soils supported the dairy farms that have grown into Taranaki's main industry today. Alpine streams feed icy-cold water across the fertile plains that surround the mountain, and snow-cooled temperatures enable the rhododendron, a gorgeously flowered Himalayan shrub, to flourish in Taranaki's gardens.

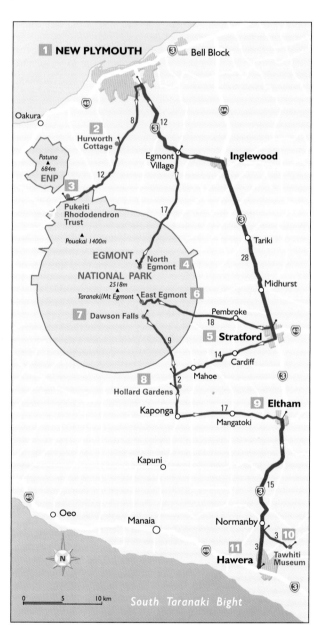

Taranaki, a dormant volcano that dominates the landscape, is 70,000 years old. Ancient Maori buried dead chiefs in caves on its snowy heights.

◼ NEW PLYMOUTH

The city's past survives in many preserved historic buildings. Regimental flags from the Taranaki Wars are on display inside St Mary's on Vivian Street, New Zealand's first stone church (1842). This architectural gem was designed by Frederick Thatcher, who was also responsible for The Gables Cottage hospital in Brooklands Park. Opposite Richmond Cottage, on Ariki Street, is the Taranaki Museum with a fascinating collection of Maori and colonial artefacts. Pukekura Park is a 10-minute walk from the city centre with 49 ha of gardens, bush walks, streams, ponds, waterfalls and a lake. In adjacent Brooklands Park you will find over 300 varieties of rhododendron and a 2000-year-old puriri tree.

◼ HURWORTH COTTAGE

From central New Plymouth drive 8 km south on Carrington Road to Hurworth at number 906, on the right side of the road.

Hurworth Cottage was built in 1856 by Harry Atkinson, who later served four terms as New Zealand's premier.

A typical Taranaki pioneer cottage in the style so commonly built in the 1850s.

Pukekura Park near the centre of New Plymouth, considered to be the finest garden in New Zealand, is full of unexpected corners and delightful walkways.

3 PUKEITI RHODODENDRON TRUST

Continue south-west 12 km on Carrington Road through farmland to Pukeiti.

The world-famous Pukeiti Rhododendron Trust gardens are set in forest between the Pouakai and Kaitake Ranges. Formed in 1951 to promote interest in rhododendrons and azaleas and the protection of native forests and birds, Pukeiti is particularly spectacular in the flowering season from late September to November. The site was selected because of the cool airflow coming off the mountain slopes, which creates ideal growing conditions for this shrub native to Nepal.

4 NORTH EGMONT

Return to New Plymouth and travel south-east 12 km on SH 3 to the Egmont Village. Turn right and drive 17 km up onto the mountain to North Egmont.

The drive to this road end passes through luxuriant rainforest that clothes the lower slopes, then climbs into the subalpine zone where tree growth is stunted by the cold air and high winds of this harsh alpine environment. Short walking tracks wind through the distinctive 'cloud forests' of dwarf kamahi with their twisted and moss-covered trunks.

The visitor centre at the top of the road provides maps and information on the mountain. Egmont National Park covers over 33,000 ha and includes the dormant volcanic cones of the nearby Pouakai Range and Kaitake Peak as well as Taranaki/ Mt Egmont, which last erupted around 1755. Taranaki's 2518 m peak is one of the most climbed in New Zealand.

5 STRATFORD

Return to Egmont Village, turn right onto SH 3 and drive 28 km to Stratford. The road passes through Inglewood where a large number of Polish, Russian and German migrants settled during its early years as a mill town.

Stratford started out as a timber town in the nineteenth century. It was named after William Shakespeare's birthplace and many of its streets bear the names of Shakespearean characters. The Patea River winds through the centre of Stratford and the town has many parks and gardens. The Taranaki Pioneer Village, 1 km south of the town on SH 3, is a very large, interesting outdoor museum with many reconstructed colonial buildings.

6 EAST EGMONT

From the centre of Stratford drive west 18 km on Pembroke Road, heading for the skifields at East Egmont.

A number of tracks signposted from the road lead into the rainforests, including the short Kamahi Walk through one of the moss-covered 'cloud forests'. From the car park at the end of Pembroke Road a well-graded 20-minute track takes you to Manganui Lodge, with good views over the ski area which features some of New Zealand's steepest runs.

7 DAWSON FALLS

Return to Stratford, turn right onto the main street and take the next turn right signposted to Dawson Falls. Drive 14 km west, turn right at the signposted junction and drive north-west 9 km up onto the mountain.

This beautiful drive climbs through the rainforest to the Stratford Mountain House and the park visitor centre, located at the end of Dawson Falls Road. The falls can be viewed from a lookout which is about 10 minutes' walk from the car park. The visitor centre provides maps for a number of other short tracks on this side of the mountain.

8 HOLLARD GARDENS

Drive 9 km down off the mountain and continue straight ahead through the next intersection for 2 km on Upper Manaia Road.

This large, rambling garden features a vast array of rare plants, rhododendrons and an unusual swamp garden.

9 ELTHAM

Continue on Manaia Road for 3 km south to Kaponga. Turn left at Kaponga and drive east on Eltham Road 14 km to Eltham.

Eltham was the home of the enterprising Chinese merchant Chew Chong, who began exporting edible fungus and then butter from the district in the 1880s. New Zealand's first co-operative dairying scheme was eventually established here, and Eltham now produces award-winning cheeses, including its famous blue vein.

10 TAWHITI MUSEUM

From Eltham take SH 3 and drive 15 km south to the Tawhiti Museum turn-off. Turn left onto Ohangai Road and drive south-east 3 km to the museum.

Perhaps the most entertaining private museum in the country, this is the brainchild of Nigel Ogle, a model-maker who has created an incredible array of lifelike figures by taking moulds from local people. These figures bring to life his fascinating displays, which are housed in an old dairy factory.

11 HAWERA

Return to SH 3, turn left and drive south for 3 km to Hawera.

The name Hawera means 'burnt place' and relates to an early inter-tribal battle when a whare (house) was incinerated along with its sleeping inhabitants. Hawera's fiery history continued, with parts of the town destroyed by blazes in 1884, 1885 and 1912. This led to the construction of the 54 m water tower which now stands empty and offers excellent views of the srrounding area. In the centre of the town King Edward Park has a willow-pattern garden with a lake surrounded by azaleas. The 400-year-old Turuturu-mokai Pa is located just north of the town on a 10 ha reserve. Nearby is the site of a redoubt where British soldiers underwent a fearsome attack by Titokowaru's war party in 1868.

Kevin Wasley's Elvis Presley Memorial Room at 51 Argyl Street houses an impressive collection. About 2 km south-east on SH 3 is the most sophisticated milk-products processing plant in the Southern Hemisphere. The Kiwi Co-operative Dairy Company's visitor centre has a revolving restaurant, and displays include a simulated ride in the cab of a milk tanker on its morning run.

A realistic dummy in the Tawhiti Museum.

29 THE WHANGANUI RIVER ROAD

DRIVING TOUR ■ 116 KM ■ 4 HOURS ■ ALONGSIDE A LEGENDARY WATERWAY

The scenic road that winds along the course of the mighty Whanganui River offers constantly changing views and passes through old battlegrounds, mission stations and tiny settlements that trace the colourful history of the river.

Rising high on the volcanic plateau in Tongariro National Park, the Whanganui River is the longest navigable waterway in the country and has been a pathway into the wilderness for both Maori and European settlers. Mission villages were established up the river during the 1840s, although poplars and willow trees planted during those early days are all that is now left of many of the settlements.

During the Hauhau rebellion in the 1860s the river was first successfully negotiated by a steam vessel when the Gundagai *carried troops and supplies as far as Koriniti. The* Moutoa *later reached Pipiriki, and by 1886 a commercial steamer service was in operation. The river cruise became internationally famous and tourists stayed at a splendid hotel called Pipiriki House and a floating hotel, the Houseboat, moored at Maraekowhai.*

Today the best way to see the river is still by boat, but for land-based explorers there are some fascinating places that can be visited on the back-country roads that venture through this beautiful wilderness area.

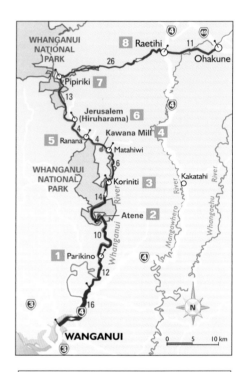

1 PARIKINO

From Wanganui drive north-east 16 km on SH 4, take the Whanganui River Road to the left and follow the river north 12 km to Parikino. One of the best views of the river is on this stretch of road heading north over the 230 m rise known as the Gentle Annie Hill. From the summit there is a panoramic view of the Whanganui Valley and the settlement of Parikino.

Parikino's quaint little Roman Catholic church serves as a reminder of Father Soulas, a priest who established several missions along the river in the late nineteenth century. During the 1860s Hauhau adherents of the Pai Marire faith travelled down the Whanga-nui River to attack Wanganui. They were defeated by other Maori at Moutoa Island and at Ohoutahi in two important battles, the government later building redoubts at Parikino, Koriniti and Pipiriki to defend the city.

2 ATENE

Drive 10 km north to Atene.

Atene is one of a series of mission stations given classical and biblical names by the Rev. Richard Taylor in the 1800s. Atene is the Maori translation of Athens. The township's meeting house, Te-Rangi-he-keiho, has the curved roof characteristic of buildings in the Whanganui River area.

3 KORINITI

Continue north 14 km to Koriniti. The seal ends after 5 km and the road is gravel from here on north to Pipiriki.

Koriniti (Corinth) has two meeting houses, Poutama and Te Waiherehere, on its marae. Poutama was transported to Koriniti from its original location across the river in 1967. Most of the important carvings from the older Te Waiherehere are now located in the Wanganui Museum. The Pepara Church was first built in 1848 and rebuilt in 1920. There is also an old mission house, a carved gateway and mounted canoe at Koriniti. To the north-west a short distance upstream lies the site of the renowned Operiki fighting pa with earthworks 3.5 m high.

4 KAWANA MILL

Drive north 6 km to Matahiwi. The Kawana Mill is on the left.

In the 1850s thousands of hectares of wheat were planted on the river flats in the Whanganui Valley by Maori farmers. The

The water-driven Kawana flour mill.

Viewed from the Gentle Annie Hill, the Whanganui River can be appreciated as a mighty 'highway'. Sweeping 290 km from its wild inland reaches to the coast, in pre-European times it was plied by hundreds of canoes.

Kawana Mill, built in 1854, is the only surviving example of over 50 flour mills that once operated along the Whanganui River. The mill was the longest operating and most successful in the valley. It fell into disrepair during the First World War but the waterwheel and grinding stones survived, allowing the mill to be completely rebuilt along with a nearby miller's cottage. Inside you can view the workings and see the old millstones originally presented by Governor George Grey (kawana is the Maori word for governor).

5 RANANA
Travel north-west 4 km to Ranana.

Ranana (the Maori translation of London) is a settlement founded by Father Soulas in the late 1880s on the banks of the Whanganui River. Nearby is the site of a famous battle of 1864 when the lower Whanganui tribes saved the township from attack by defeating an upriver Hauhau war party on Moutoa Island.

6 HIRUHARAMA
Continue 4 km north-west to Jerusalem (Hiruharama).

This photogenic little village set on a bend of the Whanganui River belies the savage history of inter-tribal war that marks the area's past. The delicate spire of the local church attracts visitors and the inside of the building features kowhaiwhai panelling and a carved altar, the legacy of the Roman Catholic mission that was re-established here in 1883 by Mother Aubert, a French nun who came to Auckland to work with Bishop Pompallier in 1860. The New Zealand poet James K. Baxter established a commune at Jerusalem in 1969, where he wrote his well-known *Jerusalem Sonnets*. He was buried here after his death in 1972.

7 PIPIRIKI
From Hiruharama drive 13 km north to Pipiriki.

When Pipiriki was one of New Zealand's busiest river ports and a major tourist centre on the main route inland and later to Mt Ruapehu, it boasted an elegant guest house that could accommodate over a hundred visitors and included a glassed-in wintergarden. The hotel burned down in 1959 but Colonial House, formerly the home of a riverboat captain, has become a museum and information centre.

From the Ranger Station a 20-minute walk up Pukehinau Hill provides views along the river valley. The hill was a Hauhau stronghold during the siege of Pipiriki in 1865 when up to 400 Hauhau warriors attacked the garrison. After heavy fighting the Hauhau surrounded and laid siege to the three redoubts in the area. The men of the garrison were short of supplies and under constant fire, and in desperation sent messages asking for help floating downstream in bottles. One of the messages eventually got through but by the time reinforcements arrived in Pipiriki they found that the Hauhau, who had run low on ammunition, had made peace the previous day.

8 RAETIHI
From Pipiriki drive 26 km east to Raetihi. The road is gravel for the first 11 km.

Raetihi was founded as a bush settlement in 1892 and almost destroyed in 1918 by a forest fire so huge that the smoke drifted to Wellington. The small Waimarino Museum on Seddon Street occupies Raetihi's old relocated railway station.

From Raetihi it is 11 km east to Ohakune.

Colonial House at Pipiriki reflects some of the elegance of the Whanganui's Victorian tourism era.

30 SOUTH-EAST FROM WANGANUI

DRIVING TOUR ■ 88 KM ■ 4 HOURS ■ A RIVER CITY AND GREEN ROLLING PLAINS

Historic farmhouses, churches and relics are scattered throughout this countryside, but many of the region's treasures lie within small museums that the local communities have carefully tended over the years.

The three main rivers that flow from the central North Island to the coastline between Wanganui and Wellington have played an important part in the development of this area. In pre-European times the coastal lowlands were mainly covered in dense forests and swamplands so for the early Maori these waterways were the easiest and most direct routes to travel inland. After European settlers arrived, the Whanganui River carried steamers north to Taumarunui, the Main Trunk Railway line followed the course of the Rangitikei, and beside the Manawatu a road and rail route was developed between the Tararua and Ruahine mountain ranges through to the Wairarapa.

■ WANGANUI

One of the oldest cities in the country, Wanganui was founded in 1841 by the New Zealand Company. The original site of the city is now the location of the historic Moutoa Gardens. The city was a frontier town during the New Zealand Wars, relics from which can be seen in the Wanganui Regional Museum in Queens Park. On display are Major Kemp's sword, Te Kooti's battle flag, and the canoe *Te-Mata-o-Hoturoa* which dates back to 1810 and may have seen battle in the attack on Te Rauparaha's fortress at Kapiti Island in 1829. The museum also features a recreation of an early Wanganui shopping street. The Sarjeant Gallery, also located in Queens Park, houses a fine collection of New Zealand art. The images captured in these nineteenth-century paintings provide a vivid glimpse into the colonial period of New Zealand's history.

Wanganui has many interesting historic buildings. One of the oldest is Tylee Cottage, on the corner of Bell and Cameron Streets, which was built in 1853 for the Commissariat of the British troops stationed in Wanganui. The old buildings at the Wanganui Collegiate School on Liverpool Street include the headmaster's house, the Big School and a pavilion, all part of a precinct of historic interest registered by the Historic Places Trust. The clock tower at Cooks Gardens, on Hill Street, stands on the site of the York Stockade and was originally built as a fire lookout tower in 1891. It was at this sporting centre that Peter Snell, the future Olympic gold medallist, recorded a world-record time running the mile in 1962. Next to Cooks Gardens is the wooden Opera House which was opened in 1899 and is among the finest buildings in the city.

The Durie Hill Memorial Tower, 33 m high

Virginia Lake in Wanganui is surrounded by enchanting gardens and picnic spots.

A distinctive folk art developed in the Ratana movement, exemplified in the twin-towered temple that is the centre of the unique community at Ratana.

and built from fossilised shell rock, provides excellent views across the city and the Whanganui River. An elevator, built in 1919, rises 66 m to the tower from a 213 m access tunnel at the base of the hill, across the river almost opposite the Wanganui City Bridge. Virginia Lake, 1.5 km north of the city on Great North Road, St Johns Hill, has a garden setting with picturesque pathways around the edge of the lake.

2 PUTIKI

From central Wanganui take SH 3 and immediately after crossing Cobham Bridge turn left into Anaua Street and travel 1 km.

The ancient pa at Putiki is one of the most historic locations in the Wanganui area. In 1829 Te Rauparaha defeated the local tribes in battle here. When one of the early missionaries, Richard Taylor, arrived 14 years later, there were still bones lying on the battlefield, which he gathered up and buried. Taylor served at the Anglican mission which was established at Putiki and was staffed until the 1880s. St Paul's Church (1937) is the fifth church built on the site and features fine Maori carvings, tukutuku and kowhaiwhai panelling. The meeting house at Putiki Pa, Te Paku-o-te-Rangi, replaced an earlier meeting house close to the river that was washed away in 1891. Many of the carvings are older than the meeting house and the pataka (sunken storehouse) at the pa dates back to the 1890s.

3 RATANA

Return to SH 3, turn right and drive south-east 16 km to the Ratana turn-off. Turn right and travel west 2 km to Ratana.

Conditions were hard for many Maori during the early 1900s. In 1918 Tahupotiki Wiremu Ratana, a Maori farmer with a gift for faith healing, had a vision of a better way of life for his people. This led to his founding the Ratana Church in 1925. The teachings of this charismatic leader were basically Christian, and his followers were mainly Maori. The unique Ratana Temple displays striking decor and symbolism. Its towers represent the two sons of Ratana, Alpha and Omega. Ratana, who died in 1939, and his wife are buried in front of the temple. The Ratana faith developed into a powerful political movement with several members holding influential seats in Parliament.

4 FEILDING

Return to SH 3 and drive south-east 26 km to Bulls via Turakina, the first European township established between Wanganui and Wellington. From Bulls continue south 6 km on SH 1 to Sanson, continue straight ahead 8 km on SH 3 to Awahuri, turn left and head north-east 6 km to Feilding.

This busy country town was named after Colonel William Feilding, who purchased land in the district in the 1870s on behalf of the Emigrants' and Colonists' Aid Corporation, whose patron was the Duke of Manchester. The town's layout was modelled on the city of Manchester, with two central squares. A number of the settlers' original cottages survive in Goodbehere and Beattie Streets, and St John's Church dates back to colonial times. A lookout on Highfield Road gives a fine view of the town and the plains beyond. Kowhai Park, on South Street, is an attractive garden with caged birds and a lake.

5 PALMERSTON NORTH

From Feilding drive 15 km on SH 54 to Newbury, turn left onto SH 3 and travel 5 km to Palmerston North.

Palmerston North, the main centre of the Manawatu region, was settled in 1870 in an area where the forest had been cleared and burned, leaving a flat expanse of featureless land. Perhaps it was the devastation that inspired the city's founding fathers to create four large areas of parkland at the heart of the town. Today these are a focal point, complemented by the Cherry Drive that is a riot of blossom in spring, and the landscaped grounds of Massey University which was established as an agricultural college in 1928.

The city's oldest surviving building, a house named Totaranui built about 1874, can be viewed along with an impressive display of historical material at the Manawatu Museum on Main Street. The house is fully furnished to give visitors a picture of how middle-class families lived in the early 1900s. The theme is continued with a reconstruction of a general store and a smithy, and an old country school house has been relocated to the site. The Maori galleries feature beautifully displayed carvings and exhibits from the Manawatu, Rangitikei and Horowhenua areas. The Palmerston North Art Gallery on Main Street West exhibits mainly New Zealand artists and the Rugby Museum on Cuba Street celebrates the national sport.

An old parish church overlooking Turakina.

Farmland near Palmerston North.

31 WELLINGTON CITY

DRIVING TOUR ■ 18 KM ■ 5 HOURS ■ AROUND THE HARBOUR CAPITAL

Wellington city nestles compactly on the harbour edge, encircled by steeply rising hills. The nation's capital is a flourishing centre of arts and culture, including a thriving film industry; the city served as the base of operations for the Lord of the Rings movie trilogy.

A huge natural harbour bounded by steep windswept hills on the southern shores of the North Island was the strategically located site chosen by the New Zealand Company in 1840 for its first settlement. During the first nine years, the number of colonists in Wellington dwindled from 436 to 85; nevertheless, the New Zealand Company had successfully anticipated the movement of the capital from Auckland. In 1865 the colonial administration, fearful that the immigrants in the South Island might break away and form a separate colony, sought a more central location and the future of Wellington was assured as government officials and diplomats began to arrive.

Wellington is regularly buffeted by the high winds that funnel through Cook Strait, the only gap in New Zealand's 1400 km chain of mountains. Located on a major fault line, Wellington experienced a severe earthquake in 1855 and in recent times has led the world in the development and application of technology to create earthquake-resistant buildings. Today the city beautifully combines modern high-rise developments along its reclaimed foreshore with gracious old homes that cling to the hillsides above the city.

Parliament Buildings sit stolidly beside the whimsical Beehive.

1 MUSEUM OF WELLINGTON CITY AND SEA

Driving south into Wellington on SH 1, turn left off the motorway onto Aotea Quay and travel 1 km south onto Waterloo Quay, continuing south 1 km onto Customhouse Quay. Take the first turn to the left onto Jervois Quay. The museum is on the left.

The magnificent old Harbour Board Bond Store on Wellington's quayside is the home of the Museum of Wellington City and Sea, which displays numerous model ships, figureheads and even the complete teak cabin from an 1879 steamship. The museum explores the city's social and maritime history, graphically presenting intriguing aspects of its earliest days. The Queens Wharf Centre is nearby, and a few minutes' walk south on Jervois Quay is the City to Sea Bridge linking an artificial lagoon with Civic Square where the City Gallery Wellington, the Edwardian style Town Hall and Michael Fowler Centre are grouped.

2 TE PAPA

Continue south-east 1 km along Jervois Quay onto Cable Street on the one-way system. The Museum of New Zealand Te Papa Tongarewa is on the left.

One of the largest new museums in the world, this exciting, futuristic multi-storeyed complex covers an area the size of three football fields and includes a canoe hall, natural history exhibits, a human cultures

Wellington's maritime history is explored in the Museum of Wellington City and Sea.

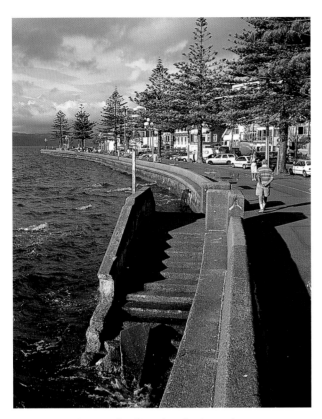

Oriental Bay, a favourite lunching place for city workers.

The Wellington cable car makes light work of Wellington's hills.

Constable Street. At the end of this street turn right into Riddiford Sreet and drive north onto Adelaide Road. At the northern end of Adelaide Road take a left turn onto Rugby Street and follow the one-way system around the Basin Reserve onto Sussex Street then turn left onto Buckle Street. Turn left again into Taranaki Street, right almost immediately into Webb Street, take the third street on the left (Thompson Street) then turn right into Nairn Street. The Colonial Cottage Museum is on the left.

This restored colonial cottage is Wellington's second-oldest building, dating back to 1858 and located on the site of an 1840 New Zealand Company Town Acre. The cottage is typical of the homes early settlers lived in during the first years of the city's development and is fully furnished with household articles from the period.

6 WELLINGTON CABLE CAR
Continue north on Nairn Street into Brooklyn Road and straight ahead into Willis Street. At the fourth set of traffic lights turn left onto Lambton Quay. The Wellington cable car is signposted on the left off Cable Car Lane.

A fun way to obtain good views across Wellington city is to take a ride on the Wellington cable car, which climbs 130 m above the commercial district past Victoria University and Kelburn Park through a series of tunnels to the Botanic Gardens. The original wooden cable cars, built in 1902, were replaced by Swiss-manufactured carriages in 1979.

7 BOTANIC GARDENS
From the cable car terminus, stroll back toward Lambton Quay through the Botanic Gardens.

The gardens cover 26 ha and feature over 300 rose varieties in the Lady Norwood Rose Garden, as well as succulents, ferns, rhododendrons, camellias, fuchsias, exotic trees and walkways through native forest.

8 GOVERNMENT BUILDINGS
On Lambton Quay, continue north to the corner of Bowen Street. The old Government Buildings are across the road on the right.

The Government Buildings, built in 1876, are one of the largest wooden structures in the world. Reopened in 1996, the buildings are open to the public with historical interpretation rooms on the ground floor and the original cabinet room on the first floor.

gallery, a national art collection and a children's learning centre. Bush City gives a taste of the New Zealand outdoors, from wetlands to glow-worm caves, and visitors can walk across a trampers' swing bridge. Awesome Forces features realistic displays that explore the volcanic power that shaped much of the country.

3 ORIENTAL BAY
Continue south-east on Cable Street, turn left onto Oriental Parade and drive 2 km east to Carlton Gore Road.

A short walk along this stretch of waterfront will take you past fashionable cafés and afford fine views of Wellington's beautiful harbour. On the hillsides overlooking the bay cluster old and new houses in a fascinating range of architectural styles.

4 MT VICTORIA
From Oriental Parade turn right into Carlton Gore Road, continue up the hill onto Grafton Road and turn right into Palliser Road. Take the first turn on the left into Thane Road, continue into Alexandra Road and take the signposted turn to the right to the Mt Victoria Lookout. It is 3 km from Oriental Parade to the lookout.

A wonderful panoramic view of Wellington city and Port Nicholson across to the Hutt Valley can be enjoyed from the lookout on Mt Victoria. The cannon on the summit was installed in 1877 and for a number of years was fired each day as a time signal.

5 COLONIAL COTTAGE MUSEUM
From Mt Victoria return to Alexandra Road, continue south 2 km and turn right onto

9 THE BEEHIVE
Continue north on Lambton Quay and turn left into Molesworth Street.

Designed by British architect Sir Basil Spence to house the executive offices of Parliament, the distinctive circular Beehive was opened in 1980. Adjacent are Parliament Buildings built in 1922 from Takaka marble and Coromandel granite.

10 THE NATIONAL LIBRARY
From the Beehive head north up Molesworth Street to the National Library of New Zealand, on the right on the corner of Aitken Street.

The National Library of New Zealand holds a rich and varied collection of research material as well as copies of every New Zealand publication. Within the building is the Alexander Turnbull Library which contains a world-famous collection of valuable historical publications including a very fine Milton collection. In the Pacific section are accounts by Pacific voyagers over a period of nearly 500 years as well as historical works by early visitors to New Zealand.

11 OLD ST PAUL'S
From the National Library continue north on Molesworth Street, turn right into Pipitea Street then right into Mulgrave Street. Old St Paul's is on the left.

The former Wellington Cathedral, Old St Paul's is a must-see for all architecture buffs. Designed in Gothic-revival style, the church was built as a temporary cathedral in 1866 from native timbers, with matai and totara floors, kauri pews, rimu framing and trusses. The beautiful natural light and stained-glass windows create a warm, peaceful atmosphere. Memorial brass plaques tell the story of early Wellington, and over the years parishioners have gifted furnishings and fittings which tell their own personal stories.

12 NATIONAL ARCHIVES
Adjacent to Old St Paul's on Mulgrave Street.

The National Archives have on display in the constitution Room of New Zealand many of the country's founding documents, including the Treaty of Waitangi, and other national treasures. New Zealand was the first country in the world to give women the right to vote and the 1893 Women's Suffrage Petition is one of the items on view.

SOUTH ISLAND
NELSON AND MARLBOROUGH

32 MARLBOROUGH SOUNDS

DRIVING TOUR ■ 237 KM ■ 1 DAY ■ SHIMMERING SEASCAPES AND LUSH BUSH

When Captain Cook reached the South Island in 1770 he anchored in Ship Cove – and stayed for three weeks. His log became almost poetic in describing the glorious sounds where travellers today experience much the same magic.

The long peninsulas that snake out into the waters of the Marlborough Sounds are the dominant feature in this extraordinary landscape. These ridgelines were the highest points in a series of ranges and river valleys that originally formed the northern tip of the South Island. At the end of the last ice age the sea level rose and the river valleys were flooded, creating the magnificent Queen Charlotte, Kenepuru and Pelorus Sounds, winding tracts of water that are bordered by narrow slivers of land stretching from the mainland out into Cook Strait.

1 PICTON

Picton, once considered as a possible site for the capital city, lies on the southern shores of Queen Charlotte Sound. As the location of the inter-island ferry terminus it is the gateway to the South Island for thousands of visitors each year.

Picton Museum, near London Quay, has a collection of Maori artefacts and a number of relics from the whaling days including one of the old harpoon guns. A short distance along the eastern shoreline of the harbour, you can go on board the coastal trader *Echo*, which was built on the Wairau River in 1905 and used to ship freight between Blenheim and Wellington until 1965, when the rail ferry service began. This old scow even saw service during the Second World War when she was used by the United States Navy as an escort vessel during the Bougainville campaign in 1943. Nearby, tracks lead along the shore to Bob's Bay and up to lookout points over Queen Charlotte Sound.

2 THE *EDWIN FOX*
About 100 metres from the ferry terminus.

For years the hulk of this clipper lay derelict on the shores of Shakespeare Bay in the Marlborough Sounds. Built in India in 1853, she carried troops to the Crimean War, took convicts to Australia and worked in the tea trade before bringing immigrants to New Zealand in the 1870s. This once-handsome vessel with its metal-sheathed teak hull is now being restored.

3 ANAKIWA
Drive west from Picton on Queen Charlotte Drive for 18 km, turn right onto the road to Anakiwa and travel 5 km north.

Anakiwa is the base of the well-known Outward Bound School which runs rigorous courses designed to build character and confidence outdoors. You can get a taste of the 71 km Queen Charlotte Track that links up with further walking routes all the way to Ship Cove, by taking a short walk through the forest on the first part of the track.

Hotels like this one on Picton's waterfront, which preserves the original façade, regularly hosted Victorian holidaymakers.

4 PORTAGE
Return to Queen Charlotte Drive, turn right and continue west 6 km to Linkwater, take the next turn to the right and travel 24 km north-east to Portage.

As the road winds above Mahau Sound and continues along the south-eastern edge of Kenepuru Sound you will have magnificent views across these sheltered forest-fringed waterways. The shop and marina at Portage cater for some of the hordes of boaties who frequent the sounds.

5 CULLEN POINT LOOKOUT
Return to Queen Charlotte Drive, turn right and drive west towards Havelock for 9 km. The Cullen Point Lookout is signposted on the right off a short access road.

From the end of the 10-minute track onto Cullen Point you can look out across both sides of the peninsula with views of Havelock tucked away beneath the hills to the south and Mahau Sound to the north.

6 HAVELOCK
Continue 3 km south-west to Havelock.

Today it is hard to believe that this quiet little town once had 23 hotels. Havelock began life as a small but busy port during the short-lived Wakamarina gold rush in 1864. It later became a sawmilling town with a wood-burning locomotive that brought timber out from the native forests from Carluke to Blackball, to the west of Havelock. Remarkably, the notable New Zealand scientists, Lord Rutherford ('father of the atom') and Dr William Pickering, of space-exploration fame, both went to primary school in Havelock. A museum occupies St John's Church. Today Havelock is an export centre for the famous Marlborough Sounds green-lipped mussels.

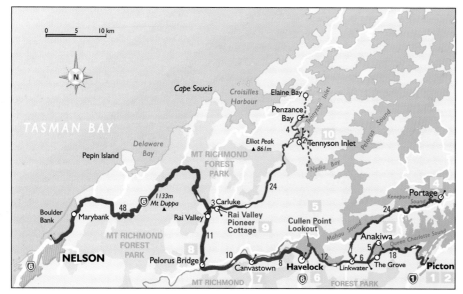

Pelorus Bridge, near the meeting point of the Pelorus and Rai Rivers.

The sparkling expanse of Tennyson Inlet, encircled with untouched forest full of native birds, looks today much as it did many centuries ago.

 **CANVASTOWN**

From Havelock drive 8 km west on SH 6 to Canvastown.

The village of Pinedale became Canvastown in the early 1860s when thousands of gold miners flocked to the area, most of them living in tents. For a short time this was the richest goldfield in the country, but by 1865 the boom was over and the miners departed as quickly as they had arrived. There are relics from the mining days near the Canvastown Hotel and the area is popular for gold panning as well as trout fishing.

PELORUS BRIDGE

Continue 10 km west on SH 6 to the Pelorus Bridge Scenic Reserve.

From the historic Pelorus Bridge there are a number of forest walks. The Totara Walk takes 30 minutes in a loop through the lush green forest made up mainly of beech, rimu, hinau and totara. One giant old totara on the track has a girth of over 7 m.

RAI VALLEY PIONEER COTTAGE

From Pelorus Bridge travel 9 km north on SH 6 to the Rai Valley township and take the turn-off to the right 2 km past the township. Drive 1 km north and turn right to Tennyson Inlet. The Rai Valley Pioneer Cottage is 2 km on the left at Carluke.

The cottage was built in 1881 by Charles Turner when the area was still cloaked in rainforest. Charles and his wife were the first Europeans to settle in the area, using locally available materials to build their home including slabs of totara for the walls, shingles for the roof and riverstones for the fireplace. The cottage was restored in 1969 and given to the Historic Places Trust in 1980. The fully furnished interior can be examined through specially designed viewing bays.

TENNYSON INLET

From Carluke continue 24 km to Tennyson Inlet. The road is sealed for the first 12 km through the valley but becomes a winding gravel road as it continues over the hills through the forest. The scenery makes the slow trip worthwhile. There is a lookout point from the top of the hills. Just before reaching the inlet the left fork of the road leads 4 km across a peninsula to a jetty at Penzance Bay and the start of the Archer Track to Elaine Bay. The right fork leads 2 km to the start of the Nydia Track.

One of the most beautiful locations in the Marlborough Sounds, Tennyson Inlet is surrounded by forested hills and features two well-graded tracks both of which are easy to explore for a short distance along the shoreline.

The Archer Track follows the western shoreline of Tennyson Inlet all the way to Elaine Bay, but it is the first section of the track that is the most scenic, passing through native forest on a gentle grade as it climbs almost imperceptibly above the water. Most of the old bridle paths in the area were built in this way, to make the climb as easy as possible for the horses.

At the south-eastern edge of Tennyson Inlet the 22 km Nydia Track heads along the coastline and across forest-clad hills to Nydia Bay and Kaiuma. Again, the first few hundred metres provide beautiful views through the forest across the still waters of this idyllic inlet.

After exploring Tennyson Inlet return to SH 6 for the 48 km journey west to Nelson.

Pioneers made extensive use of local trees to build homes like this one at Carluke.

33 AROUND NELSON

DRIVING TOUR ■ 73 KM ■ 4 HOURS ■ ARTS AND CRAFTS AND GOLDEN SANDS

The Nelson region is one of the sunniest in New Zealand. This, together with its superb local food and wine, innovative arts, relaxed lifestyle and idyllic unspoiled coastline make it an enchanting place to visit.

In 1841 Edward Gibbon Wakefield's New Zealand Company founded the settlement of Nelson, part of a grandiose scheme to systematically colonise the whole country with small farms clustered around centrally located towns. The idea was to transplant a selection of migrants from all of the English social classes to found the new colony, but in reality 'too few gentlemen with too little money' took on the challenge. Land in the towns was distributed early but the farmland remained unallocated, forcing the settlers to live in the towns and use up their capital. The New Zealand Company's entitlement to the land was under dispute, Captain Wakefield was killed in the Wairau Affray and the New Zealand Company was later declared bankrupt. The infant colony almost foundered in its early years for lack of money but the favourable climate and much hard work enabled the settlers to establish themselves and eventually prosper.

Today the city is renowned for its parks and gardens, and boasts a number of stately old homes and restored cottages dating back to the 1860s. A flourishing arts and crafts movement is represented in numerous galleries, craft and pottery trails, markets and museums.

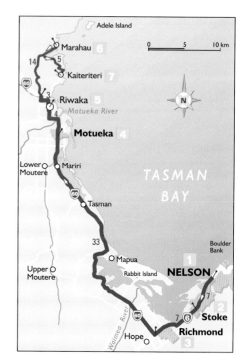

1 NELSON

Many small and large town residences survive from the early days of Nelson's settlement, including workmen's cottages in South Street and Richmond Avenue, and the rather grand mansion Melrose on Brougham Street. Bishop's School in Nile Street East has a display of textbooks and items dating back to 1844, when it first opened. Nelson's Christ Church Cathedral on Trafalgar Square – the third church to be raised on the site – was built over a 40-year period from 1925 and is an imposing presence in the middle of the city.

Founders Park on Atawhai Drive replicates a colonial town. This museum park, which also features an audio-visual display on the Port of Nelson and a maze, is set in two separate sections connected by an operating railway. Nearby are the Miyazu Japanese Gardens.

The Suter Art Gallery on Bridge Street houses a permanent collection of important paintings and lithographs including works by Lindauer, Van der Velden and Woollaston, with exhibitions covering a diverse range of subjects including sculpture and fibre crafts. Nelson is renowned for the quality of its local

clay and is famous for its pottery. Glass-blowing, wood-carving and other arts and crafts are much in evidence.

The Visitor Information Centre on Trafalgar Street has an Arts Trail and Gallery Guide showing the location of the numerous galleries and studios, as well as information on the vineyards in this area which is noted

An early cottage, Nelson.

The Nelson region offers some of the finest horse trekking in New Zealand.

Broadgreen, one of the oldest houses in Nelson, has elegantly stood the test of time. Many of the trees in its extensive gardens were planted by the original owner.

for the quality of its grapes and distinctive wines. Fine views over the city can be obtained by driving up onto Botanical Hill.

2 STOKE
From Nelson take SH 6 and drive 7 km south to reach Stoke.

At Isel Park on the main road in Stoke rhododendrons and azaleas grow under the shelter of century-old trees brought to the area from all over the world by sea captains at the request of wealthy landowner Thomas Marsden. The two-storey stately home built of stone is Isel House. It has been restored and is used as a gallery and museum. Behind it is the Nelson Provincial Museum, the oldest in the country, with a large collection of Maori artefacts and an extensive array of historical photographs from the area.

Stoke is also the location of Woodstock, a notable cob house built in the 1850s and Broadgreen (1855), which is one of the largest rammed-earth cob houses in the country. Set in beautiful gardens, Broadgreen has been restored and furnished with careful attention to period detail as a fine example of a gentleman's residence. McCashin's Brewery, the home of the fabled Black Mac beer, is on the right on SH 6 as you leave Stoke.

3 RICHMOND
Continue south 7 km on SH 6 to Richmond.

Named after Richmond-on-Thames in England, this town boasts one of New Zealand's finest country churches, the Holy Trinity, a traditional English-style church built in timber and consecrated in 1872. The huge gum tree that stands at the entrance to the racecourse was planted by Francis Otterson, one of the earliest settlers who arrived on the *Lord Auckland* in 1842.

4 MOTUEKA
From Richmond take SH 60 and drive north-west 33 km to Motueka.

Motueka is the main centre in a horticultural area famous for its hops, green tea and fruit growing. The tall hop vines are trained onto poles and wire frames, and the scaly cone-like fruit is kiln-dried and used in brewing beer. The main fruit-picking season is from March through to June for apples, kiwifruit and grapes.

Motueka was founded in 1842 and today retains its small port on the Moutere Inlet, a short distance from the main street. Te Ahurewa, on Pah Street, is one of the South Island's few Maori churches. Built in 1897, the small church contains a number of interesting relics and Maori decorations.

5 RIWAKA
Continue north-west 4 km on SH 60 to Riwaka.

The quaint old port at the mouth of the river is now largely unused but the area has remained an important centre for research in the growing and processing of hops.

6 MARAHAU
Continue north-west 3 km from Riwaka on SH 60 and turn off right to Marahau, 14 km north on the inland road.

Marahau is the southern access point to the Abel Tasman National Park and also the starting point for the renowned Abel Tasman Coastal Track. The track is 55 km long, but visitors can take a short walk on the start of the track through forest above small bays and numerous beaches divided by rocky granite headlands.

The Tinline Walk is a short coastal track that runs through forest near the start of the Abel Tasman Track. Many of the native tree species including beech, kahikatea, rimu and pukatea have been labelled on this 30-minute loop track.

This part of the bay is named the Astrolabe Roadstead because the French navigator Jules d'Urville anchored his corvette the *Astrolabe* here in 1827. Adele Island, close offshore, was named after d'Urville's wife.

7 KAITERITERI
From Marahau drive south-east 5 km to Kaiteriteri on the coast road.

One of the most popular beaches in the South Island, Kaiteriteri has picture-postcard appeal with its clear blue water and the golden sands that are typical of this region. The sands derive from granite rock that runs from the hills to the coastline. Granite is a very hard rock formed deep within the earth's crust under extreme heat and pressure. As it cools, tiny cracks called 'joints' form. Large areas of granite that have been uplifted to the earth's surface are subjected to weathering. Weak acids from vegetation combine with rainwater and eat their way into the joints, breaking apart the crystals of quartz, feldspar and mica that make up the granite. The glittering gold mica particles turn into iron compounds and are eventually washed down the rivers along with the hard quartz crystals to form magnificent golden beaches.

The golden sands of Kaiteriteri Beach.

34 NORTH OF NELSON

DRIVING TOUR ■ 222 KM ■ 1 DAY ■ EXPLORING GOLDEN BAY

In an unspoiled wilderness outcrops of marble hide a honeycomb of caves and underground rivers, and steep granite country sweeps down to a coastline of pristine golden beaches fringed with lush forest.

In 1642 the Dutch explorer Abel Tasman became the first European to reach New Zealand when he sailed into Golden Bay. The coastline of the National Park that bears his name holds the same enchantment for visitors today as it did for those early explorers. This is paradise. Golden-sand beaches enclosed by rocky granite headlands separate the forest-clad hills from the crystal-clear water.

The forests cover a mountain range formed by a huge granite dome over 100 million years old. The granite runs beneath even older formations of marble which have survived immense changes including submersion beneath the sea, but have been uplifted and are now weathering high in the hills where an intricate system of underground rivers and caves lies beneath the rock. Roads and tracks lead to huge drop shafts that fall deep inside the mountain and to natural springs where the water wells up onto the plains below. This is all part of the karst landscape of weathered rock formations that make up this fascinating area.

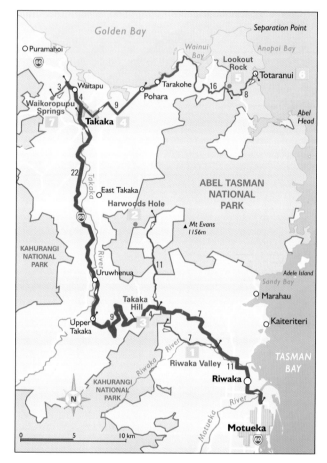

1 RIWAKA VALLEY

The trip starts at Motueka. Drive north-west 11 km on SH 60 to the Riwaka Valley turn-off on the left and follow the unsealed road that runs west along the Riwaka River for 7 km.

The Riwaka Valley has a bush reserve and some good swimming pools in the river which issues from a spring fed by water from the labyrinth of tunnels inside the Takaka Hill.

2 HARWOODS HOLE

Return to SH 60 and drive 7 km up onto Takaka Hill. Turn right onto the unsealed Canaan Saddle Road and drive 11 km north to the start of the Harwoods Hole walking track. The road passes through an impressive karst landscape with weathered limestone rock outcrops bordering dried-up stream beds where the rivers have long since disappeared underground.

A half-hour walk through the beech forest leads to the edge of the largest drop shaft in the Southern Hemisphere. The track passes a number of sinkholes or dolines, some covered in moss and others filled up with water.

Carved out of the limestone rock by a river that cut deep into the hillside and created a huge waterfall into an underground cave system, Harwoods Hole is 50 m across and 200 m straight down. Experienced cavers abseil down the sheer face into a cave system that emerges at Gorge Creek. Be extremely cautious near the edge of the drop shaft especially in wet weather. A short side track climbs to a viewpoint above the shaft from where you can also see out to the coast.

3 TAKAKA HILL

Return to SH 60 and drive 4 km up to the Takaka Hill summit, 791 m above sea level. The Ngarua Caves, not far from the summit, have fascinating limestone formations and moa bones have been found inside. The lookout point at the Takaka Hill summit is on the right.

The Takaka Hill summit provides views right across the plains towards Nelson and the distant Marlborough Sounds. Known locally as the Marble Mountain, the hill features distinctive weathered outcrops of fluted rock which can be seen from the lookout point.

4 TAKAKA

Continue west 9 km down from Takaka Hill to Upper Takaka in the river valley below and drive north 22 km following the Takaka River to Takaka.

Takaka is the last major township as you head north. You will notice large stretches of dried-up riverbeds in this part of the countryside where streams have cut their way underground into the limestone rock. These have created extensive subterranean river systems, some of which emerge out at sea off the coast of Golden Bay.

5 LOOKOUT ROCK

Take the road from Takaka signposted to Totaranui and head north-east 9 km to Pohara on the coast. A few kilometres past Pohara the seal ends. Travel 16 km north-

The rocky coast near Pohara on the way to Totaranui.

The view looking east from Takaka Hill with Tasman Bay in the distance.

east on the dusty road which continues around the headlands to Anatimo before crossing forest-clad hills to reach Lookout Rock Track signposted on the left.

The first part of the track provides an interesting 20-minute walk through rainforest along the Pigeon Saddle in Abel

Remote Anapai Bay is a corner of paradise with golden sands and clear turquoise water.

Tasman National Park. In this section of forest there is great diversity. Instructional material posted along the walk identifies the forest species and enables you to recognise tangled supplejack vines, miro, kamahi, red beech, rata and old rimu and matai covered in epiphytes (perching plants), as well as find out how all these grow and adapt in the forest. A further 10 minutes' walk beyond the forest brings you to Lookout Rock which has superb views out to the coast.

6 TOTARANUI

Continue north-east 8 km to Totaranui.

With its magnificent stretch of golden beach, Totaranui is one of the most attractive locations on the northern coastline of the South Island. There are a number of walking tracks from Totaranui, including the famous Abel Tasman Coastal Walk, but the best track for visitors on a day trip is the 20-minute walk to Anapai Bay. The track crosses a ridge-line then heads down to the coast through subtropical rainforest where huge tree ferns and nikau palms fill the valley. The knowledge gained on the Lookout Rock forest walk (above) will give you an appreciation of this stretch of forest. Anapai Bay is an

idyllic, small golden-sand beach framed by unusual granite rock formations, the lush rainforest and clear blue water.

7 WAIKOROPUPU SPRINGS

Return 33 km to Takaka and turn right onto SH 60. Drive 4 km north-west and turn off left just past Waitapu, then travel south 3 km to the Waikoropupu Springs Scenic Reserve.

The 'Pupu' Springs, as they are usually known, are the largest springs in New Zealand. A series of tracks lead around the 16 main springs in the reserve. From two large vents that make up the biggest spring, incredibly clear, cold and slightly salty water bubbles up out of sand, while several smaller vents make up the 'Dancing Sands' group of springs. The springs are tidal, but the cycle indicates earth rather than sea tides. Researchers believe the enormous volumes of water come from the Takaka River which dries up most summers at a point near Lindsays Bridge, on the way to Waikoropupu Springs. Water is also fed in from Gorge Creek on the Canaan Plateau, where the stream runs underground below Harwoods Hole.

Tracks from the springs lead through a goldmining area that dates back to 1901. Still in evidence are the water races and 'working faces' where men from the Takaka Sluicing Company washed river material over riffle boards to trap the particles of gold. Large boulders were stacked neatly to one side while the finer sands and gravels were removed by a tail race. The company processed nearly 4000 ounces (112 kg) of gold, making it one of the most successful Golden Bay companies, but by 1909 the gold and the enterprise had come to an end.

Return to Takaka and travel 53 km back to Motueka.

35 THE NELSON LAKES

DRIVING TOUR ■ 222 KM ■ 1 DAY ■ JEWELS HIDDEN IN THE MOUNTAINS

The main road west from Blenheim follows the Wairau River, skirting the Richmond Range, to two deep lakes carved by glaciers set within the rugged mountains and bird-filled beech forest of the Nelson Lakes National Park.

Early British immigrants came to New Zealand to build houses and churches and to run sheep and cattle on flat grasslands, so most of the European explorers in the South Island were looking for a large inland plain. For over a hundred years the main route from Nelson south for the coaches and farmers driving stock lay along the river valleys to Tophouse and the Wairau River. The route between the Wairau and Nelson was discovered in 1842 by a young surveyor named John Cotterell, who was later killed in a skirmish after joining a group of settlers attempting to arrest Te Rauparaha and his warriors. Cotterell had got as far south as the Nelson Lakes and had climbed the St Arnaud Range hoping to see an inland plain. He was dismayed to find instead rows of mountain ranges stretching as far as the eye could see. The dream of finding flat pasture lands was soon replaced by the quest for gold and miners worked their way around the river valleys to Lakes Rotoroa and Rotoiti.

The beauty of this wilderness area touched even seasoned explorers like Julian Haast who commented in 1859, 'I am sure that the time is not far distant when this spot will become the favourite abode of those whose means and leisure will permit them to admire picturesque scenery.'

Haymaking time on the Wairau Plains.

1 RENWICK
From Blenheim take SH 6 and drive west 11 km to Renwick via Woodbourne where the aerodrome was the starting point for the first east to west crossing of the Tasman by plane, on 13 October 1928. Charles Kings-ford-Smith made the flight in the Southern Cross, having already completed the first west to east crossing when he landed at Wigram in Christchurch a few weeks earlier.

The Renwick museum, located on the main road, features a reconstruction of an old tavern and houses relics from the early days of European settlement in the area. Some of the historic homesteads in Renwick date back to the early days of sheep farming in Marlborough, including the Langly Dale Station where the original homestead and outbuildings still survive. You can also visit the Cork & Keg on Inkerman Street, styled after an old English pub, with its own brew of 'Renwick' beers and cider.

2 TOPHOUSE
From Renwick take SH 63 and drive 87 km south-west along the Wairau Valley to the Tophouse turn-off on the right. Drive 3 km north to the Tophouse which is signposted on the right.

This detour is the start of a long winding route that was used to drive sheep from Nelson through to the Wairau Valley during the early days of European settlement. The cob-walled Tophouse was one of the first hotels in Marlborough and a staging post for horse-drawn coaches. To the north the Douglas fir and radiata pine that make up the Golden Downs State Forest cover large parts of the catchment areas of the Motueka, Wai-iti, Tadmor and Sherry Rivers.

3 LAKE ROTOITI
Return to SH 63, turn right and drive west 4 km to St Arnaud. Turn left off the main highway and follow the access road past the

<hr />

MARLBOROUGH WINE TRAIL
Marlborough is the largest grape-growing region in New Zealand. About 20 wineries near Blenheim produce a variety of wines but the area is internationally acclaimed for its sauvignon blancs. Most wineries are open daily and can be found easily with the Marlborough Winemakers Wine Trail Guide available from the Blenheim I-Site in the Railway Station on State Highway 1. Visitors can learn about wine-making, sample wine at the cellar door or enjoy it with the best of local food at the wineries' restaurants.

Montana's Brancott Estate hosts the famous Marlborough Food and Wine Festival each year during the second weekend in February.

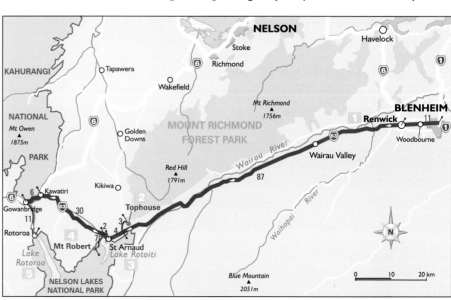

Park Headquarters 1 km down to the edge of Lake Rotoiti.

Once a mining centre, St Arnaud is now the headquarters for Nelson Lakes National Park. An old sluice gun stands as a reminder of the miners who worked their way up the river valleys in search of the 'mother lodes'. Several walks lead along the luxuriant shores of Lake Rotoiti. This lake is popular for swimming and yachting, and carries plentiful stocks of brown trout.

The Nelson Lakes are a product of thousands of years of glaciation. The rocks that make up the surrounding mountains are sandstone and greywacke that was uplifted from the sea floor 200 million years ago. During the ice ages ancient glaciers gouged and carved away the rock, creating the steep valley walls and the deep depressions that later filled to become lakes.

Today much of the area's beauty lies in the native forests that cover the river valleys and stretch into the mountains. A good way to experience these forests is on some of the short walks that run from the lakeside. Two interesting walks that each take about an hour and a half are the Loop Track that runs through moss-covered beech forest on the edge of the lake, and the Peninsula Nature Walk leading through the forest across a moraine formed by the glacier that created Lake Rotoiti. The glacier carried rock debris down from the mountains, piling it up into a huge natural rock wall that was left behind when the glacier retreated. This glacial moraine created a natural dam behind which the lake formed and which now makes up the peninsula at the edge of Lake Rotoiti.

⁴ **MT ROBERT**
Return to SH 63, continue west 2 km and turn left onto the road leading south 7 km to the base of Mt Robert.

Lake Rotoroa, more isolated than Rotoiti, lies in the mountains of Nelson Lakes National Park.

Mt Robert rises above the south-western shoreline of Lake Rotoiti. A huge fracture in the earth's crust known as the Alpine Fault runs right through this area. Over many thousands of years the continents have moved along these fault lines which separate the earth's crust into vast plates that float like islands on the underlying mantle of molten rock.

It was on the slopes of Mt Robert that German geologist Julius von Haast stood when he made his observation that the landforms to the west had moved. He arrived at his own theory of an alpine fault line to explain the movement of the land, coming to this conclusion more than a hundred years before the theory of plate tectonics and continental drift had been developed.

⁵ **LAKE ROTOROA**
Return to SH 63 and drive north-west 30 km to Kawatiri, turn left onto SH 6 and travel west 6 km to Gowanbridge. Turn left here onto the 11 km unsealed road south to Lake Rotoroa.

The Flower Walk and the Short Loop Track are two easy 10-minute walks through the forest near Lake Rotoroa. The forest canopy is alive with a wonderful variety of birds including tui, robins, frolicsome bush parrots and inquisitive little fantails that often flit along beside humans on the forest trails. In the low light that filters through to the forest floor many kinds of insects and lizards live among luxuriant mosses and lichens.
Return 11 km to SH 6 and head east 38 km back to St Arnaud.

Expansive vineyards thrive in the well-drained alluvial soils of the Wairau Valley.

36 ALONG THE BULLER RIVER

DRIVING TOUR ■ 216 KM ■ 1 DAY ■ GOLD TOWNS, SPECTACULAR SCENERY

Much of the route on this trip follows the course of the mighty Buller River, through sleepy little towns that were once busy goldmining centres, to a dramatic gorge where the road is cut into a vertical cliff face.

When Nelson was founded in the 1840s, bureaucratic difficulties prevented the first settlers from taking up land to farm as they had expected and many almost gave up hope of making a living. However, when industrious German immigrants arrived and planted grape vines and fruit trees that flourished in the sunny climate they showed the way to prosperity. Horticulture became a thriving industry and many of the unemployed established themselves on smallholdings. The early settlers worked hard developing farms inland and opening up routes through to the Wairau River and along the Buller River to the West Coast. The discovery of gold in the area drew fresh hordes of prospectors and gold diggers seeking to make their fortunes, and further enriched the towns.

There is little left of many of these towns today, but the region remains lushly planted with stonefruit, berries, hops and vines, supplying the rest of the country with its rich harvest.

Myriad small streams feed the mighty Buller River.

1 HOPE
From Nelson drive 18 km south-west on SH 6 through Richmond to Hope.

Hope was founded by German settlers and originally named Ranzau. The town retains links with its German past. St John's Lutheran Church on Ranzau Road has a graveyard with the headstones of some of the early immigrants inscribed in German. Further along the road is a two-storeyed cob house built in 1863.

2 BRIGHTWATER
Continue 5 km south-west on SH 6 to Brightwater.

The name describes the sparkling waters of the Wairoa River and was given to the district by Alfred Saunders, who established a flour mill here in the 1850s. St Paul's Anglican Church was built in 1857 and the young wife of Nelson's first bishop, Bishop Hobhouse, was buried in this churchyard when she died in childbirth. Brightwater was the birthplace of Lord Rutherford, the founder of nuclear physics and winner of the 1908 Nobel Prize for Chemistry.

A refreshment stop on SH 6.

3 WAKEFIELD
Continue south-west 7 km on SH 6 to Wakefield.

The oldest surviving Anglican church in the South Island can be found by making a short detour signposted 'Pig Valley' to St John's Anglican Church (1846). A little west of Wakefield, the signposted Pigeon Valley Steam Museum is a fascinating collection of steam-driven machinery.

4 GLENHOPE
From Wakefield drive 24 km south-west on SH 6 to Kohatu then continue for a further 24 km south-west across the hills to Glenhope.

A cairn beside the road records the contributions of early pioneers in the settlement of the Hope Valley. One of these, George Fairweather Moonlight, was a flamboyant character who retired in the Murchison area after making a number of significant discoveries of gold in Otago and became a local legend as self-appointed sheriff and extravagantly costumed publican.

5 MURCHISON
Continue for 40 km on SH 6. From Kawatiri the road follows the course of the Buller River. Kawatiri, the Maori name for the Buller River, means 'river flowing swiftly through a narrow gorge', an accurate description of this impressive waterway. The Nelson Lakes act as a buffer in times of heavy rainfall, collecting huge volumes of water from the mountains. This is then released into the

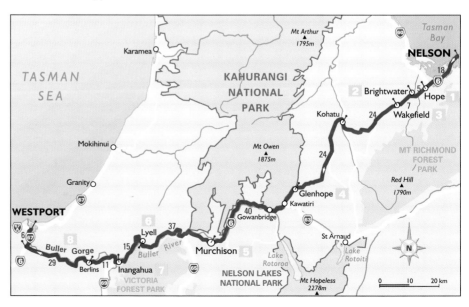

South of Wakefield, sheep graze peacefully around derelict buildings that a hundred years ago bustled with the busy daily life of a prosperous farm.

GOLD PANNING

A shovel and a pan are all you need to go in search of gold in many of the South Island's rivers. The gold-bearing shingle, known as pay dirt, is placed in the pan and submerged in water. A side-shaking or circular swirling motion causes the gold to sink, then the pan is quickly tilted to spill the stones over the rim. On the West Coast the gold is usually mixed with heavy black sand which is dried and then blown away, leaving, if you are lucky, small flakes of gold.

track follows an old dray road to the Croesus stamping battery. New Zealand's largest gold nugget was found near here, and the lure of gold still attracts people wanting to try their luck panning in local streams.

INANGAHUA

From Lyell drive 15 km south-west on SH 6 to Inangahua.

Here the Inangahua River joins forces with the Buller. Inangahua was once an important centre in the movement of quartz-crushing equipment brought up the Buller River from Westport en route to Reefton. It lies a short distance to the west of the Alpine Fault and the township has experienced numerous earthquakes over the years including one in 1968 that led to the evacuation of its inhabitants. The area has impressive limestone caves, including a system that burrows 5 km through a hill.

BULLER GORGE

Drive 11 km west on SH 6 to Berlins, which marks the beginning of the lower Buller Gorge, then continue 29 km west to the junction with SH 67.

The spectacular Buller Gorge is famous for its mist-shrouded forests and the notable section of roadway at Hawks Crag where the road has been blasted into a vertical cliff face, providing just enough space for buses to squeeze through. The crag is named after Robert Hawks, an early prospector who came to the area in search of gold.
Turn right onto SH 67 and drive north 6 km to Westport.

Buller, which swiftly becomes a raging torrent. Near Gowanbridge the road passes through impressive gorge scenery, then across the river flats to Murchison.

Located on an alluvial gravel plain formed by the Buller and Matakitaki Rivers, Murchison lies close to the Alpine Fault, where two sections of the earth's crust grind slowly past each other until they generate enough pressure to create an earthquake. On 17 June 1929 a powerful quake that was felt throughout New Zealand was centred on Murchison, with aftershocks continuing for 2 weeks. At the Murchison Museum on Fairfax Street you can see in graphic detail the devastation caused by the quake. The town was evacuated, but 17 lives were lost and the surrounding area was left in ruins. The earthquake changed much of the form of the land and caused the Maruia River to gouge out a new channel, creating a waterfall. Some of the upheaval created by the earthquake on the

landscape is still clearly visible, but the scars caused by extensive gold dredging, which continued on the Matakitaki River until the 1940s, have now been largely covered by scrub.

LYELL

Continue west on SH 6 for 37 km to Lyell.

Driving along this scenic highway, beside the forest-clad banks of the Buller River, it is hard to imagine that several thousand people lived here in the mid-1800s, lured by the prospect of finding gold and striking it rich. A short distance along the 3 km Lyell Walkway is a fascinating pioneer cemetery hidden in the bush. The

A lofty bridge spanning the Buller Gorge.

SOUTH ISLAND

THE WEST COAST AND ALPINE PASSES

37 THE PUNAKAIKI COAST

DRIVING TOUR ■ 136 KM ■ 1 DAY ■ RAINFORESTS AND SCULPTURED ROCKS

On one side of the highway that skirts Paparoa National Park are rocky beaches pounded by booming surf, on the other side dense, fern-filled forest interspersed with tiny neglected settlements that once housed the miners who flocked here.

Charles Heaphy and Thomas Brunner were the first Europeans to explore the Paparoa region, in 1846. Until then it had been visited only by Maori and the crews of sealing ships. It took Heaphy and Brunner almost three weeks to traverse the coastline, in incessant rain, crossing swollen rivers and scaling cliffs at Perpendicular Point on rope ladders made of flax and rata. Other than the scenic highway that spans this beautiful stretch of coastline, the Paparoa coast has changed little since the pioneering days. Mining for gold and coal, then logging the lush forests, have left their marks on the landscape, but within the boundaries of Paparoa National Park and the many scenic reserves along the coast are areas of untouched wilderness, a host of caves and sinkholes surrounded by dense bush in an intricate 'karst' landscape, where the limestone rock has been carved by water into elaborate natural rock structures. The Paparoas owe much of their beauty to these limestone cliffs and rock formations, but they are also distinguished by the beautiful coastal rainforests that cloak the landscape.

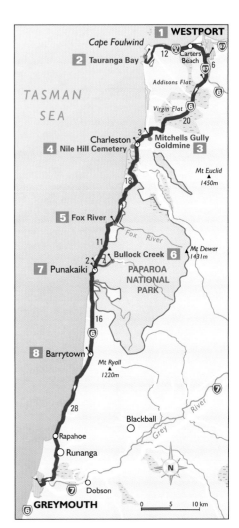

The Punakaiki Coast highway is sandwiched between the surging Tasman Sea and rainforest.

1 WESTPORT

Westport's growth was fuelled by the early Buller goldfields then, as a river-mouth port, the town became a centre for exporting coal, with over 800,000 tonnes a year shipped out until 1914. Coaltown, located in an old brewery on Queen Street, traces the history of coalmining in the area and includes a walk through a mine simulation complete with sound effects.

2 TAURANGA BAY

From Westport drive 12 km west on SH 67A out to the coast and the Tauranga Bay seal colony.

Seal pups are born from November until late December, and usually remain with their mothers on the rocks for a month before they begin heading out to sea. The males become fiercely territorial after the pups are born, so visitors to the colony should take care not to place themselves between the seals and their escape route to the sea. It takes 5 minutes to walk to the seal colony, and if you have time you can continue on the Cape Foulwind Walkway, which leads from the bay 4 km along the coast out to the lighthouse on Cape Foulwind. A replica of Abel Tasman's astrolabe, a navigational instrument used to measure the angle of the sun, overlooks Tauranga Bay.

3 MITCHELLS GULLY GOLDMINE

Return 12 km towards Westport then drive 6 km south on SH 67, take SH 6 and travel for 20 km south-west towards Charleston. Mitchells Gully is on the left.

In 1869 there were over 200 stamping batteries and crushers operating in the Charleston area. The gold-bearing sedimentary rock was mined by hand, then fed through a stamping machine powered by a

Fishing boats, Westport.

Limestone rocks in Paparoa National Park have been sculptured in fanciful forms by centuries of exposure to the weather.

waterwheel. The crushed sands were then washed over copper plates coated in mercury, separating the gold from the sand. The mercury amalgamated with the gold during this process so the next step was to evaporate the mercury in a retort for reuse, leaving only the gold. You can see the process and the equipment in action at Mitchells Gully and explore old mine workings and miners' huts.

4 NILE HILL CEMETERY
From Mitchells Gully drive south-west 3 km on SH 6. The Nile Hill Cemetery is signposted down a short access road to the right.

At the height of the gold rush Charleston was the largest of the West Coast gold settlements, with shanties located all along the pack route into the town, which boasted 80 drinking houses, a hospital, a library and a population of 12,000, most of whom were gold diggers with claims on the Nile (Waitakere) River. Charleston was one of the towns that grew and died within a few short decades during the gold rush years on the West Coast. Today most of what remains of the town has disappeared amongst the scrub, but a 5-minute walk will take you to a fascinating old cemetery on Nile Hill where gravestones bear the names of many of the early settlers. Many of those laid to rest here came from Unst in the Shetland Islands to spend their final days searching for elusive gold in the sands of Nine Mile Beach.

5 FOX RIVER
From Nile Hill cemetery return to SH 6 and drive 18 km south to the Fox River.

From the Fox River Bridge a track heads east inland through the forest. Visitors can spend 20 minutes on the first part of this trail. This is the old Inland Pack Track that leads from the Fox River south to the Punakaiki River. Originally known as Razorback Road, the track was cut from 1867 to 1868 and provided an inland route around the rugged headlands and cliffs on the Punakaiki Coast for the next 40 years. The coast road was not opened until 1929.

6 BULLOCK CREEK
Continue 11 km south on SH 6 to Bullock Creek, signposted to the left, and drive 4 km east.

This short drive along the narrow rocky road along Bullock Creek is an excellent way to experience the 'karst' landscape of the Paparoas. About two-thirds of the way along the road the river dries up and feeds into the subterranean caves that connect Cave Creek and the Pororari River. Exploring a little in the forest along the roadside will reveal the distinctive fluted limestone rock that has been eroded into intricate patterns by the natural acids in the leaf litter on the forest floor.

7 PUNAKAIKI
Return to SH 6 and drive south-west 2 km to Punakaiki.

Outcrops of stratified limestone along the Punakaiki coast have created the distinctive Pancake Rocks at Dolomite Point, with their spectacular blowholes and tunnels that can be visited via a short boardwalk from the road.

The unusual formations were created by the wind and waves eating into the softer layers of rock sandwiched between harder layers of stratified limestone. The sedimentary rock was formed on the sea bed millions of years ago, before being uplifted and eroded into the distinctive fragmented rock pattern that can be seen today. The blowholes, with jets of seawater propelled high into the air are particularly impressive but operate only under specific conditions: a strong south-westerly wind pushing up a big ocean swell creates the blowhole action from 2 hours before high tide.

8 BARRYTOWN
Continue 16 km south on SH 6 along a beautiful stretch of coastal highway to Barrytown. The road skirts rocky headlands and sweeping beaches set against bush-clad hills.

Originally known as Seventeen Mile Beach, Barrytown is yet another old mining settlement. Gold was found in the sands along the coastal flats as early as 1866, but it was not until 1879, when larger deposits were discovered in the mountains, that miners flocked to the area and the Croesus Track was cut to provide access from Barrytown across the Paparoa Range to the diggings in the Grey Valley. Trampers still walk this old trail, which leads to many of the former gold workings in the hills.

From Barrytown continue south 28 km on SH 6 to Greymouth.

The famous limestone Pancake Rocks near Punakaiki are a curious example of sea-sculpting.

38 LEWIS PASS

DRIVING TOUR ■ 355 KM ■ 1 DAY ■ ALPINE TARNS AND ANCIENT ROCK DRAWINGS

A couple of hours after leaving the coast at Greymouth the highway winds through a subalpine zone where cold mountain lakes glimmer through the trees and hot-water springs provide unexpected oases.

Although Lewis Pass (863 m) is not as high as the alpine passes further south, the traverse is a wonderfully scenic journey on an excellent road through the mountains and characteristic beech forests of the Southern Alps. The pass separates the Maruia and Waiau watershed areas, marking the boundary between Canterbury and Nelson.

Rediscovered by Europeans in 1861 and named after surveyor Henry Lewis, the pass was originally used as a route to the West Coast by generations of Ngai Tahu Maori in search of greenstone. Food was scarce on the West Coast, so the Maori took slaves captured in battle to carry food and supplies on the long journeys across the mountains. With food running low on the return trip the slaves were frequently killed and eaten on the pass and their remains flung into Cannibal Gorge. The Maori name for the gorge was Kapai-o-kai-tangata, meaning 'a good feed of human flesh'.

For the energetic, there are some outstanding mountain walking tracks in the area.

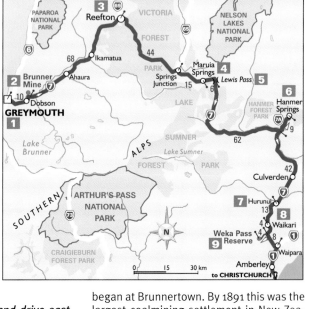

1 GREYMOUTH

The largest town on the West Coast, the port of Greymouth is located on the Grey River and is a main centre for coal and timber industries. The History House Museum, on Gresson Street, has an extensive photographic collection as well as fascinating displays relating to the town's history. The historic Monteith's Brewing Company, on the corner of Turumaha and Herbert Streets, offers tours that include sampling their award-winning beers.

The Left Bank Art Gallery and the Jade Boulder Gallery, both in Tainui Street, feature displays of greenstone (New Zealand jade). Greenstone is found mainly in the West Coast region, in a belt of rocks in the Southern Alps that are more than 200 million years old. These rocks are washed down rivers to the coast in places. For many centuries Maori from both Islands braved the alps and the wild coast to seach for this precious stone they called pounamu, which had a central part in their culture. The hard stone could be worked to a razor-sharp edge and was used for tools and weapons. It was also intricately carved into tribal emblems and ornaments to which great prestige was attached.

One of Greymouth's features is a huge rock breakwater along the river, built in 1991 after two disastrous floods. The wall protects the town from floodwaters and directs the force of the river currents against the sand bar at the river mouth, reducing the amount of dredging needed to keep the channel free. A walk along the top of the wall provides an interesting perspective of the town.

2 BRUNNER MINE

Take SH 7 from Greymouth and drive east 10 km following the Grey River. From the left side of the road you can cross the river to the old mine workings on a suspension bridge erected in the 1860s.

Thomas Brunner first reported coal seams in the area in 1848, but it was not until the 1860s that production of firebricks and coke

began at Brunnertown. By 1891 this was the largest coalmining settlement in New Zealand, and with a population of 2231 was the third-largest town on the West Coast.

In 1896 Brunner was the scene of the country's worst mining disaster when a gas explosion killed 67 men and boys working underground. Although the last coal was brought out of the mines in 1906, the coke

A triumph of nineteenth-century engineering, a suspension bridge crosses the Grey River to the Brunner Mine. The bridge has recently been upgraded.

The band rotunda evokes relaxed Sunday afternoons in the small town of Reefton.

The Hurunui Hotel has one of the longest continuous tenures in the country with its licence dating back well over a century. This fascinating old building was constructed from blocks of limestone and pitsawn timber in 1869. John Hastie's original licence for this hotel included the provision that horses had to be provided for travellers to ford the river.

8 WAIKARI
Continue 13 km south to Waikari on SH 7.

The small township of Waikari, located just off the main highway, has commemorated with a marble statue the local doctor Dr Charles Little, who died during the influenza epidemic in 1918 while trying to save the people of the town.

9 WEKA PASS RESERVE
Travel 4 km south on SH 7 towards Weka Pass. A side road signposted on the right leads 4 km west to the Weka Pass Historic Reserve.

Visitors to the reserve can examine some remarkable examples of early Maori art. The drawings on the limestone walls of an overhanging rock face date back over 500 years to when the site was used as a natural rock shelter by groups of Maori hunting moa and other birds that were abundant in the area. The drawings include human figures, fish and dogs, which the artists drew in charcoal from their fires and a red ochre.
Return to SH 7 and drive 8 km south to the next major junction, then take SH 1 and travel 57 km to Christchurch.

ovens and brickworks were kept in production until the 1930s with coal from the St Kilda mine further up the river. Today you can walk around the historic reserve and explore the pit-head machinery and many of the old kilns and tunnels.

3 REEFTON
From the Brunner Mine, the journey north-east on SH 7 to Reefton is 68 km through river valleys covered with forest.

Reefton came into prominence in 1870 with the discovery of rich gold-bearing quartz reefs in the hills and valleys around the town, which was soon nicknamed Quartzopolis. Reefton prospered – it was the first town in Australasia to get electric lighting – but when the gold dwindled, so did the settlement's fortunes, although miners continued to extract coal from the hills for many years. Interesting historic buildings in the town include the courthouse (1872) on Church Street, Sacred Heart and St Stephen's Churches (1878) on Walsh Street and the School of Mines (1886) on Shiel Street. A number of gold workings in the hills nearby can be visited and there is a replica of a gold mine in the Reefton Visitor Centre on Broadway.

4 MARUIA SPRINGS
From Reefton drive south-east 44 km on SH 7 to Springs Junction and continue for 15 km, still on SH 7, to Maruia Springs.

Maruia Springs thermal resort features a Japanese-style bath-house and naturally heated outdoor rock pools. The complex is a luxuriously relaxing place to break the journey, especially in winter after the first snowfalls.

5 LEWIS PASS
Continue on SH 7 for 6 km to the Lewis Pass.

The road climbs through forests of red and silver beech into the subalpine zone, where you will see small alpine tarns and stunted, moss-covered vegetation. Near the summit of Lewis Pass on the left side of the road, a 30-minute walking track, the Tarn Nature Walk, loops through the mountain beech forest near the start of the St James Walkway.

6 HANMER SPRINGS
Continue 62 km south then east on SH 7 to the Hanmer Springs turn-off. It is 9 km north on SH 7A to Hanmer Springs. The road crosses the historic Waiau Ferry Bridge, built in 1886–87 to replace the original wooden bridge which blew down in the 1870s.

Already known to Maori, these thermal springs nestled in the mountains were discovered by Europeans in 1859 and Hanmer was developed as a health resort with its own sanatorium. Today hydrotherapy has given way to relaxing in hot pools for pleasure, and the exotic forests that surround the area provide a number of walks through the handsome stands of trees, some of which were planted a century ago. Few of the original buildings have survived in the township, but the wooden post office dates back to 1901.

7 HURUNUI
Return to SH 7 and turn left. Drive 24 km south-east to the Red Post Corner and continue 18 km south-west to Hurunui.

Fly fishing on the Inangahua River, east of Reefton.

39 ARTHUR'S PASS

DRIVING TOUR ■ 240 KM ■ 1 DAY ■ FORMIDABLE PEAKS AND ALPINE FLOWERS

Over more than a century explorers and workmen braved the precipitous slopes and icy conditions to establish first a bridle path then a coach road on the spectacular route that is now a major highway.

The highway across Arthur's Pass in the Southern Alps passes through a magnificent national park. Huge braided rivers define its borders: the Waimakariri and Poulter to the south, the Otira and Taramakau to the north. These river valleys are popular tramping routes through the mountains, while the road across the pass provides many opportunities for visitors to explore and experience this beautiful alpine environment. Moss-covered forests line the roadsides and short tracks venture onto mountain slopes covered in alpine flowers.

The surveyor Arthur Dobson first heard from Maori of the pass at the head of the Otira Valley, and in 1864 he explored the route while seeking a way to supply West Coast gold diggers from Christchurch. Dobson reached the pass and later returned to make the descent into the Otira Valley, but his brother who was also a surveyor reported that building a road over 'Arthur's pass' would be too expensive. However, the next year construction began and hundreds of workers braved the extreme conditions to complete the road in a year. This heralded the start of a new era for the West Coast, the beginning of a coaching service and, later, a railway line across the Alps. A monument to Arthur Dobson stands at the top of the pass.

1 JACKSONS
From Greymouth take SH 6 and drive south 18 km to Kumara Junction, turn left and continue 46 km south-east on SH 73 following the Taramakau River to Jacksons, where the valley begins to narrow.

The old Jacksons tavern once provided accommodation and fresh horses for the coach parties who made the arduous trip over the alps.

2 ARTHUR'S PASS LOOKOUT
Continue east and then south for 19 km on SH 73 to Otira where the gorge closes in and the highway hugs the sheer rock faces of the mountains that tower above. The journey continues south 10 km on SH 73 up the steep winding road that climbs to Arthur's Pass and a lookout point.

From the lookout there are superb views back across the valley, but also pay attention to the kea that hang around the car park. These cheeky alpine parrots are capable of stripping the windscreen wipers and other rubber fittings from a vehicle while other members of the flock distract the car owners.

3 DOBSON NATURE WALK
Continue south 2 km on SH 73 to the Dobson Nature Walk signposted on the right.

An interesting 30-minute exploration can be made from the road near the summit, on the Dobson Nature Walk which circles through tussock and marshland on a series

Alpine flowers, Arthur's Pass.

Mt Rolleston rises majestically above the beech forest.

Trout-filled Lake Pearson is set in a dramatic, desolate landscape.

of boardwalks, providing a close-up look at exquisite alpine flowers surrounding a beautiful alpine tarn named Lake Misery. During the gold rush days, sheep and cattle grazed these fields when they were being driven across the pass to feed the hungry miners on the West Coast.

4 ARTHUR'S PASS TOWNSHIP
Continue 4 km south on SH 73 to reach the township.

At the DOC visitor centre in the Arthur's Pass township you can view one of the old Cobb and Co. coaches that used to regularly cross the pass to service the gold towns of the West Coast. These leather-sprung vehicles covered the 270 km of road in 37 hours. Passengers crammed inside and also rode on the roof, often glad to get off and walk up the steeper grades where the wheels were sometimes perilously close to the edge of a sheer drop. Runaway horses, broken brakes, flooded rivers, snowstorms and

---

TRANZALPINE EXPRESS

Work began on a rail crossing of the Southern Alps soon after the road across Arthur's Pass was completed. The major obstacle was the completion of the 8.5 km long Otira Tunnel, which by the time it was finished in 1923 was the longest in the Southern Hemisphere and the seventh longest in the world. The 233 km of narrow-gauge single track on the Midland line uses six viaducts and 16 tunnels to reach the station at Arthur's Pass before descending through the Otira Tunnel to Greymouth. The line drops from 620 m above sea level on the Canterbury side to 483 on the Westland side of the tunnel, a gradient of 1:33. Riding the TranzAlpine Express is one of the world's great railway adventures and is especially dramatic in winter.

---

drunken drivers all took their toll, but the coaches kept running until 1923, when the Otira tunnel was opened and the Midland Railway completed.

About half a kilometre north of the township a short walk leads to the Devils Punch-bowl Falls, named by Arthur Dobson, which plunge 131 m into a steep-sided valley. It is an easy 10-minute walk to the lookout point and 30 minutes if you want to go to the base of the falls. The last part of the walk can become an icy and difficult scramble during winter but the sight and sound of the falls plunging into the valley at close quarters is an impressive spectacle.

5 THE COACH ROAD
Continue south 5 km on SH 73 to the Coach Road Track signposted on the right.

This easy 20-minute track leading from the roadside follows a section of the old coach route. Throughout the exceptionally cold winter of 1865 over a thousand men toiled with picks and shovels, digging and blasting their way through the main divide. This road – considered a major engineering feat for its time – was opened in 1866 for drays and, following more preparation, was used by horse-drawn coaches.

6 LAKE PEARSON
The journey continues south-east on SH 73 following the Waimakariri River, famous for its fishing, jet boating, tramping and good picnic and swimming spots. The Waimakariri is also the gateway for classic tramping routes leading deep into the Arthur's Pass National Park. The river flows through alpine gorges before winding its way on braided lowland flats for 150 km across the Canterbury Plains to the sea. It is 26 km along this stretch to Lake Pearson.

Lake Pearson is set against erosion-torn hillsides, burnt off by early runholders, and is teeming with rainbow and brown trout. It also harbours the sleek crested grebe, a tailless waterbird with a long slender neck and pointed bill.

7 CASTLE HILL
Drive 19 km south on SH 73 to Castle Hill.

The limestone country and fascinating rock outcrops of Castle Hill can be clearly seen from the road. These distinctive formations were created by weathering over centuries to produce the smooth rounded forms that can be seen today. Maori hunting parties who used these rocks as shelter about 500 years ago drew pictures using charcoal on the smooth limestone, sometimes mixing the charcoal with fat or oil. Four hundred years later Castle Hill became a staging post for the Cobb and Co. coaches that provided transport from Christchurch to Hokitika. From the road you can follow a 10-minute walking track down to a limestone cave and if you have time, cross onto the boulder-strewn slopes to explore Castle Hill.

8 YALDHURST
Continue south 11 km on SH 73 to Lake Lyndon, which often freezes over in winter to the delight of skaters, then drive 44 km south-east, crossing Porters Pass, to Dar-field. Stay on SH 73 and travel a further 33 km east to Yaldhurst.

This long stretch of the journey passes through dramatic scenery and the highest point on the route, Porters Pass, which at 944 m is a few metres higher than Arthur's Pass. From here there is a sharp descent toward the more gentle country of the Canterbury plains. The eastern side of the alps is famous for extraordinary cloud formations.

At Yaldhurst the Transport Museum on School Road, set in the grounds of an 1876 homestead, has a collection which has grown from a single 1910 Renault to include many types of vintage cars, motorcycles, racing cars, steam engines, aircraft and horse-drawn vehicles.

It is 3 km further on SH 73 to Christchurch.

Unusual rock formations on Castle Hill.

40 THE WEST COAST

DRIVING TOUR ■ 258 KM ■ 1 DAY ■ GOLD, GREENSTONE AND GLACIERS

The rugged length of 'the Coast' has always been a challenging living environment, described in fearful terms by early explorers, but the lure of its natural wealth and beauty has captivated its hardy inhabitants and proved irresistible to tourists.

During the ice ages huge frozen rivers gouged their way down from the mountains of the Southern Alps and across the western coastal plains, carving out steep-sided valleys and depositing rock along their paths to the sea. Today some of the glaciers remain, locked in a series of advances and retreats determined by variations in seasonal weather patterns. This spectacular landscape is now cloaked in the luxuriant rainforests that gradually covered the land following the last major ice age, 15,000 years ago.

For most of its existence, Westland's coastline has been deserted, with only small parties of Maori venturing across the mountains in search of greenstone (New Zealand jade) along raging rivers. The discovery of gold in the 1860s brought a rapid end to the Coast's isolation as thousands of miners established gold-rush towns and worked the easily accessible alluvial deposits, before the emphasis moved to mining the quartz veins deep in the mountains.

1 SHANTYTOWN

From Greymouth drive 8 km south on SH 6 and take the turn-off left to Shantytown which is 3 km inland heading south-east. The wild stretch of coastline south of Greymouth is the resting place for piles of driftwood washed down from inland rivers.

Shantytown is a reconstruction of a nineteenth-century goldfields town, incorporating a number of relocated buildings such as the old Notown Church and the Ross Borough Council Chambers. The town also features period shops, a gaol, post office, hotel, livery stables, a working sawmill and stamper battery. Visitors can try panning for gold and ride on an 1897 locomotive or a horse-drawn vehicle.

2 HOKITIKA

Return to SH 6, turn left and drive 32 km south to Hokitika.

In the 1860s Hokitika became a goldmining 'metropolis', with a lively population of over 6000 and many more miners living on nearby diggings. The port was one of the busiest in the country - 19 ships arrived or left in a single day in 1865 and up to 40 sailing ships used to moor at the quayside at any one time after running the treacherous sand bar at the entrance to the harbour. Spectators would line the shore to watch vessels negotiate this hazard by sailing broadside on to the seas. A ship ran aground once every 10 days on average between 1865 and 1867. More than 40 were wrecked completely, and the rest were raised by screwjacks and dragged across the bar to the river in an operation that became known as 'making the overland trip'.

You can retrace the history of the town in the West Coast Historical Museum on Tancred Street, and visit the old Custom House and the restored historic wharf on Gibson Quay. The memorial clock tower on the main street was built in 1901–02 to commemorate the South African War and King Edward VII's coronation. Headstones in the cemetery at the northern end of the town provide individual snippets of history. Across the road from the cemetery is a dell with the largest outdoor colony of glow-worms in the country. A recent Hokitika attraction is Water World, an aquarium on Sewell Street with giant eels that are fed by divers wearing steel mesh gloves. You can also pan for gold at Phelps' gold mine, 2 km south of the township.

3 LAKE KANIERE

From Hokitika drive east 2 km to the Kaniere township and follow the road east for another 15 km to the attractive picnic area on the edge of the lake. The road then continues 23 km around the lake, passing a number of sandy bays and forest walks before returning to Kaniere via Kokatahi. An 8 km stretch along the eastern shore of the lake is unsealed.

Lake Kaniere is a scenic gem set in the forest. The depression that formed the lake

An operating water wheel in a realistic setting at Shantytown.

On the lonely, windswept coastline south of Greymouth piles of driftwood silver in the sand.

was carved out by a glacier during the ice ages, the rock wall created at the end of the glacier forming a natural dam through which the Kaniere River flows.

4 LAKE MAHINAPUA
Return to Hokitika, take SH 6 and drive 9 km south to Lake Mahinapua.

A walkway leads from the roadside through lowland rimu forest along an old tramline built in the 1920s in the Lake Scenic Reserve, which was gazetted in 1907. It takes about 15 minutes to walk to the lake, where you can often see black swans, bitterns and white herons. Mahinapua was once a coastal lagoon, but centuries of sand accumulation in a belt of dunes eventually cut off the access to the sea, creating this tranquil lake surrounded by forests of tall kahikatea, miro, matai, totara, rata and rimu.

5 ROSS
Continue 18 km south on SH 6 to Ross.

This historic gold town lies on New Zealand's richest alluvial deposits and was one of the earliest goldfields on the West Coast. Among the few original buildings that have survived are St Patrick's Church on Aylmer Street, built in 1866 and one of the oldest buildings on the Coast, the old gaol, and on the corner of St James and Bond Streets a solid little miner's cottage, built in 1885 by a Belgian couple who had struck it rich in the goldfields. Near the cottage, the Ross Historic Goldfields Walkway has tracks leading to historic dams, sluice gates, mine shafts, tunnels, mining machinery and an old cemetery.

6 OKARITO LAGOON
From Ross travel south 96 km on SH 6. The road passes through Harihari, which made the news in 1931 when Australian pilot Guy Menzies made the first single-engined flight across the Tasman and landed in a swamp near the town, safely, but upside down. Continue through Whataroa and along the shoreline of Lake Wahapo. A short distance past the lake, turn right onto the road to Okarito Lagoon and drive north-west 13 km to Okarito and the coast.

This lagoon, comprising tidal flats and shallow open water surrounded by forests of kahikatea and rimu, is the largest unmodified wetland area in New Zealand and is a feeding ground for numerous wading birds including the rare kotuku (white heron). The black sands south of Okarito were a significant source of gold in the nineteenth century.

7 FRANZ JOSEF GLACIER
Return to SH 6, turn right and continue south 13 km past the forest-fringed shores of Lake Mapourika to Franz Josef township. Turn left onto Glacier Access Road and drive south for a further 5 km inland towards the mountains along the Waiho River.

Two walks can be made from Glacier Access Road to obtain good views of the glacier. The first and easiest starts approximately 4 km up the road on the left, a 10-minute climb to Sentinel Rock, a distinctive outcrop of schist bedrock rounded off by the glacier. When Julius Haast explored the valley in 1865, Sentinel Rock had just emerged from beneath the receding glacier, and although it has advanced nearly 2 km since 1985 it is still several kilometres back from the position it occupied a hundred years earlier.

For a closer look at the glacier, continue to the end of the road and the start of a flat, 45-minute walk to the spectacular terminal ice face. From the safety of the terminal viewing point you can often see and hear huge blocks of ice breaking from the sheer face of the glacier, crashing into the riverbed below.

Return 5 km to Franz Josef township.

This old farm near Ross basks in the splendour of the Southern Alps.

41 HAAST PASS

DRIVING TOUR ■ 295 KM ■ 1 DAY ■ A ROAD THAT TOOK 100 YEARS TO COMPLETE

Although lower than the other alpine passes, Haast is the mightiest, surrounded by looming peaks and brooding forest, with waterfalls close to the highway. The drama of the western approach contrasts with the eastern descent into the bare tussocklands of Central Otago.

The Haast Pass highway is one of the most magnificent alpine scenic routes in the country. Maori had long used this 564 m pass through the main divide on greenstone-gathering trips into Westland before Te Puoho, a northern chief, led a raiding party down the West Coast and across the pass to attack Ngai Tahu settlements in Otago in 1836. A gold prospector named Charles Cameron was the first European to cross, in 1863, and a few weeks later Julius von Haast led a party of four to the Coast and named the pass after himself. A narrow pack track had been completed by 1876, but work didn't begin on the road until the 1920s. Finally completed in 1965, the Haast Pass Highway opened up the West Coast by creating a link between Westland and Central Otago.

The highway runs through the Mt Aspiring National Park with its impressive mica-schist mountains sculpted by glaciers during the ice ages and some of the most interesting alpine vegetation to be found anywhere in the world. The Aspiring region has always held a fascination for explorers, climbers, trampers and for anyone with a love for the mountains.

1 FOX GLACIER TOWNSHIP

You can arrange to join a guided walk onto the Fox Glacier from the township or explore one of the forest walks in the area. The Minnehaha Walk on the left just south of the township, off SH 6, loops through lush rainforest made up of moss-covered kamahi. The 20-minute walk enables you to experience the magic of these forests.

Fox Glacier is a vast river of ice.

2 LAKE MATHESON

Leaving Fox Glacier township on SH 6, turn right onto Cook Flat Road and drive 7 km west to Lake Matheson.

It takes only 15 minutes to walk from the car park to forest-fringed Lake Matheson, but if you have the time you can spend an hour and follow the track around the lake, which in the early hours of the morning produces picture-postcard reflections of the Southern Alps in its dark, mirror-like waters.

3 FOX GLACIER

Return to SH 6 and travel south about 2 km, turn left onto Fox Glacier Access Road and drive 5 km east.

From the end of the road it is an easy 20-minute walk to the impressive terminal face of the Fox Glacier where the river surges from a huge cavern under the ice and enormous blocks of ice tumble into the water. To the south lies Cone Rock, a 277 m sheer rock face which rises dramatically from the valley floor.

4 MORAINE WALK

Return to SH 6, turn left and drive 1 km south across the Fox River Bridge, then turn left and travel 1.5 km east on Glacier View Road.

The 20-minute Moraine Walk leads from the right-hand side of the road through a dark moody forest covering ancient rock moraines deposited by the Fox Glacier at the end of the ice ages. The boulders that cover this part of the valley are over 200 million years old and many of the giant rata and rimu trees on the older parts of the moraine have been growing for more than 1000 years. With its moss- and fern-covered floor and subdued light filtered by the canopy, this ancient rainforest has a haunting character. The loop track rejoins the road 5 minutes' walk from the starting point.

5 LAKE PARINGA

Return to SH 6 and turn left. The 46 km stretch of SH 6 from Fox Glacier south passes

Stands of kahikatea, New Zealand's tallest tree, line the road near Lake Paringa.

through beautiful stands of forest to the coast at Bruce Bay before heading inland again for another 23 km to Lake Paringa.

Popular for trout fishing, this tranquil lake right beside the road is surrounded by forest on the old main route between Otago and the West Coast, once a well-used cattle track.

6 LAKE MOERAKI
Continue south-west 17 km on SH 6 to Lake Moeraki.

This peaceful forest lake is not far from the sea. While it takes 40 minutes to walk to the coastline at Monro Beach, home to seals and a breeding colony of Fiordland crested penguins, there are several shorter walks from the lake.

7 THUNDER CREEK FALLS
From Lake Moeraki drive 35 km south-west on SH 6 towards Haast following the coastline south from Knights Point, which features impressive rock stacks off the shore. After crossing the longest single-lane bridge in the country, SH 6 turns inland to follow the Haast River deep into the mountains of the Southern Alps. Haast township is the last place to get petrol before you drive across the Haast Pass. Continue south-east 45 km from Haast to the Thunder Creek Falls.

It is just a 5-minute walk from the right-hand side of the highway to the Thunder Creek Falls which plummet 28 m over a sheer rock face. Haast explored the lower parts of the valley in 1863, finding the forests alive with kakapo and other ground-dwelling birds. Today you are likely to see kea, kaka and parakeets in the forests of Mt Aspiring National Park.

8 HAAST PASS
Continue 4 km south on SH 6 to the Gates of Haast, where an iron bridge spans the river that surges with tremendous power across the huge boulders on the riverbed. Continue south 6 km to the Fantail Falls which can be seen to the right of the road, set in forest-clad slopes below Mt Armstrong. It is another 6 km south on SH 6 to the top of the Haast Pass.

At the summit an old bridle track leads down through the forest to Davis Flat. This track was well established by 1880 but remained unimproved until 1929, when work on the Haast Pass highway began in stages, reaching Haast in 1960 with the final section to Knights Point in Westland completed in 1965.

A few minutes spent exploring along this track close to the roadside will give you an idea of the conditions experienced by early travellers on this route.

9 MAKARORA
Continue south on SH 6 for 18 km to Makarora.

This area, once covered with thick forests, was extensively logged from 1861 to provide timber for local buildings, and when the gold boom reached Central Otago the logs were rafted across Lake Wanaka to the Clutha River.

Today the forests cloaking the valley are made up almost entirely of silver beech; however, near the Mt Aspiring park visitor centre at Makarora a 15-minute walk passes through podocarp forest containing a wide variety of tree species. Halfway along the walk is a pitsaw display showing how the logs used to be cut by hand.

From Makarora continue south 49 km on SH 6, alongside Lake Wanaka, traversing high bluffs to a narrow stretch of land known as The Neck, where the road crosses to Lake Hawea. Lakes Wanaka and Hawea were gouged out by huge glaciers during the ice ages. From Lake Hawea township it is another 12 km south-west on SH 6 to the junction with SH 84. Turn right onto SH 84 and travel west 3 km to get to Wanaka.

Knights Point where the rainforest meets the sea south of Lake Moeraki.

SOUTH ISLAND
QUEENSTOWN AND BEYOND

42 WANAKA AND THE MATUKITUKI

DRIVING TOUR ■ 112 KM ■ 5 HOURS ■ EXPLORING MT ASPIRING NATIONAL PARK

The Matukituki Valley route offers a rare and relatively easy opportunity to drive deep into the mountains, covering a fairly short distance yet leaving the bustling town of Wanaka and its commercial operations far behind.

According to Maori legend the great chief Te Rakaihautu carved out the beds of Lake Wanaka and Lake Hawea with his mighty ko (digging stick), piling up the debris to form the mountain ranges. Wanaka, the third largest of the southern lakes, is fed by the Makarora and Matukituki Rivers and is the source of the Clutha River. The Matukituki, which flows from the west into Lake Wanaka, was known as 'the white destroyer' in Maori legend, although literally translated, Matukituki means 'raging stream'.

The government surveyor James McKerrow was probably the first European to visit the Matukituki Valley, in 1862, while searching in vain for a pass across to the west coast. The following year James Hector crossed a high saddle now known as Hector Col to the Waipara and Arawhata Rivers. The 28-year-old had already received a Royal Geographical Society gold medal for his explorations in North America and was later to become director of the Geological Survey.

The first sheep runs were established at Glenfinnan and Cattle Flat Station in the Matukituki Valley in 1876. During the cold winter of 1878 the snow lay more than a metre deep in the valley for four months. Glenfinnan lost nearly 8000 sheep. Heavy rain also falls frequently on the upper reaches of the valley, the Mt Aspiring Station recording up to 2700 mm annually with up to 138 days of rain. The snow and rain is an integral part of the character of this beautiful alpine environment in Mt Aspiring National Park.

Beech forests, both silver and red, predominate, but a wonderful variety of shrubs, tussocks, ferns, vines and alpine flowers flourish in the harsh environment. Several tracks are used by seasoned trampers to traverse the valley and day visitors can explore a comfortable distance along the start of some of these routes.

1 WANAKA

Lake Wanaka is 45 km long, up to 311 m deep and covers 181 sq km. The lake was carved out by ancient glaciers, vast rivers of ice that once extended from the mountains across the plains as far south as the junction of the Clutha and Lindis Rivers. The glaciers carried and deposited huge quantities of rock which made a natural dam behind which the lake has formed.

Located on these glacial deposits on the southern shores of the lake, Wanaka township is the headquarters for the Mt Aspiring National Park and a modern and charming resort catering for summer holidaymakers as well as skiers arriving in winter to take on the challenges of Treble Cone and Cardrona. The visitor centre has current information on roads, tracks and weather conditions which should be checked before you venture into the mountains.

2 GLENDHU BAY

From Wanaka drive north-west 11 km to Glendhu Bay. The snow-covered, pyramid-shaped spire of Mt Aspiring comes into view to the north-west from the road 10 km past the Wanaka township.

Against the glorious mountain backdrop, Glendhu Bay comes to life in spring with the golden flowers of the kowhai and the rich budding greens of poplars, willows and maples. In autumn these trees turn to a blaze of red and yellow before they lose their leaves.

3 DIAMOND LAKE

Continue west 8 km from Glendhu Bay. The turn-off to the Diamond Lake Track is signposted on the right. Drive 1 km to the car park.

From the car park a walking track leads along the edge of Diamond Lake which is fringed with raupo and overhanging willows. You can usually see mallard, black teal and paradise shelduck on the lake. It is a 20-minute walk to a clifftop viewing platform that looks out across the lake, the track climbing through a forest of fuchsia and wineberry where you are likely to see numerous friendly fantails and hear bellbirds singing. A further 10 minutes' walk brings you to a second viewpoint overlooking Lake Wanaka.

4 TREBLE CONE SKIFIELD

Return to the main road, turn right and go west 2 km, passing the 60 m Twin Falls on the winding gravel road to Treble Cone

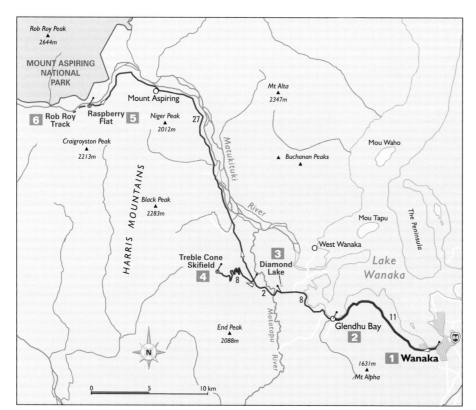

Native and exotic trees along the shoreline of Glendhu Bay dress Lake Wanaka in changing colours with the seasons.

Skifield Road, signposted on the left. It is a steep but exhilarating 8 km drive to the skifield car park.

Even if you are not visiting Wanaka to ski, the drive up to Treble Cone skifield is very rewarding, especially in summer. From the road there are excellent views across Lake Wanaka and the mountain ranges to the north but the views from the car park at the top of the road are simply stunning – almost as good as from a scenic flight.

5 RASPBERRY FLAT

Return to the main road, turn left and continue 15 km on the gravel road north-west to Cameron Flat. Here the road runs close to the base of Niger Peak, opening up dramatic views of Mt Avalanche to the north-west with its jagged ridgelines and spectacular ice faces. The road fords some small streams on the last 12 km to Raspberry Flat and this is where the scenery is most magnificent. To the north across the river is Hells Gate, towering bluffs that rise above the entrance to the west branch of the Matukituki; to the south is the sharp 2094 m pinnacle of Sharks Tooth. Make sure you engage low gear when crossing the Niger Stream and the stream at Glenfinnan. The fords have a rock base so there is little chance of getting stuck as long as you exercise caution.

Raspberry Flat is the starting point of a 4WD and walking track to the Aspiring Hut in the West Matukituki Valley which is the main access route for mountaineers to Mt Aspiring. The scenery on the drive to this point is unforgettable but when you arrive at Raspberry Flat you can fully appreciate the peace and tranquillity of this beautiful location deep in the mountains.

6 THE ROB ROY

The Rob Roy Track starts from the end of the road at Raspberry Flat.

This walking track offers a chance to experience the Matukituki River at first hand by following the first 25-minute section of the track to the Rob Roy swing bridge across the Matukituki River. The track was opened in 1987 as part of the National Parks Centennial Year celebrations. The flat glacial valley provides easy walking, the track crossing a footbridge over Big Creek before heading out across the grassy river flats with mountains on all sides.

The river valley was covered in beech forest until the late 1800s when milling and grazing began in the upper reaches of the Matukituki. Today the forest covers the steep sides of the valley, scoured clean in places where small avalanches have crashed down from the snowfields and glaciers above. If you stop and listen you can hear the crack of breaking rock and the sound of thundering rockfalls in the distance.

The birdlife in Mt Aspiring National Park is prolific. The forests are the home of species of parrot, including the cheeky kea, and many smaller birds. The tiny rock wren, New Zealand's only true alpine-dwelling bird, manages to shelter in freezing rock crevices.

As you get closer to the river you may come across the paradise shelduck and from the banks of the river or the swing bridge you can see the huge mica-schist boulders that make up the riverbed of the Matukituki. Across the river is the Rob Roy Valley, cloaked in beech forest, and beyond lies the 2606 m Rob Roy Peak with its snowfields and glaciers.

From Raspberry Flat it is 33 km to Glendhu Bay on the unsealed road and a further 11 km on sealed road to return to Wanaka.

The road leading deep into the Matukituki Valley penetrates a wilderness where mountains disappear into clouds and the silence is broken only by rushing streams.

Not for the faint-hearted, the Rob Roy swing bridge above the Matukituki River.

113

43 WANAKA TO QUEENSTOWN

DRIVING TOUR ■ 135 KM ■ 5 HOURS ■ GOLDMINING TOWNS AND A GIANT PUZZLE

The feverish hunt for gold in Central Otago in the nineteenth century created many small towns that boomed and died, and scarred the landscape. Today the ghostly remains of the gold rush are already softened, if not obliterated, by the grandeur of the natural environment.

Long before the arrival of the Europeans, Maori roamed the shores of Lake Wanaka, coming to the area to fish, hunt moa and occasionally to make the journey west for greenstone. From the early 1850s European settlers began to arrive in the area. In 1853 a 23-year-old settler from Southland, Nathaniel Chalmers, persuaded an old Maori chief named Reko to take him inland. They reached the junction of the Clutha and Hawea Rivers on foot then set off down the Clutha, spending four days rafting through the gorges to Balclutha on a craft built from dried flax stems.

By the 1860s sheep were being driven into the area and surveyors exploring it, while miners worked the gold deposits. The men who searched for gold in the mountains of Central Otago left behind many areas desolated by sluicing, dredging and mining. Introduced plants including wild thyme now grow in many of these places, the wonderful fragrance of these flowers filling the cool air when they are trodden on. Other plants like the matagouri are hardy enough to survive winter snows as well as summer heat and have sharp spikes which provide a natural defence against rabbits, grazing sheep and trampers' boots.

⬛ MT IRON
From Wanaka drive east 2 km on SH 84. The Mt Iron Reserve is signposted on the left.

From the summit of Mt Iron there are panoramic views of Lake Wanaka and beyond. The Mt Iron track is a loop, but the easiest and fastest way to take advantage of the viewpoint is to take the track leading to the left from the car park and climb the gentle grade on the western slopes of the hill,

then return the same way. It takes about 30 minutes to reach the top on the well-marked track through tussock and manuka. The best views are from the lookout point above the bluffs on the eastern side of the summit towards the Clutha and Cardrona Valleys. Lakes Wanaka and Hawea were formed by glaciers during the last 15,000 to 20,000 years and the landscape visible today features many glacial landforms. Among the most prominent are the hummocky mounds of rock on the plains below. These are moraines which were created as the glaciers retreated, leaving piles of rock which had been carried down from the mountains on the ice flows during the periods of glacial advance.

⬛ PUZZLING WORLD
From Mt Iron Reserve continue 1 km east on SH 84 to Puzzling World on the right.

New Zealand's original three-dimensional maze, Puzzling World features a 1.5 km long complex of passages that are entertaining and challenging for both adults and children to negotiate, and separate sections with hologrammatic and more conventional puzzles to be tackled.

⬛ WANAKA WARBIRDS
Continue east 5 km on SH 6 to the Wanaka Airport on the left.

The collection of restored aircraft in the New Zealand Fighter Pilots' Museum includes a P51 Mustang, Spitfire, Kittyhawk, Grumman Avenger and SE5A biplane. A recreated briefing room screens authentic newsreel footage from the Second World War. The nearby Wanaka Transport Museum displays 150 vehicles including old British

Mt Iron overlooks the plains behind Wanaka.

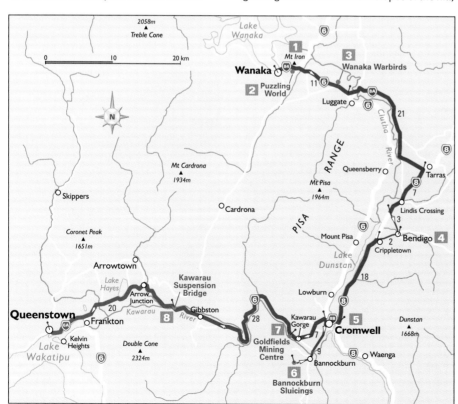

The ghostly remains of goldminers' cottages rise from the slopes at Bendigo.

cars and motorcycles, as well as aircraft ranging in size from the tiny Flying Flea to the huge Russian Antonov. There are also 7000 toys on display.

4 BENDIGO
Continue 3 km east on SH 6 and turn left onto SH 8A which crosses the Clutha River and heads 21 km south-east to join SH 8. Turn right onto SH 8 and drive 7 km south to the Bendigo turn-off on the left. It is a 3 km drive on an unsealed road up to the old gold-mining settlement of Bendigo.

Bendigo was mined for over 50 years and was one of the few successful quartz mining areas in Otago. The road leads up through the scrub past dozens of old crumbling stone cottages in this fascinating mining area. Enjoy the scenery from your car and the roadside or spend 20 minutes exploring the area on a well-defined walking track. Some of the old mine shafts in the area drop up to 170 m deep so make sure you stay on the track.

5 CROMWELL
Continue 2 km on the Bendigo loop road back down to SH 8, turn left and continue south 18 km to the Cromwell turn-off. Turn right onto SH 8B and drive 1 km to Cromwell.

In the 1970s Cromwell became the site of a hydroelectric power scheme that involved creating the huge Clyde Dam to harness the Clutha River. Lake Dunstan, which formed behind the dam, submerged much of the area in 1992 but a number of historic buildings were relocated and can be seen at 'Old Cromwell Town'. Cromwell is famous for its fruit, in particular apricots, which thrive in the gold-bearing alluvial soils.

6 BANNOCKBURN SLUICINGS
From Cromwell drive south on Bannockburn Road 5 km to the Bannockburn bridge which crosses the Kawarau Arm of Lake Dunstan. Continue south 1 km past the bridge and turn right into Felton Road, then drive another 2 km to the Bannockburn Sluicings which are part of the Otago Goldfields Park.

Set in the midst of the Pisa, Carrick and Dunstan Mountains, the Bannockburn Sluicings were created between 1862 and 1910 by more than 2000 men who came here in search of gold. The miners channelled water from streams high in the Carrick Mountains along races into storage areas far below. The water was released under pressure through sluice guns to create strong jets that were used to loosen and wash away the gold-bearing gravels.

The mining operations created a ruined landscape, but one which has its own stark beauty, emphasised by its position within the solitude of the surrounding mountains. It is a 10-minute walk to the amphitheatre where you can see the the full effect of the sluicing operations on the landscape. The track continues higher to Menzies Dam, 1 km from the road and a 15-minute walk from the amphitheatre. This is where the miners stored their water and on the nearby slopes are the remains of the mud brick houses of Stewart Town and the fruit trees planted by the miners. This is the high point of the track and from here you can return the way you came or continue down on the loop track along an old water race.

The men who built the dams and water races often made more money than the miners by selling the water needed for the sluice guns. One of the largest channels was the Pipeclay Gully Sludge Channel which was used to wash waste material over 2 km down to the Kawarau River. Construction started in 1877 and took 10 years to complete. The miners paid sixpence a day to feed water and tailings into the channel.

7 GOLDFIELDS MINING CENTRE
Return to Cromwell and continue west 1 km to SH 6, turn left and drive 7 km to the Goldfields Mining Centre signposted on the left.

You can try panning for gold in the Kawarau Gorge at the Goldfields Mining Centre. From the road, the goldmining area across the river is reached via an old suspension bridge. Guided tours explore the tailings and some impressive restored mining equipment on a site overlooking the river. There are demonstrations of hydraulic sluicing and a fully operational stamping battery.

8 KAWARAU SUSPENSION BRIDGE
Continue west on SH 6 for 28 km through the Kawarau Gorge to the Kawarau Suspension Bridge on the right. The road follows almost the same route as that used by the packhorses and drays and, from the 1860s, by coaches. It was always a hazardous journey and today, especially during winter, sections of the road are prone to icing up.

The 43 m high Kawarau bridge was built in 1880 to provide access to the goldfields around Lake Wakatipu, and remained in use until 1963. In 1988 it became the location for the world's first full-time commercial bungy jumping operation.
From the bridge it is another 20 km west on SH 6 and SH 6A to Queenstown.

Goldfields Mining Centre.

Bungy jumping from the Kawarau bridge.

44 QUEENSTOWN HIGHLIGHTS

DRIVING TOUR ■ 64 KM ■ 5 HOURS ■ ADRENALINE RUSHES AND NOSTALGIA

The features for which the Queenstown area is most famous are all included in this short trip. Visitors can jump, jet boat, shoot rapids, ski, or simply enjoy watching all this happening, then absorb the atmosphere of an old gold town.

Although Queenstown is the self-styled 'adventure capital of the world', after all the bungy jumping, white-water rafting, parapenting and jet boating it is the magnificent scenery that emerges as the real attraction. Nestled on the shores of Lake Wakatipu, Queenstown occupies one of New Zealand's most scenic locations, set against the majestic Eyre Mountains and the snow-capped splendour of the Remarkables.

The discovery of gold at Arrowtown in 1862 brought an influx of prospectors and Queenstown became the port for sailing vessels and paddle steamers crossing the lake with supplies and carrying out gold via Kingston to the south.

The Shotover gained a reputation as the 'richest river in the world' because of stories such as that involving a pair of prospectors who set out to rescue their dog from a rock crevice and discovered over 11 kg of gold in a single day. By the early 1900s, however, sightseers were arriving in increasing numbers to make trips out on the lake on the paddle steamers and take the buggy ride out to Skippers Canyon to see the miners at work. The modern Queenstown is a Mecca for tourists who come for its spectacular scenery, skiing and snowboarding, hiking and any number of exciting outdoor adventure activities.

1 SKYLINE GONDOLA
The Skyline Gondola on Brecon Street in Queenstown can be reached from the information centre on the corner of Camp and Shotover Streets by driving north-west up Camp Street, turning left into Man Street, taking the first right and continuing to the end of the street.

The Skyline Gondola climbs 450 m to a viewing complex overlooking Queenstown, Lake Wakatipu and the Remarkables, giving a panoramic view of the whole area. If you want to get outside for some mountain air you can also make a 20-minute walk along the Ben Lomond Track which starts behind the complex. The track leads through a Douglas fir forest onto the open subalpine grasslands on a long ridgeline running towards the 1748 m Ben Lomond Peak.

2 SHOTOVER RIVER
Return down Brecon Street, turn left into Isle Street and continue into Robins Road then onto Gorge Road which heads north 7 km to Arthurs Point on the Shotover River. The Shotover Jet operates from a jetty on the riverside, on the left of the road across the bridge.

The fabulously rich Shotover River still yields gold but is now better known as the venue for one of New Zealand's most popular jet boating experiences. The Shotover Jet skims the sheer faces of the canyon walls in an exhilarating trip that takes visitors 14 km downstream from the bridge at Arthurs Point and back. It is worth stopping to watch the jet boat coming through the canyon even if you don't have the nerve to make the trip.

3 SKIPPERS CANYON
Travel north 2 km to the next junction, take the left fork and continue 7 km on the winding road up to Coronet Peak. Take the turn-off to Skippers Canyon on the left and drive a short distance along this notorious dirt road to get views of the impressive Skippers Canyon.

One of the main mining locations of the last century, Skippers Canyon is reached on a twisting road that took 8 years to build with funds accumulated from a levy placed on gold brought out of the area. The scenery in the canyon is dramatic, with sheer drops of over 100 m beside the road in some places. A sign at the top of the hill advises travellers that hire-car insurance is invalid on the next stretch of road. However, you can safely take

One of New Zealand's most notorious back-country roads winds through Skippers Canyon.

Arrowtown captures the atmosphere of a gold town in the 1800s.

4 CORONET PEAK SKIFIELD

Return to the main road, turn left and travel 4 km to the Coronet Peak skifield.

Coronet Peak offers a range of runs for all levels of ability, the highest run starting at 1620 metres above sea level. The drive up to the skifield is interesting at all times of year with impressive views across the valley below.

5 ARROWTOWN

Go down the hill from Coronet Peak, drive 11 km and turn left onto the road to Arrowtown. It is 12 km north-east to Arrowtown.

The Arrow River became famous as one of the richest sources of alluvial gold in the world in 1862 when William Fox discovered gold only a few hundred metres from where the town now stands. Today this is the most picturesque of Otago's gold towns with a number of carefully preserved wooden cottages on its tree-lined streets. A visit to Arrowtown will take you back in time to the days of the gold rush. Many of the historic buildings on Buckingham Street have been converted to tourist shops, the old Bank of New Zealand (1875) is now a museum and you can visit the old gaol built in 1875. The museum also serves as an information centre and provides booklets and directions for visitors who would like to wander around the streets of Arrowtown learning about its history and buildings. You can also try your luck panning for gold in the Arrow River.

6 CHINESE SETTLEMENT

In Arrowtown, head north-west along Buckingham Street towards the Arrow River. The walking track to the Chinese Settlement follows the river west.

Near Bush Creek a 15-minute track leads

Chinese miner's hut on the Arrow River.

through a small Chinese settlement including two miner's huts and a store that were reconstructed following excavations carried out in 1983. The hardworking Chinese 'diggers' often worked the tailings left by other miners, sifting out the fine particles of gold that had been overlooked.

7 LAKE HAYES

From Arrowtown head south 3 km to Lake Hayes. A short access road signposted to the right leads to a picnic area among the willow trees on the northern edge of the lake.

Surrounded by exotic trees and farmland, this small lake is renowned for its perfect reflections. It was known to the Maori as Waiwhaka-ata – 'water that reflects objects' – and is a favourite subject for artists and a popular spot for trout fishing. Pukeko, scaup and the secretive marsh crake live around the lake which is also a breeding ground for the Australian coot. Although Lake Hayes was thought to have been discovered by the Australian stockman Donald Hay in 1859, it is named after the 'Bully' Hayes, a notorious blackbirder and pirate who made his name on the Arrow goldfields in 1863.

Continue south 2 km, turn right onto SH 6 and drive south-west 16 km to Queenstown.

in the scenery by travelling less than the first kilometre and if you want to see more, guided trips into Skippers Canyon can be arranged from Queenstown. At the head of the canyon lie mining relics, including the remains of the old township with a restored schoolhouse and dwellings. Skippers is also the starting point for a wild and unforgettable rafting experience on the Shotover River, which culminates in a hair-raising ride through a narrow tunnel cut by the miners. You can also watch bungy-jumpers leaping 72 m from the Skippers suspension bridge into a narrow gorge.

In the still surface of Lake Hayes the landscape is mirrored in astonishing detail.

45 NORTH ALONG LAKE WAKATIPU

DRIVING TOUR ■ 174 KM ■ 1 DAY ■ STEAMSHIP, FOREST TRAILS AND WATERFALLS

In the mountains at the head of Lake Wakatipu lie the remains of one of the region's most famous gold mines, the Invincible. Nearby in the silent forest nestles gem-like Lake Sylvan, home to a colourful variety of water birds.

The first Maori settled in the area around Lake Wakatipu over a thousand years ago, but once the moa had been hunted to extinction they moved to the east coast, returning occasionally on long journeys in search of greenstone on an ancient route from the head of Lake Wakatipu across the mountains and along the Hollyford Valley to the sea.

William Rees explored Lake Wakatipu in 1859 and laid claim to a run on the eastern shoreline on what was to become the future site of Queenstown. Gold was discovered near Queenstown the following year. By 1863 the surveyor James McKerrow had journeyed up the Rees Valley, followed by Patrick Caples who crossed the Rees Saddle the following year in search of gold. By 1882 a quartz battery was in operation on the lower Rees and gold was being brought out of the mountains, but a more sustainable long-term industry was about to begin. An Irishman, the Rev. W. S. Green, made a mountaineering attempt on Mt Earnslaw that year, and from this grew a successful tourism industry based on guided climbs and excursions into the wilderness.

Today Queenstown is a busy year-round tourism centre, catering for thousands of skiers over winter as well as sightseers and trampers heading into the mountains to explore the old gold and greenstone trails during summer. The diversity and accessibility of its beautiful surroundings make it a not-to-be-missed travellers' destination.

1 QUEENSTOWN

Originally the site of a remote sheep station, Queenstown boomed with the discovery of gold in 1863 and the influx of thousands of diggers. The town has a number of interesting historic buildings, including Williams Cottage (1866) on the waterfront, Eichardt's Tavern in the Mall and the Old Stone Library on Ballarat Street, which was built in the 1870s and is framed by two tall sequoia trees. Queenstown Gardens were planted in 1867 on a small promontory jutting out into the lake. On Brecon Street the Queenstown Motor Museum is packed with motoring

The Old Stone Library, Queenstown.

memorabilia, old cars, motorcycles and a Russian Mig 21 jet. Also on Brecon Street is the Kiwi and Birdlife Park where kiwi can be seen in nocturnal conditions as well as the rare black stilt and other native birds. The park is involved in a programme to raise endangered species.

2 THE STEAMER WHARF
On the waterfront of Queenstown Bay.

The Steamer Wharf is the hub of much activity in Queenstown and the home of the steel-hulled *Earnslaw* which was built in Dunedin and then completely dismantled before being hauled by rail to Kingston, where it was reassembled and launched on Lake Wakatipu in 1912. The last of the many steamships that once plied the waters of the lake, she burns a tonne of coal per hour and is capable of 13 knots. The *Earnslaw* carries passengers across Lake Wakatipu to the Walter Peak Farm, founded in the 1860s and one of the oldest sheep and cattle stations in the country.

From the main jetty you can also visit the Underwater World Aquarium where trout, eels and New Zealand's only diving duck, the scaup, can be observed at eye level through special viewing windows.

3 BOB'S COVE
From Queenstown take the road to Glenorchy and drive south-west 13 km. Bob's Cove Track is signposted on the left.

Bob's Cove, named after an early Lake Wakatipu boat skipper, became a popular location for steamer excursions. A lime industry operated here from 1880 to 1900, with the lime shovelled into kilns and fired before being shipped to Queenstown where it was used in the construction of many of the old buildings including the Queenstown Library.

Originally known as Te Punatapu, the cove was a stopping point for Maori walking the trail along the lake into the mountains in search of greenstone. Today Bob's Cove is a peaceful place to stop for a swim or relax beside the cool waters of the lake and can be reached on a well-graded 15-minute walk.

4 INVINCIBLE MINE
From Bob's Cove continue south-west then north 34 km to Glenorchy at the northern end of Lake Wakatipu. The views of the lake and the surrounding mountains from the road are magnificent but more scenic wonders lie ahead in the mountains at the head of the lake. Drive north from Glenorchy

On the road to Glenorchy, ever-changing views unfold of the northern arm of Lake Wakatipu and the Humboldt Mountains beyond.

8 km on the Glenorchy–Paradise Road and turn right to Rees Valley then continue north 10 km to McDougalls Creek and the Invincible Mine track signposted on the right.

In 1879 a quartz reef was discovered at this site in the Richardson Range and the Invincible Quartz Mining Company began crushing in 1882, the first stone yielding 325 oz (9 kg) of gold. By 1884 large quantities of tailings were being produced by the operation and tests showed that the discarded crushed rock still contained significant amounts of gold. A 679 m wooden chute was built to carry the tailings down into a wooden building on the valley floor where a water-powered turbine drove machinery that was used to further process the tailings and extract gold.

By 1887 the mining was coming to an end and the mine was abandoned in 1889. Other hopeful syndicates tried to work the mine between 1902 and 1922 but this part of the Richardson Range has numerous faults and the elusive quartz reef was never rediscovered.

It is an easy 30-minute walk up to the Invincible Mine on a well-formed track. The remains of a huge waterwheel, as well as seven large cast-iron bowls known as berdans used to grind the ore, along with the framing and camshaft from the stamping battery, can all be found at the site. Quartz ore was extracted from several levels on the mountainside. Only the lower partially collapsed level is still open, where a shaft was driven 230 m horizontally into the mountain to reach the vertical quartz reef. The quartz was blasted and dug out by hand, then the ore was pushed out by hand in trucks weighing up to a tonne running on tram rails.

5 LAKE SYLVAN

Return south 10 km and turn right onto the Glenorchy–Routeburn Road. After 9 km the road crosses the Dart River and continues north-west 6 km to the Lake Sylvan turn-off on the right. Travel 1 km to the start of the track to the lake.

It is a pleasant 30-minute walk through the forest to the edge of Lake Sylvan. The lake was formed at the meeting point of the Rees and Dart Glaciers which once covered the valley floor. In the forest are the remains of an old tramline built to haul out beech trees which were milled here in the 1920s and 1930s. Today these peaceful forests are the home of the delightful bush robin and on the lake you will find little shags, and paradise, mallard and grey ducks.

6 DOUBLE BARREL FALLS

Return to the Glenorchy–Routeburn Road, turn right and drive 6 km to the road end and Routeburn Shelter, where the Double Barrel Falls Track starts.

This is a loop track but you can take a 30-minute walk on the first section and return the same way, through the beautiful red beech forest in the Lower Routeburn Valley, the foliage appearing a vivid green as the light filters through the forest canopy. The sound of the Double Barrel Falls grows louder at the halfway point of the walk and views of the rock faces of Mt Momus and the Sugarloaf Saddle appear.

7 ROUTEBURN TRACK

The track starts from the end of the Glenorchy–Routeburn Road.

A short walk at the start of the world-famous Routeburn Track will take you through towering beech forest and across small streams.

The Routeburn Track follows the path of one of the old greenstone trails across the mountains from the Mt Aspiring National Park into Fiordland, where it joins the Hollyford Track out to the West Coast. Early European explorers saw this trail as a route from the goldfields around Lake Wakatipu across the mountains to the West Coast, where the gold could be shipped directly to Australia. The track was cut into the mountains following an easy grade that could be negotiated by horse-drawn drays laden with gold, which makes it an easy walk for visitors of all ages.

The journey back to Queenstown is 76 km.

TSS Earnslaw, *the 'Lady of the Lake', is the last of dozens of steam-driven vessels that once plied Lake Wakatipu.*

46 WAKATIPU TO TE ANAU

DRIVING TOUR ■ 235 KM ■ 1 DAY ■ LONELY PEAKS, TAKAHE AND A CLASSIC TRAIN

The road south from Queenstown skirts the lower arm of Lake Wakatipu at the feet of the towering Remarkables and then the Hector Mountains, affording the traveller a real sense of the grandeur of this region, before heading west to the gateway of the Fiordland wilderness.

The name Wakatipu means 'place where the demon lies'. According to Maori legend the curiously shaped Lake Wakatipu was created when a giant demon captured the daughter of a Maori chief and took her to his home in the mountains. After struggling against a 'nor-easter' the exhausted demon lay down to sleep with his head near Glenorchy, his knees at Queenstown and his feet at Kingston. The girl's lover had followed the trail into the mountains, crept up to the sleeping demon and set it on fire, and the demon's fat burnt its way deep into the earth. All that remained was its heart, beating within a gigantic trench which gradually filled with rain and snow to form an enormous lake in the shape of the demon. The changes in the level of the lake were said to be the pulsing of the demon's heart.

Today the natural surge in the lake that travels from one end to the other, taking over 50 minutes, is attributed to a phenomenon known as a transverse seiche. Although Lake Wakatipu is not big enough to be tidal, the level of the lake alters as part of a natural fluctuation in the water level caused by the wind or atmospheric pressure variations.

The second largest lake in the South Island after Lake Te Anau, the Z-shaped Lake Wakatipu has a total length of 77 km and covers 293 sq km. Surrounded by steeply rising mountains and carved out by ice-age glaciers, the lake is 378 m at its deepest, dropping to a point that is below sea level. The natural rock dam formed at the edge of the glacier that shaped Lake Wakatipu lies at Kingston, with the terminal moraine blocking the flow of water into the Mataura River Valley.

The swift-flowing waters of the Kawarau River at Frankton.

1 FRANKTON ARM

From Queenstown drive north-east 7 km on SH 6A and turn right onto SH 6. Drive south 2 km to Frankton. The road crosses the outlet to Wakatipu on a control structure that was built in 1926 to dam the Kawarau River and allow further gold recovery downstream. Across the bridge, turn right and drive west 7 km out onto the Frankton Arm.

The Frankton Arm is a narrow peninsula stretching out into Lake Wakatipu and the location of one of New Zealand's most picturesque golf courses. There are beautiful views of the Remarkables, the snow-clad range that rises steeply from the eastern shoreline of Lake Wakatipu. The highest point on the skyline is the 2343 m peak of Double Cone.

2 REMARKABLES SKIFIELD

Return to SH 6, turn right and drive 4 km to the Remarkables Skifield Road. Turn left and travel 10 km on the winding gravel road to the skifield. The views from this road, which is also used for rally events, are amazing.

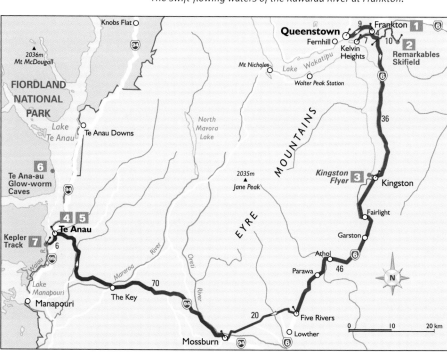

The Remarkables are an exciting place to visit even if you are not skiing. The views from the skifield road are spectacular, but taking the chairlift to the Wakatipu lookout will provide truly awesome views across Lake Wakatipu and Queenstown into the mountains beyond. This is one of the most outstanding alpine scenic viewpoints in the country and can easily be reached by road and chairlift without involving any serious climbing.

3 THE KINGSTON FLYER
Return to SH 6, turn left and head south 36 km along the shoreline of Wakatipu under the peaks of the Remarkables to Kingston at the southern end of the lake. Take the turn-off on the right and travel west 2 km to the Kingston Station.

This is the home of the *Kingston Flyer*, which ran as a crack express to Gore from 1902 to 1937. Over the summer months you can ride on this historic steam train from the charming little station at Kingston to Fairlight and back. This marvellous old engine with its immaculately restored coaches is fascinating to inspect, even if you don't have time to take a ride.

4 TE ANAU
Return to SH 6, turn right and drive 46 km south to Five Rivers. Turn right here and travel 20 km on sealed back roads to Mossburn. From Mossburn take SH 94 and drive north-west 70 km to Te Anau.

With its three long arms stretching west into the forest-clad lower slopes of Fiordland's mountains, the glacier-gouged Lake Te Anau is 53 km long, covers 345 sq km, and is up to 417 m deep. Te Anau township, the gateway to Fiordland National Park, lies on the shores of the lake at the start of New Zealand's most famous scenic highway, the road to Milford Sound (see Tour 47). The DOC visitor information centre, near the lakefront on the road to Manapouri, can supply inform-

At the Remarkables skifield the slopes are gentle and even non-skiing visitors can go exploring in the snowy landscape.

ation on walks in the area and features most interesting displays on Fiordland's wilderness areas and wildlife. Te Anau is the start point of several spectacular walking tracks.

5 TE ANAU WILDLIFE CENTRE
Located on the outskirts of the town on the road to Manapouri a short distance from the DOC visitor centre.

At the centre you can see native birds in aviaries and natural enclosures, including the takahe, a large flightless bird with striking blue and green feathers and a huge red beak. It was by the end of the nineteenth century thought to be extinct but in 1948 a pair was found in the Murchison Range. These rare birds are now bred in captivity and released back into the wild.

6 TE ANA-AU GLOW-WORM CAVES
The Te Ana-au Caves, after which Lake Te Anau was named, lie at the base of the Murchison Mountains and can be reached by boat trips that leave regularly from the pier at the end of Milford Road.

These caves, part of Maori legend, were rediscovered in 1948 by a local explorer, Lawson Burrows. The caves are still young in geological terms, having formed over the last 15,000 years, and the flow of the Tunnel Burn Stream continues to carve away the rock. Inside the caves a series of walkways and two short boat trips will take you past underground waterfalls and whirlpools into a magnificent glow-worm grotto.

7 KEPLER TRACK
From Te Anau drive 3 km south on SH 95 and turn right onto the access road to the Waiau River Control Gates 3 km from the main road.

The control gates at the head of the Waiau River are the starting and finishing point for the Kepler Track. An ideal way to experience the wilderness of the forests that border Lake Te Anau is to take a 25-minute walk along the start of the track as far as Dock Bay. This well-formed walkway leads through a forest made up of red and mountain beech with kamahi in the subcanopy, and the occasional rimu growing along the shoreline.
Return to SH 95, turn left and drive 3 km back to Te Anau.

The Kingston Flyer *revives the excitement of steam-train travel.*

47 THE ROAD TO MILFORD

DRIVING TOUR ■ 224 KM ■ 1 DAY ■ LAKES, RAGING RIVERS AND SILENT FIORDS

The road to Milford Sound is a magnificent scenic highway that travels from the shores of Lake Te Anau, across the mountains beyond, to emerge in the glacier-carved splendour of Milford Sound, the focal point of Fiordland National Park.

Beneath the mysterious waters of Milford Sound lies an ancient valley carved from the rock by glaciers over two million years ago. During successive periods of advance and retreat, the glaciers pushed their way down from the huge ice caps covering Fiordland's mountains and extended out to sea. The glaciers were thousands of metres thick and their enormous weight was enough to grind away the rock as they moved across the land, carving out steep-sided valleys. When the glaciers began to melt at the end of the last ice age, 15,000 years ago, the sea rose and flowed into the glacial valleys along the coastline, creating fiords. These silent waters are sheltered by huge underwater moraines – large piles of rock carried down from the mountains and deposited by the glaciers as they began to retreat. This is an awe-inspiring landscape, where waterfalls plummet over high cliffs and vegetation clings to sheer rock walls above the deep sounds.

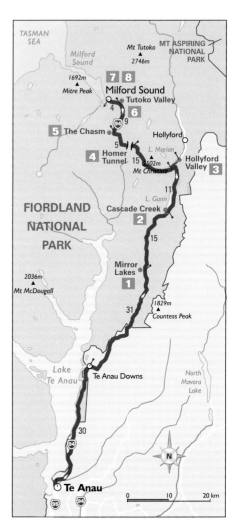

Lake Fergus is one of two small lakes that border the road to Milford shortly past Cascade Creek.

1 MIRROR LAKES

From Te Anau head north 30 km on SH 94 across the plains to Te Anau Downs where you can stop at the jetty to see the historic SS Tarawera *which carries trampers across the lake to the start of the world-famous Milford Track. The road continues north along the Eglinton Valley for another 31 km through patches of beech forest to the Mirror Lakes signposted on the left.*

A 5-minute boardwalk leads through moss-covered beech trees to viewing platforms at the Mirror Lakes where picture-perfect images of the surrounding snow-capped peaks are reflected in the still water.

2 CASCADE CREEK

Continue north on SH 94. Ahead lies a stretch of road signposted as 'the avenue of the disappearing mountain', which provides the illusion that a peak ahead is sinking out of sight as you drive directly towards it. It is 15 km to Cascade Creek signposted on the left.

An easy 30-minute loop walk leading from Cascade Creek circles through the forest to Lake Gunn. The lake was known to Maori as O Tapara and its shores were a resting place for parties heading to Anita Bay on the West Coast in search of greenstone. Paradise ducks and scaup can often be seen on the lakes while the surrounding red beech forest is alive with forest birds, including tomtits, fantails, bellbirds, parakeets, kereru and the tiny rifleman. You may also catch sight of the long-tailed bat, which, along with another species of bat, are New Zealand's only native land mammals.

3 HOLLYFORD VALLEY

Continue north 11 km on SH 94 and turn right into Hollyford Road. Drive north-east 1 km to the start of the Lake Marian Track signposted on the left.

The best walk in the Hollyford Valley is the first 15-minute section of the track to Lake Marian. The track crosses a swing bridge over the wild waters of the Hollyford River then leads through the forest to an exciting boardwalk perched above a series of rapids where the river rages down through the forest.

4 HOMER TUNNEL

Return to SH 94, turn right and drive along the upper reaches of the Hollyford River. The road runs past a thundering waterfall on the left, with rapids on the right as the valley steepens on its winding path towards the Homer Saddle. It is 15 km driving north-west to the Homer Tunnel which descends 1 km through the mountain to emerge in the Cleddau Valley.

In the Upper Hollyford Valley beech trees overhang the turbulent Hollyford River.

The waters of Milford Sound are sheltered from the wild ocean by an underwater moraine, a natural barrier deposited by a long-departed glacier.

Named after Harry Homer, who discovered the saddle in 1889, the tunnel was begun in 1935 as a project for the unemployed and took another 18 years to complete. The rough-hewn rock walls of the Homer Tunnel, dripping water and lit only by your headlights, present an eerie sight as you drive downhill towards the western portal. Just past the exit, a 15-minute nature walk climbs from the right side of the road through the forest beneath the towering rock face of the Homer Saddle and surrounding valley walls. On a rainy day the mountain comes alive with dozens of waterfalls cascading down the sheer rock faces from the Homer Saddle.

5 THE CHASM
Continue north-west 5 km on SH 94 down the winding road through the Cleddau Valley to the Chasm, signposted to the left.

A 10-minute walking track leads from the road to the impressive Chasm, a series of falls where the water has spun small rounded stones that have cut fluted channels into the rock. The upper falls tumble 22 m through a series of cascades under a natural rock bridge to another waterfall.

6 TUTOKO VALLEY
Continue 9 km north-west down through the forest-covered Cleddau Valley on SH 94 to the Tutoko Bridge. The Tutoko Walking Track is signposted on the right.

You can take a short walk into the forest on the Tutoko track, but good views of 2746 m Mt Tutoko can be obtained from the road bridge. The peak was first climbed by Samuel Turner, an eccentric Englishman who led several expeditions in the 1920s, modelled on the classical mountaineering expeditions made in the Himalayas, complete with guides, porters and carefully selected companions. He finally reached the peak of Fiordland's highest mountain on his sixth attempt.

7 MILFORD SOUND
Continue west 4 km on SH 94 to Milford Sound.

No photographs or travel reports can adequately prepare the visitor for the first glimpse of Milford Sound, a scenic wonder dominated by the distinctive form of Mitre Peak. As the climate warmed at the end of the ice ages, huge amounts of ice melted and the sea level rose, flooding many of the deeply cut glacial valleys to create the fiords that now make up this magnificent stretch of coastline.

8 BOWEN FALLS
The track to the Bowen Falls is clearly signposted from the end of the road and the ferry jetty.

You can walk to the 160 m Bowen Falls in less than 10 minutes, the track rounding a rocky bluff and skirting through a small patch of forest onto the rocky fan below the falls which explode in two tiers from a hanging valley high above.

After heavy rain the falls are even more dramatic. The volume of water increases and a single vast curtain of water and spray thunders into the sea.
From Milford Sound it is 121 km back to Te Anau on SH 94.

CRUISING MILFORD SOUND
Milford Sound has two distinct characters. On a clear day it is a picture of tranquillity, but during rain the fiord is transformed, revealing the power of water as countless falls erupt into life from sheer rock walls. High winds often blow the huge volumes of water that cascade from the 146 m Stirling Falls back up into the air.

The tranquil waters of Milford Sound are best experienced on one of the scenic cruises that cover the full length of the sound out to the sea. A variety of cruises run daily, some of which include a trip to the underwater observatory at Harrison Cove. The sound is a diver's paradise, where deep-water species such as black coral exist in unusually shallow depths. This is due to the huge volumes of water that flow into the fiords, creating a layer of fresh water over the salt water that filters out sunlight and creates conditions normally found at much deeper levels. Bottle-nose and dusky dolphins can be seen in the clear waters, along with Fiordland crested penguins, and the now-protected fur seals have returned.

SOUTH ISLAND

THE DEEP SOUTH

48 SOUTHLAND

DRIVING TOUR ■ 250 KM ■ 1 DAY ■ PRIMEVAL FOREST AND A DINOSAUR RELATIVE

On this trip the traveller reaches the bottom of the New Zealand mainland and the last city before the vast sweep of the Southern Ocean and Antarctica. This land is dramatic, but the friendly folk who live here take it all for granted.

The World Heritage site of Fiordland National Park, the largest in New Zealand, covers 1.2 million hectares along the remote south-western coastline of the South Island. It contains 14 fiords, from Milford Sound south along the coast to Preservation Inlet, some stretching as far as 40 km inland as they trace the paths of the ancient glaciers that created them. These glaciers carved out New Zealand's deepest lakes and created the rock faces over which some of the highest waterfalls in the country plunge.

Captain Cook recorded large numbers of seals at Dusky Sound in 1773, and a major sealing enterprise flourished in the region in the early 1800s. East of the Fiordland wilderness, Southland's rich river lowlands began to attract the region's first farmers, hardy Scots who trekked south from Otago. The settlement that was to become Invercargill was founded in 1856 and its streets were named after Scottish rivers. Today the soft 'burr' of Southland speech, the only regional accent in New Zealand, is a reminder of the pioneers.

A gold rush in the 1890s brought miners to Preservation Inlet, where two townships flourished then died and were reclaimed by the forest. Surveyors, prospectors and explorers made their way inland during the early 1900s, among them Sir Thomas McKenzie, later to become Premier of New Zealand. As early as 1894 McKenzie advocated that Fiordland should become a public park, and 10 years later most of the land had been reserved, though the park was not created until 1952.

1 RAINBOW REACH
From Te Anau drive south 11 km on SH 95 to the Rainbow Reach Track which is accessible from a short road signposted to the right off the main highway.

The track, reached by crossing a swing bridge over the river, leads to Shallow Bay, but you can take a delightful walk along the first few hundred metres through beautiful stands of tall red and mountain beech trees on the banks of the Waiau River.

2 MANAPOURI
Continue south-west 10 km on SH 95 to Manapouri.

New Zealand's largest power station is sited on the western shores of Lake Manapouri and in the 1970s it was proposed to increase the level of the lake by 12 m to provide more water storage for the station. The prospect of irreparable damage to this most beautiful lake, originally called by Maori 'lake of a hundred islets', outraged New Zealanders. Nationwide protests and a petition with over a quarter of a million signatures eventually led to the scrapping of the project.

Manapouri covers over 43 sq km and is the country's second-deepest lake. One of the more easily accessible of the southern lakes, you can walk down to the water's edge from the roadside.

3 CLIFDEN SUSPENSION BRIDGE
Drive east 5 km on SH 95, turn right, then travel south 64 km to the old suspension bridge at Clifden. A short access road leads to the right off the main road to the bridge.

The wonderfully engineered old Clifden suspension bridge on the Wairaki River dates back to 1899. Near the beginning of the bridge are the remains of an even earlier settlement.

The Kepler Mountains, sombre sentinels above Lake Manapouri.

Lake Hauroko, wide and peaceful-looking in its forest surroundings where red deer graze, plunges to a glacier-gouged depth of nearly half a kilometre.

4 LAKE HAUROKO

Turn right a short distance south of the Clifden Bridge and travel west 32 km on a gravel road to the shore of Lake Hauroko.

There is a 10-minute nature walk along the edge of Lake Hauroko, New Zealand's deepest lake and the site of a well-preserved Maori burial cave which was discovered on Mary Island in 1967. A woman believed to be of high rank was buried sitting upright in this tapu (sacred) place in about 1660. A recreation of the burial is featured in the Fiordland National Park Visitor Centre at Te Anau.

James McKerrow was the first European to see the lake during his third reconnaissance survey of Southland in 1863. From the western end of the Takitimu Mountains he caught a glimpse of the lake, 'Shining like a great mirror from the depths of the bush at the base of the Princess Mountains'.

5 TUATAPERE

Return to the main highway, turn right and travel south 13 km on SH 99 to Tuatapere.

Known as the 'Hole in the Bush', Tuatapere can trace its development back to its early days as a sawmilling centre for the bushmen cutting their way through the beautiful lowland forests that once covered Te Tua, Te Waewae, Waihoaka and Orepuki. Today the town hosts a national wood-chopping carnival each year on New Year's Day and also is the self-proclaimed 'Sausage Capital' of New Zealand. Tuatapere Domain is an attractive bush reserve in the heart of the town that serves as a reminder of the forest that once cloaked the countryside.

6 OREPUKI

From Tuatapere drive 10 km south on SH 99 to the cliffs above Te Waewae Bay, where you can occasionally see Hector's dolphins and southern right whales. Orepuki Beach is a further 8 km south-east on SH 99. Along the roadside, stands of macrocarpa have been dramatically clipped by the strong southerly winds that buffet the shoreline.

Although gold was found at Orepuki Beach in the 1860s, the very fine dust proved too difficult to extract. Coalmining was tried then abandoned, and a huge shale works was built in the 1890s, but that operation also failed, along with later plans to extract iron and platinum from the sand. Monkey Island Beach, signposted to the right off the main road, provides a safe place to swim and a chance to glimpse a little gold dust.

7 RIVERTON

Continue south-east 16 km on SH 99 to Colac Bay where early Maori quarried the argillite rock that breaks through on the eastern shoreline of this long, sweeping beach, and fashioned it into cutting implements. Continue east 13 km on SH 99 to Riverton.

Southland's oldest community, Riverton was established by whalers in the 1830s. Many original cottages have survived in good condition since their construction in the 1860s. The harbour, located on the mouths of the Aparima and Pourikino Rivers, is now a busy fishing port. In the Riverton Early Settlers Museum on Palmerston Street you will find a sledge used by Sir Edmund Hillary in Antarctica, portraits of the Howells, Riverton's founding family, and an impressive exhibition of local watercolours.

8 INVERCARGILL

Drive 30 km east on SH 99 and turn right onto SH 6, then travel south 6 km to reach Invercargill.

Invercargill, the second southernmost city in the world, is spread across wide-open plains near the bottom of the South Island. The early pioneers came here to establish a flax industry, but it was the rich Southland grasslands that were to establish the city and fund the substantial civic legacies that have survived to the present time. Among the city's most impressive buildings is the huge brick water tower, on Leet Street, built in the 1880s. The Southland Museum and Art Gallery is at Queens Park, an 81 ha public reserve which can be reached off Gala Street. Founded more than a hundred years ago, the museum was roofed over with a massive pyramid in 1990 and features displays on early colonial settlers, Maori stone toolmaking and jade carving. In a state-of-the-art tuatarium, more than 40 of these spiny-backed reptiles that have survived since the dinosaur age are part of a successful captive breeding programme. When the tuatara hatchlings are old enough, they are released on predator-free offshore islands.

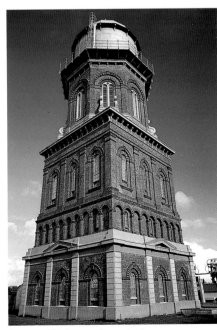

Invercargill's impressive water tower.

49 THE CATLINS

DRIVING TOUR ■ 311 KM ■ 2 DAYS ■ A REMOTE SOUTHERN COASTLINE

The Southern Scenic Route from Te Anau to Dunedin through the Catlins Forest Park leads to one of the least-known corners of the country. Visitors to the Catlins have a chance to travel through an area almost frozen in time, one of New Zealand's last true frontier districts.

The Catlins district is quieter today than it was a century ago, when up to 30 sawmills operated here. Sealers arrived in 1810, whalers in the 1830s, and in 1840 the first settlers arrived, intent on farming. By the 1870s Hinahina, on the Catlins River, was one of the busiest timber ports in the South Island. Work on the railway from Balclutha began in 1879 as settlers moved into the cleared valleys, but by 1915 only 68 km of rail line had been laid, as far as Tahakopa, and townships were dwindling as the easily reached timber was cut out. Despite the destruction, the pioneers recognised the beauty of these forests, and some areas were reserved as early as 1905. Today the forests are slowly regenerating, healing the land.

Oyster boats at Bluff, at anchor after returning from stormy Foveaux Strait.

1 BLUFF
From Invercargill take SH 1 and travel 30 km south to Bluff.

SH 1 ends at the Stirling Point signpost, which shows distances to the South Pole and other significant locations around the world. The port is usually full of fishing and oyster boats, and is the departure point for the catamaran to Stewart Island. The Foveaux Walkway runs along the shoreline of the Bluff Scenic Reserve and the lookout point on Bluff Hill, affording panoramic views, can be reached by road from near the wharf.

2 CURIO BAY
Return north 30 km on SH 1 and turn right onto the main road to the Catlins. Drive east 46 km to Fortrose, continue east for a further 28 km then turn off right to Curio Bay which is 16 km south on an unsealed road.

Curio Bay features the extensive fossilised remains of a 160-million-year-old Jurassic-age forest which can be seen embedded in the rocks at low tide. The forest was petrified after being buried by a volcanic eruption. Over time the wood has been replaced by silica but the structure of the trees remains. The prehistoric cyads, tree ferns and ancestors of the matai and kauri resemble fossils found in South America, confirming that New Zealand was once part of the great southern supercontinent of Gondwanaland.

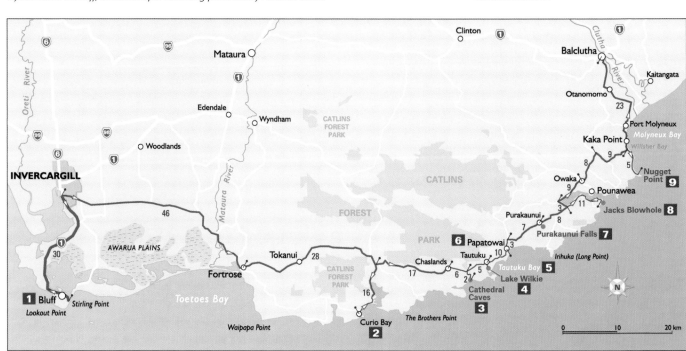

The Cathedral Caves on Waipati Beach return amazing echoes from deep within the rock face.

3 CATHEDRAL CAVES

Return north to the main road, turn right and drive east 17 km to Chaslands. The road is unsealed after the first few kilometres. Continue 6 km east and turn right into the Cathedral Caves access road which runs 2 km south. The caves are accessible only at low tide, so check the tide-table posted at the turn-off.

It takes 15 minutes to walk down through the coastal forest to Waipati Beach and another 10 minutes to walk north along the beach to the Cathedral Caves. The first cave is the largest, with its roof over 30 m high. You can walk barefoot on the sandy floor of the cave through to the second cave which joins the first in a V formation. After emerging from the second cave, another small group of caves can be visited just around the next corner.

Purakaunui Falls.

4 LAKE WILKIE

Return to the main road, turn right and drive east 5 km to the Lake Wilkie Track signposted on the right.

During summer, the rata that fringe the 5-minute track to Lake Wilkie are covered in scarlet flowers. The lake fills a small depression behind the coastal sand dunes, where you can observe the succession of plant species from the edge of the lake into the dense stands of mature forest trees. There are some large rata, rimu, miro and totara in this part of the forest.

5 TAUTUKU BAY

Continue 1 km east to the Tautuku Bay track on the right opposite the Outdoor Education Centre.

The 15-minute walk down to the dunes and the beach leads through a magnificent section of forest that has been protected as part of a reserve since 1902. Sadly, much of the fine coastal podocarp forest in the area was cut, from the turn of the century through into the 1960s when the last sawmills closed.

6 PAPATOWAI

Continue north-east 10 km over the hill to Papatowai. The Florence Hill Lookout provides views back across Tautuku Bay before you reach Papatowai.

It is an easy 20-minute walk through the coastal forest to Picnic Point and another 10 minutes to Kings Rock. If you make the return trip along the beach you will be rewarded with panoramic views of the forest-fringed Tahakopa Bay across the estuary to the north. From the north side of the Tahakopa River Bridge at Papatowai, a second track, the Old Coach Road, leads through the coastal podocarp forest to a moa-hunter archaeological site near the river mouth. An easy 30-minute walk on this track provides access to Tahakopa Bay.

7 PURAKAUNUI FALLS

Continue north 3 km, turn right onto the road signposted to the Purakaunui Falls and drive north-east 7 km. The track to the falls is signposted on the right.

The falls are reached on a 20-minute walk through podocarp and beech forest to a platform at the base of the cascades. This beautiful place was made a reserve in 1905.

8 JACKS BLOWHOLE

Continue 19 km north-east to Jacks Bay near the mouth of the Catlins River.

From the wild and windswept Jacks Bay a marked route leads 25 minutes across farmland above the coastal cliffs to an impressive 55 m deep blowhole, which is connected to the sea by a cavern 200 m long. Offshore lies Tuhawaiki Island, named after the famous Maori chief 'Bloody Jack Tuhawaiki' who swam to the island in the 1830s to escape the massacre taking place at Cannibal Bay by Te Rauparaha and his raiders from the North Island.

9 NUGGET POINT

Return south-west 11 km and turn right, then drive west 3 km to the main road. Turn right and travel north-east 9 km to Owaka. Continue north-east 8 km and turn right onto the Karoro Stream Road, which is unsealed, heading east 9 km to Willsher Bay on the coast. Turn right and drive south 5 km to Nugget Point.

A short track leads from the end of the road to a stone lighthouse that was built in 1869 on this wild and remote rocky headland. On the shoreline below this exposed point, fur seals bask on the rocks, along with Hooker's sea lions and elephant seals, the only place on the mainland where these species coexist. Yellow-eyed penguins, sooty shearwaters, gannets and shags breed here, so take care not to disturb them – keep to the track and use binoculars.

Return north 5 km to the sealed road and continue 2 km north to Kaka Point, a further 3 km north to Port Molyneux and 11 km to Otanomomo, then turn right onto the main road and travel north 7 km to Balclutha.

Beneath the Nugget Point lighthouse seals often come ashore.

50 OTAGO'S GOLDFIELDS

DRIVING TOUR ■ 413 KM ■ 2 DAYS ■ RELICS OF A FEVERED PAST

The desolate, subalpine tussock-country of Central Otago, desert-like in summer and shrouded in snow in winter, daunted would-be farmers, but attracted thousands of gold diggers who rushed to uncover the treasure beneath the bleak landscape.

In 1861, when the province of Otago was in its infancy, news arrived of the discovery of gold on the Tuapeka River. Within weeks the goldfields attracted more than 6000 miners, many of whom had deserted their homes, work and families. Otago became the scene of social turmoil, the likes of which had already been experienced during earlier gold rushes in California, New South Wales and Victoria. The fever was fuelled by further rich finds in the Dunstan (Cromwell) Gorge. This rush petered out by 1862, but miners were already on the move to the Arrow and Shotover Rivers, while several smaller strikes occurred at St Bathans, Hogburn, Mt Ida and other localities. Many reminders of those gold-crazed days still exist. The dry Central Otago climate has helped preserve the mud and stone buildings, old mining equipment, mine shafts and tunnels that tell of the toil and hardships faced by those seeking to make their fortunes in gold. The old miners' trails in Otago's goldfields allow modern-day travellers to experience a little of those heady days.

Arched steel bridge at Alexandra.

1 LAWRENCE
From Balclutha go north-east 21 km on SH 1, at Clarksville turn left onto SH 8 and drive north-west 33 km to Lawrence.

Gabriel Read discovered gold 4 km north of Lawrence in July 1861. Read's discovery, in what became known as Gabriel's Gully, sparked off a gold rush that created a boomtown at Tuapeka (later Lawrence), which soon had a population of over 11,000, double that of Dunedin. Many of the buildings in Lawrence date back to those days, and you can make an 8 km round trip north from the town on unsealed roads through the old gold workings. At one of these, the Blue Spur, New Zealand's first hydraulic elevator enabled gold-bearing gravels to be flushed by water pressure. In this much-eroded spot you can see large tunnels and extensive water races and cuttings.

2 ROXBURGH
Continue north-west 51 km on SH 8 to Roxburgh.

Roxburgh is the centre of a large fruit-growing district, but like many Central Otago towns it first flourished in the gold-rush era. After itinerant diggers had taken the easier pickings, some 20 gold dredges kept working the alluvial gravels in the Clutha River.

3 ALEXANDRA
Continue north 30 km on SH 8 to Gorge Creek where a monument stands to the unknown number of miners who perished in 1863 in the snow on the Old Man Range. It is another 4 km north on SH 8 to the art gallery at Fruitlands which occupies an 1866 stone building that, as the Speargrass Hotel, once hosted weary travellers. Nearby, Symes Road leads to the restored Mitchell's Cottage, a superb example of the skills of Shetland Islands stonemasons. Continue north 13 km on SH 8 to Alexandra.

The first gold dredge was invented in Alexandra in the 1890s, creating a new boom and attracting world-wide attention. Today the town is an oasis of trees in a barren rocky landscape. A courthouse built in 1879 has survived, and more relics are on display in the Alexandra Historical Museum on the corner of Thompson and Walton Streets.

4 CLYDE
From Alexandra travel 10 km north-west to Clyde on SH 8.

Clyde was once the centre of the Dunstan goldfields, and stone buildings dating back to the 1860s line the streets of this small town which now lies in the shadow of the huge Clyde Dam. There are two museums in Clyde: the historic Magistrate's Courthouse on Blythe Street, featuring exhibits that depict domestic life on the goldfields, and the Stationary Engine Display on Upper Fraser Street, which has a range of rural machinery.

5 OPHIR
From Clyde take the road heading east towards Springvale, drive east 8 km to the

The old post and telegraph office at Ophir is one of the town's more graceful buildings.

junction with SH 85, turn left and travel 19 km on SH 85 north-east to Omakau. Turn right and cross the picturesque stone suspension bridge built in 1880 over the Manuherikia River to Ophir.

Once a bustling goldmining settlement known as Blacks, Ophir is now a peaceful town that has preserved its past in a number of buildings, including a delightfully restored post and telegraph office built in 1886 using schist masonry and plaster quoins. The building retains most of its Victorian fittings.

6 ST BATHANS

Return across the bridge to SH 85 and continue north-east 17 km to Becks. Turn left and take the road north 16 km to St Bathans.

In its heyday St Bathans had a population of over 2000 and supported a dozen hotels. The gold diggers and dancing girls are long gone, but you can visit the surviving pub, the original gold office and town hall. Nearby is the Blue Lake, where miners dug away a 120 m hill to create a 70 m hole, once the site of the deepest hydraulic mining lift in the world.

7 GOLDEN PROGRESS MINE

Continue south-east on 8 km of unsealed road from St Bathans back to SH 85. Drive south-east 9 km on SH 85 to Idaburn, turn right and drive 5 km south-west on an unsealed road to the Golden Progress Mine which is accessible off Reefs Road on the left.

In its day, the poppet head at the Golden Progress Mine, Oturehua, was an important technological component of the goldmining operation.

The Golden Progress mine site, a 10-minute walk from the road, features the only remaining poppet head in the Otago goldfields. This 14 m high structure stands over a 46 m deep mine shaft and supports wheels over which ropes were run to haul ore to the surface. The reefs here were worked from the 1860s through into the 1890s then again from 1928 to 1936. A massive twin boiler stands near the poppet head.

8 HAYES ENGINEERING WORKS

Continue south-west 3 km through Oturehua to the Hayes Engineering Works signposted on the right.

Originally stablished by Earnest Hayes in 1895, the Hayes Engineering Works manufactured rural machinery. Hayes' inventions included the world-famous Hayes wire strainer. The remarkable water-powered workshop comes to life occasionally on demonstration days, but even when it is not

in operation it is fascinating to explore this collection of mud-brick and corrugated-iron buildings.

9 RANFURLY

Return north-east 8 km to Idaburn, turn right onto SH 85 and travel south-east 21 km to Ranfurly.

Ranfurly is the main population centre of the Maniototo Plain and the rural Art Deco Capital of New Zealand, lying between the aptly named Rough Ridge and the Rock and Pillar Range. At the old Ranfurly Station, a display traces the history of the railway line, now converted into a mountain-bike trail.

10 MIDDLEMARCH

Drive east 15 km on SH 85 to Kyeburn, turn right and head south 41 km along the Taieri River on SH 87 to Middlemarch.

On the side of the road at Middlemarch you will see distinctive sun-dried brick buildings and stone-walled sheep yards on the Taieri Lake Station. The woolshed and homestead date back to the 1860s. The nearby river is full of trophy-sized trout and there are good places to swim.

11 MOSGIEL

Continue 52 km south on SH 87 to Outram, then head east 13 km to Mosgiel.

Mosgiel is located on the level expanse of the Taieri Plain, which was reclaimed from swampland. The settlement was named after a farm owned by Robert Burns, the immortal son of Scotland whose nephew led the first pioneering settlers to Otago. Mosgiel achieved prominence through its woollen mills, which began production in 1871. The mills, Invernay Homestead, East Taieri Presbyterian Church and Holy Cross College are fine examples of Victorian architecture, and the town's first flour mill (1864) still stands.

From Mosgiel drive south-east 2 km to SH 1, turn left and travel east 14 km to Dunedin.

The beautiful Blue Lake at St Bathans now fills an ugly excavation left by goldminers.

51 HISTORIC DUNEDIN

WALKING TOUR ■ 2 KM ■ 4 HOURS ■ CENTRAL-CITY ARCHITECTURAL GEMS

The founders of Dunedin had a firm and lofty vision of the city they wanted to create. This, and the wealth accrued from gold, inspired designers and leading citizens to erect magnificent buildings that encapsulated Victorian architecture.

The first Scottish migrant ships, sponsored by the Free Church of Scotland, set sail for New Zealand in 1847 with the aim of establishing a 'New Edinburgh' in the Pacific. The community was eventually named Dunedin, the ancient name for Edinburgh. Although the Scottish pioneers were soon outnumbered by later arrivals, they made an indelible mark on the city, which prospered throughout the 1860s with the discovery of gold in Central Otago. The boom generated rapid growth, and Dunedin became New Zealand's largest and most influential centre with a population in 1874 that was bigger than Auckland's.

Leading architects from around the country as well as overseas were drawn to the city. Many grand public buildings were erected, including the first university in New Zealand, and the city also had the first cable-operated tramway outside the United States. Today Dunedin has the most interesting collection of Edwardian and Victorian architecture of all New Zealand's cities, with numerous stately homes reflecting the aspirations of miners who retired to the city after they had struck it rich. The Scottish influence is still evident in the city: it possesses the only kilt store in the country and boasts a statue of the poet Robbie Burns presiding over the Octagon, the heart of the city.

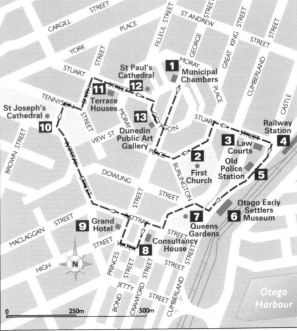

1 MUNICIPAL CHAMBERS
The trip starts in the Octagon, the centre of Dunedin, near the statue of Robbie Burns.

The best view of the Municipal Chambers is from the statue of Robbie Burns on the north side of the Octagon. The bronze statue of Scotland's national poet was erected in 1877. Over 2000 people gathered in the Octagon in 1878 for the laying of the foundation stone for the Municipal Chambers designed by R. A. Lawson. The building was completed in 1880 and faithfully restored in 1989.

2 FIRST CHURCH
Head south from the Octagon on Princes Street and turn first left into Moray Place. Follow Moray Place across Burlington Street to First Church.

Melbourne architect R. A. Lawson was only 29 years old when he won a competition to design the First Church. Lawson designed many of Dunedin's buildings, including Otago Boys High School, the Knox Church and the ANZ Bank in Princes Street. Churches were his specialty and by the time construction of the First Church started in 1867, Lawson had considerable experience in working with the local materials. The result is an inspirational church with a beautifully proportioned tower and spire. Set amongst trees in spacious grounds, the church is a masterpiece of Gothic revival. It is worthwhile walking around the church to fully appreciate its architecture. The interior and exterior stone carvings are the work of Louis Godfrey whose work can also be seen at Larnach Castle (see Tour 52).

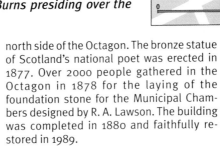
The severely Gothic Law Courts.

3 LAW COURTS
Continue along Moray Place and turn right at the next corner into Lower Stuart Street. The Law Courts are on the right on the corner of Dunbar Street.

This Gothic-style building in Port Chalmers stone was opened in 1902 complete with blunt pillars, battlements and a marble statue of Justice with a sword in one hand and a set of scales in the other. The designer was government architect John Campbell.

4 RAILWAY STATION
Continue along Lower Stuart Street across Castle Street to the Railway Station directly ahead.

The grandiose Railway Station was built in Flemish Renaissance style of basalt with Oamaru limestone facings. It features copper domed towers, lions perched on the clock tower and elaborate stonework around the arched windows. Inside the booking hall the spacious foyer is decorated with Royal Dalton majolica tiles with an amazing porcelain mosaic floor. The building was completed in 1906 and its designer, George Troup, earned a knighthood for this remarkable edifice.

5 OLD POLICE STATION
Across the road south of the Railway Station is the old red brick Police Station on Castle Street.

Completed in 1895, the Police Station, like the Law Courts, was designed by John Campbell. The building bears a strong resemblance to Scotland Yard, designed by English architect Norman Shaw who had a strong influence on Campbell's work.

6 OTAGO EARLY SETTLERS' MUSEUM

Continue towards Cumberland Street to the Otago Early Settlers' Museum on the left.

The museum features two distinctive steam locomotives in glass-fronted display rooms facing the street. The double-ended *Josephine*, the oldest steam locomotive in New Zealand, pulled passenger coaches between Dunedin and Port Chalmers. Inside the museum are displays of a remarkable range of colonial household items, furniture, paintings and photographs in an Edwardian setting. Exhibits also cover early Maori history and tell the story of the early European and Chinese gold diggers.

7 QUEENS GARDENS

Cross the road to the Queens Gardens opposite.

The gardens feature a white marble cenotaph dedicated to the fallen soldiers in the First and Second World Wars, a statue of Queen Victoria and one of the Reverend D. M. Stuart, the first minister of Dunedin's Knox Church.

8 CONSULTANCY HOUSE

Turn left into Crawford Street then right into Rattray, and first left into Bond Street. Consultancy House is on the left.

Although it has had a number of different owners and names, Consultancy House, formerly the old Express Company Building, has retained its unmistakable character. The seven-storey structure was hailed as New Zealand's first skyscraper when it was completed in 1908. It is a copy of the Auditorium Building in Chicago, designed by Louis Sullivan, the 'inventor of the skyscraper'.

9 GRAND HOTEL

Continue along Bond Street and turn right into Water Street. A plaque in the pavement on the right of the road marks the location where the first settlers stepped ashore in 1848 after their arrival on the sailing ship John Wickcliffe. *Turn right into Princes Street. The Grand Hotel is on the opposite side of the road on the corner of High Street.*

Completed in 1883, the Grand Hotel was the finest in the city, opening to a crowd of over 6000 people. The interior decoration is particularly elaborate with carved brackets supporting fluted columns on the first floor. It is now part of the Southern Cross Hotel, which houses Dunedin's casino.

10 ST JOSEPH'S CATHEDRAL

Continue north on Princes Street, turn left into Rattray Street and walk up the hill to St Joseph's Cathedral.

Many of Dunedin's churches were built

Terrace houses on Stuart Street. The domestic as well as civic architecture of early Dunedin looked back to the settlers' homeland.

from Oamaru limestone. An example is St Joseph's Cathedral with its magnificent stained-glass windows crafted in Munich. The internal stone carvings include lizards, birds, flowers, leaves, vines and grapes. The building was designed by Frank Petre and was completed in 1886. He also designed St Dominic's Priory next to the cathedral, which was completed a year later in 1887.

11 TERRACE HOUSES

Past the cathedral turn right into Tennyson Street and then left into Smith Street. Turn right and head down Stuart Street towards the Octagon. The Terrace Houses are on the right.

The Victorian terrace houses, with bay windows and balconies, were more modest homes built in the style of those in British cities.

12 ST PAUL'S CATHEDRAL

As you return to the Octagon, St Paul's Cathedral is on the left side of Stuart Street.

Dating to 1919, St Paul's Cathedral has the only stone-vaulted nave roof in New Zealand. The cathedral was built of Oamaru stone on land donated by Johnny Jones, an early Otago trader and whaler. The location is a prime site and feathers were ruffled when it was given to the Church of England, as at the time Presbyterians outnumbered Anglicans by nearly five to one.

13 DUNEDIN PUBLIC ART GALLERY

At the southern side of the Octagon.

The Dunedin Public Art Gallery, founded in 1884, is New Zealand's oldest art gallery. The gallery houses a significant collection of New Zealand and international pieces, including over 40 works by Frances Hodgkins and paintings by Constable, Reynolds, Durer, Gainsborough and Monet. One of the earliest acquisitions was Petrus Van der Velden's *Waterfall in the Otira Gorge*, considered to be New Zealand's finest nineteenth-century landscape painting.

St Paul's Cathedral is the second to stand on this site. The first was hurriedly built in 1862 and proved structurally unsound.

52 OTAGO PENINSULA

DRIVING TOUR ■ 87 KM ■ 1 DAY ■ GRACIOUS HOMES AND ANTARCTIC WILDLIFE

The road along the Otago Peninsula offers superb vistas of Otago Harbour and leads to one of the most accessible wildlife areas in the South Island, with stops at historical sites along the way.

Dunedin is renowned for its historic buildings, marine wildlife and magnificent natural setting. Surrounded by hills, Dunedin's 22 km harbour is one of Otago's finest assets. Captain Cook missed the entrance when he sailed past in 1770, but in 1809 sealer Captain Daniel Cooper entered the harbour and by 1831 a whaling station, store and farm had been built at Otakou, trading in whale oil, seal skins, potatoes and flax. In 1848 the Otago Harbour saw the arrival of two ships, the John Wickliffe and the Philip Laing, carrying 340 colonists from Scotland. About 12,500 immigrants arrived during the 1850s, most of them Presbyterian Scots who brought their families with them.

The settlement was isolated and for a time remained the smallest and poorest in the country. However, the discovery of gold in 1861 brought massive change. A total of 256 ships arrived that year, mostly carrying gold diggers. Otago's civic leaders, the Rev. Thomas Burns and Captain William Cargill, were worried that the influx of single men would bring social and moral decline. The town developed into a 'bustling, rowdy, raffish outpost of the goldfields' as one historian summed it up. Commerce thrived and Dunedin developed rapidly, adding distinctive architecture to its natural beauty and becoming a seat of learning. Today Dunedin is a university city with a large academic population fostering its special character.

Glenfalloch, a colonial dream house.

1 UNIVERSITY OF OTAGO
The tour starts on SH 1, on Cumberland Street at the University of Otago.

The University of Otago, founded in 1869, comprises a number of Gothic-style buildings added over the years, including the distinctive clocktower built in 1879 and the School of Mines which was transferred to the new building in 1909 from its original location in a tin shed. The two Professorial Houses built in 1879 were considered outrageous at the time, drawing criticism in a local newspaper, the *Otago Witness*, for their 'extraordinary complications and inclinations of roof' as well as for the colour of the brick which was described as an 'inflammatory red'.

2 GLENFALLOCH
From Otago University, drive south on one-way Gowland Street into Castle Street and Cumberland Street which are all part of

SH 1. *Turn left into Jetty Street and cross the railway bridge, then right into Wharf Street and travel south onto Portsmouth Drive. This 5 km section of the journey follows the southern shoreline of the Otago Harbour across a causeway onto Portobello Road*

and the Otago Peninsula on the left and then heads north-east 10 km to Glenfalloch.

Originally the home of George Gray Russell, the old kauri Glenfalloch homestead dates back to the 1870s. Russell, a Dunedin businessman, turned the surrounding 40 ha property into a botanical wonderland. The gardens feature azaleas and rhododendrons which thrive in Dunedin's cool climate and are at their best in September and October.

3 NZ MARINE STUDIES CENTRE
Continue north on Portobello Road 2 km to Macandrew Bay. Long stretches of distinctive stone walls divide green fields and

The Professorial Houses at the University of Otago.

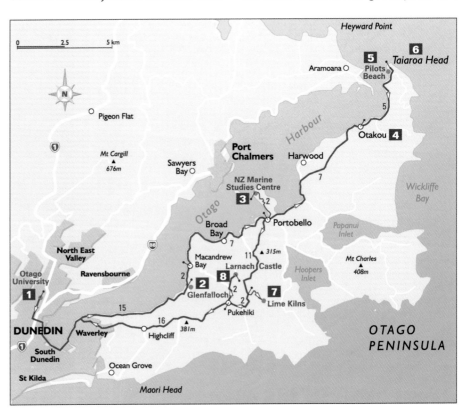

The lighthouse at Taiaroa Head.

border roadsides on the Otago Peninsula. *The road and rock walls at Macandrew Bay were built in the 1860s by prisoners housed in the floating hulk of the* Success, *which was dragged along the harbour as the workers slowly moved along the bay. It is another 7 km to Portobello. Turn left at the store into Hatchery Road and drive north 2 km to the NZ Marine Studies Centre.*

The University of Otago's NZ Marine Studies Centre and aquarium at Portobello is open to the public and offers the chance to explore an amazing array of life from the southern oceans, Otago and New Zealand's coastal waters. There are touch tanks where you can pick up crabs and encounter starfish and anemones.

4 OTAKOU
Return to Portobello, turn left onto Harington Point Road and continue north-east 7 km to Otakou. The access road to Otakou Marae is signposted on the right.

The name Otago is derived from Otakou which was the site of a whaling station in the 1830s. The church at the Otakou Marae was opened in 1941 to commemorate the centenary of the signing of the Treaty of Waitangi. Moulded concrete simulating wood-carvings adorn the church and also the meeting house which was opened in 1946.

5 PILOTS BEACH
Return to Harington Point Road and continue 4 km north-east. The access road to Pilots Beach is signposted on the left.

Southern fur seals can usually be seen at the northern end of this sheltered sandy cove where harbour pilots once joined the ships entering the channel.

6 TAIAROA HEAD
Continue north-east on Harington Point Road less than 1 km to Taiaroa Head.

The Royal Albatross colony at Taiaroa Head is the only albatross colony in the world established on a mainland site and provides a unique opportunity to view these giant birds, with a wingspan of more than 3 m, that soar over the spectacular headland near the entrance to the Otago Harbour. The birds, which normally breed in Antarctica, arrive in September, mate in October and lay eggs in November, incubating the chicks until January. Between March and September the parents are busy collecting food for the chicks until they are ready to fly.

Guided tours can be arranged to concealed viewing areas of the albatross colony and through some of the restored underground tunnels, magazines and gun emplacements that were part of the Taiaroa Head defences.

Near the albatross colony is the Taiaroa Head lighthouse and a restored Armstrong 'disappearing' 6-inch gun installed in 1888 because of fears of a Russian invasion. This is the only weapon of its type that is still in working order. Served by a crew of 10, the 6-inch gun was capable of firing a 100-pound shell every 60 seconds to a range of 8 km.

7 SANDYMOUNT LIME KILNS
Return 13 km south-west on Harington Road and turn left onto Highcliffe Road. Drive 11 km on this winding road into the hills and turn left into Sandymount Road. After less than 1 km the lime kilns are visible on both sides of the road.

The three old lime kilns in the area, the best preserved of which is close to the road, date back to the 1860s. Limestone was a precursor of cement. It was burnt and made into mortar that was used in brick and stone construction work, an essential component of much of the building in early Dunedin. The circular tower of the kiln rises above arched brick fireplaces with a large tunnel at a lower level providing access for removing the burnt lime.

8 LARNACH CASTLE
Return to Highcliff Road, turn left and drive 2 km west, then turn right into Camp Road and travel north 2 km to Larnach Castle. On this high ridgeline, century-old dry-stone farm walls stretch into the distance.

Construction began in 1871 on this extraordinary neo-Gothic home of politician and financier William Larnach and continued for 15 years. He spent a fortune on its interior, which includes a huge ballroom with a sprung floor, Georgian-style hanging staircase, elaborately carved ceilings and Italian marble fireplaces. The views across Otago Harbour from the battlements, 330 m above sea level, are superb.
Return to Highcliff Road, turn right and drive 16 km south-west back to Dunedin.

Dry-stone walls were common farm features on the hills of the Otago Peninsula.

135

SOUTH ISLAND

OTAGO AND SOUTH CANTERBURY

53 DUNEDIN TO OAMARU

DRIVING TOUR ▪ 137 KM ▪ 5 HOURS ▪ OTAGO'S FARMING HERITAGE

The wealth that many early Dunedinites lavished on their homes often came from farming estates that occupied a large part of Otago. These farms used innovative technology and paved the way for New Zealand's agricultural economy.

When European whalers arrived on the Otago coast early in the nineteenth century, many married into long-established Maori communities. By the 1840s the first farming settlement had been established, near Waikouaiti. Missionaries and increasing numbers of settlers began to arrive, followed by a sudden influx of miners after gold was discovered further inland. The region prospered, and the wealth generated by the gold is still evident in the many fine Victorian buildings that grace Dunedin and Oamaru. Substantial income was also generated by the huge farming estates developed in North Otago, where the export of frozen meat to the United Kingdom was pioneered. Dunedin became the largest and most influential centre in the country. Dunedin people still maintain that the North Island was built with Otago money. The history of the region is proudly preserved in a number of museums along the coastal plains.

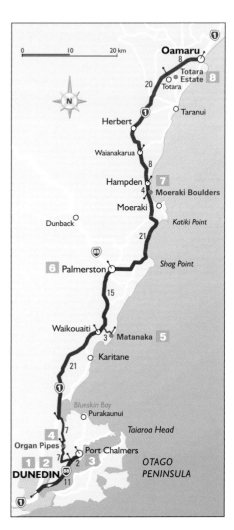

For more than 100 years Wilson's distillery in Dunedin made New Zealand's only whisky, in the tradition of the Scots who founded the city they originally called 'New Edinburgh'.

1 OLVESTON
The trip starts at Olveston a few minutes' drive from the Octagon in Dunedin's city centre. Drive north-west up Stuart Street and take the fourth turn on the right into London Street, turn left into Royal Terrace and left into Cobden Street.

Olveston, a Jacobean-style mansion built in 1906 by David Theomin, was bequeathed to the city in 1966. Left virtually untouched since 1933 it is preserved as a gallery of domestic art, its interior crammed with a treasure trove of artefacts. Designed by Sir Ernest George, a prominent British architect, it was built with double brick walls faced with Oamaru stone and Moeraki gravel. The building had every interior comfort including electricity, inter-communicating telephones and even central heating. The staircase in the Great Hall, as well as the elegant oak balcony, were both prefabricated in England.

2 WILSON'S DISTILLERY
Return to Royal Terrace, turn left and drive down the hill and turn left onto Heriot Row. Continue north onto Park Street and turn left onto George Street. It is 2 km to the Wilson's Distillery which can be reached by turning right into Duke Street then left into Willow-bank Street on the banks of the Water of Leith, a small stream that runs down from the city's green belt through the city and the university grounds.

Although the distillery is now closed, it is still fascinating to see where whisky was made from local malted barley and pure water piped from the Lammerlaw Range.

3 PORT CHALMERS
Return to Duke Street, turn left, then turn right onto Cumberland Street. Continue south 1 km, turn left into Albany Street and then left at the T-junction into Anzac Avenue.

Drive north-east 1 km onto Ravensbourne Road. Continue north-east 13 km along the northern shoreline of the Otago Harbour to reach Port Chalmers.

Port Chalmers, where Otago's pioneering settlers arrived in 1848, has retained a number of interesting buildings that have changed little since the 1880s, when New Zealand's first shipments of frozen meat to England left from the port. A museum with an appropriately nautical flavour is located in the old post office building in Beach Street, with photographs of the port in the days of sail when the harbour was a forest of masts. There are also relics on display from when Captain Scott left Port Chalmers on his expeditions to Antarctica in 1901 and 1910. Flagstaff Lookout on Aurora Terrace provides excellent views across the port and along the harbour where today a large fishing fleet is based.

Buildings surviving from Otago's first farm, at Matanaka, sit picturesquely in a paddock that overlooks a long sweep of coastline.

4 THE ORGAN PIPES

Return south-west 2 km and turn right onto Upper Junction Road. Drive west 3 km and turn right onto Mt Cargill Road. Head north 4 km to the Organ Pipes track signposted on the left.

It is a 30-minute walk up the hill to this basalt rock formation on a track well provided with steps and boardwalks. The track passes through patches of forest with mountain cedar and broadleaf before reaching a viewing platform below the 10-million-year-old columnar lava rock formation. From the track there are expansive views out to the coast.

5 MATANAKA

Continue north 7 km along Mt Cargill Road to SH 1. This is the old main route into Dunedin. Turn right and drive north-east 21 km on SH 1 to Waikouaiti. Continue north 1 km and turn right off SH 1 onto the gravel road that heads east 3 km out to Matanaka on the coast.

Waikouaiti was Otago's first harbour and the site of a whaling station established in 1838 by Sydney-based trader and ship-owner Johnny Jones. A few years later he established a permanent farming settlement. The buildings at Matanaka, including a stable, storehouse, granary, schoolhouse and a three-seater loo, are among the oldest surviving in the South Island. It is a 5-minute walk out to these fascinating old buildings perched high above the sea.

6 PALMERSTON

Return to SH 1, turn right and drive 15 km north to Palmerston.

Palmerston was the starting point for the long journey into the mountains made by early gold prospectors heading out on the 'Pigroot' into the Otago hinterland. This was the preferred route into the Maniototo, as it was more sheltered than the Dunstan Trail. On the crest of a hill above the town is a monument to Sir John McKenzie, who started out as station manager on the Shag Valley run and rose to become Minister for Lands in the Liberal Government of the 1890s. He was an enthusiastic advocate of the small farmer and worked to break up the monopoly held by the large estates.

7 MOERAKI BOULDERS

Continue 21 km north on SH 1 towards Hampden. The Moeraki Boulders are signposted on the right off a short access road.

The large spherical boulders scattered along the beach at Moeraki are concretions formed over a period of 4 million years, around a central limestone crystal core, and have been washed out from the bluffs along the shore. Two of these boulders were found to contain dinosaur bones, from a 7 m long plesiosaur and a smaller mosasaur. According to Maori legend, the boulders were gourds that fell out of the voyaging waka (canoe) *Araiteuru*, which was wrecked nearby. A reef at Shag Point, at the southern end of Katiki Beach, is said to be the hull of this canoe. Seals and penguins can be seen along this beautiful stretch of coastline.

8 TOTARA ESTATE

Continue 4 km north on SH 1 to Hampden and a further 8 km to Waianakarua where the highway passes over an arched stone bridge built in 1874. The old Mill House (1879), located on the left-hand side of the road, was a working mill until 1940 and has been converted into a restaurant. Continue north-east 20 km on SH 1 to the Totara Estate signposted on the right.

At the Totara Estate, sheep carcasses were processed before being sent by rail south to Port Chalmers for the first refrigerated shipment from New Zealand to England on the clipper *Dunedin* in 1882. It was the beginning of a multi-billion dollar industry that was to form the basis of New Zealand's economy for the next century. The 1860s limestone farm buildings were restored by the Historic Places Trust and feature displays tracing the development of this historic farm. *Continue 8 km north-east on SH 1 to Oamaru.*

The legendary Moeraki boulders.

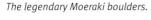

Historic Totara Estate.

54 OAMARU TO THE ALPS

DRIVING TOUR ▓ 256 KM ▓ 1 DAY ▓ HYDRO DAMS AND GLACIAL LAKES

The Waitaki Valley route from the east coast through to the mountainous interior was used for hundreds of years by Maori hunting parties. This trip retraces their steps and visits a series of spectacular constructed and natural lakes.

Oamaru, with its graceful white stone buildings, was a pleasing sight to nineteenth-century sailors who called it 'the white lady by the sea'. By the time Governor Grey visited in the 1870s the bustling port had become a gateway for entrepreneurs busy exporting produce from the rich stations of North Otago. The city remains a gateway to North and Central Otago and the Mackenzie Country.

Central Otago covers a great fragmented schist plateau with broad tussock covered basins and gently graded hills rising 600 m and more from the coast. This is a region of climatic extremes with dry, hot summers and cold, frosty winters. Today much of the land is covered only in tussock, but up to 1500 years ago there were still forests of matai and totara. From the tenth century the forests were gradually ravaged by the fires of the ancient moa hunters and the erosion continued into the twentieth century as the early runholders brought sheep onto the landscape and an ever-increasing population of rabbits took its toll on the vegetation.

Today Central Otago is one of the most frequently travelled regions in the South Island yet one of the least known, as most tourists simply pass through these lonely plains on their way to the mountain resorts.

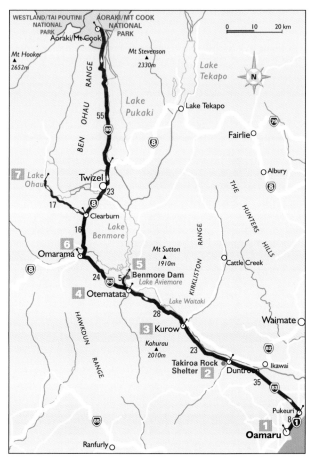

1 OAMARU

'The white stone city' boasts the best-preserved collection of historic commercial buildings in the country, with more than 20 in the Harbour–Tyne Street precinct alone. The city was officially founded in 1858 but did not grow substantially until the local limestone became a valuable commodity after it was discovered that it could be sawn after it was quarried. The rock hardens when exposed to air, which made it perfect for use as a building material in an area where timber was in short supply and expensive. The rock comes from the outskirts of town, at a limestone quarry near Weston.

Notable examples of Oamaru stone include a number of buildings on Thames Street: the 'Old Post Office' (1864) and the 'New Post Office' (1884), the Courthouse (1883), the National Bank (1870) and the Brydone Hotel. The Brydone Hotel, a survivor from the time when Oamaru had 18 hotels and 30 grog shops, was built during the 1880s but was not able to sell liquor for 60 years after a change in licensing laws in 1905. Thames Street was made exceptionally wide to allow turning space for the bullock teams hauling heavy drays laden with wool down to the docks.

A short distance from Thames Street is the historic precinct of Harbour and Tyne Streets. On Harbour Street you will find Meeks Elevator Building (1883) which was used for grain storage, the National Mortgage Building (1880) built for a stock and station agency, the Harbour Board Building (1876), Lanes Emulsion Factory (1907) and the Loan and Merchantile Co. building built in 1882.

St Patrick's Basilica, Oamaru.

Tyne Street features the Customs House (1884), the Exchange Chambers (1889) and the *Oamaru Mail* building (1900).

Each evening the Oamaru Blue Penguin Colony return to shore to nest a few minutes' walk from town. This amazing spectacle is enhanced by grandstand seating for a close encounter with these enchanting birds.

2 TAKIROA ROCK SHELTER

From Oamaru take SH 1 and drive north-east 8 km, turn left onto SH 83 and travel north-west 35 km to Duntroon. The Takiroa Rock Shelter is signposted on the left a short distance north of the town.

Named by Robert Campbell, an early runholder, after his hometown in Scotland, Duntroon lies on the confluence of the Waitaki and Maerewhenua Rivers. The hills in the area feature cragged limestone bluffs, many of which contain prehistoric fossil beds and more recent remnants left by moa hunters. The most significant find was made in 1852 at the Takiroa rock shelter where you can view examples of 500-year-old Maori rock

Hundreds of years ago a Maori hunter painted this figure on the Takiroa rock shelter.

The cliffs above the Ahuriri River near Omarama have taken on the appearance of a forest of giant needles as the clay has weathered over time.

art. After centuries of exposure to the open air the drawings have faded considerably and some were removed by an American rock art enthusiast in 1916. However, those that remain offer a fascinating insight into a time when the area was cloaked in forest and the now extinct giant eagle soared above the landscape. Small family groups travelling in search of moa and other food sources used the natural shelter provided by the over-hanging bluffs at Takiroa as a campsite and it was here that they recorded what they had seen on their journeys.

3 KUROW
Continue 23 km north-west on SH 83 to Kurow.

Kurow is strategically located near the confluence of the Waitaki and Hakataramea Rivers, both renowned for their trout and salmon fishing. The Vicarage of St Albans was built in 1892 along with its associated chapel featuring a kauri and limestone interior and a large stained-glass window.

4 OTEMATATA
Continue 28 km north-west on SH 83 passing Lake Waitaki on the right, on the road to Otematata. The dam at Lake Waitaki was completed in 1938 and was the last hydro-electric dam in New Zealand to be built using the labour-intensive pick and shovel earth-moving methods that had prevailed before the widespread use of excavators and bulldozers.

Now a picturesque holiday village near the tree-lined shores of Lake Aviemore, Otematata was originally built in 1958 to provide accommodation during the Aviemore and Benmore power projects. The concrete Aviemore Dam was completed in 1968.

5 BENMORE DAM
From Otematata turn right off SH 83 and drive 5 km to the Benmore Dam. The road

runs through a wildlife reserve where deciduous trees on the edge of the water provide a golden border in autumn.

It is a short but impressive drive up onto the ramparts of the Benmore Dam which holds back a 7900 ha lake, the largest artificial lake in the country, greater in volume than the entire Wellington Harbour.

6 OMARAMA
Return to SH 83, turn right and drive north-west 24 km. As you travel towards Omarama at the head of the Waitaki Valley you will see distinctive clay pinnacles in the distant cliffs on the left-hand side of the road. These are formed by the active Osler fault line which continually exposes the clay and gravel cliffs.

The rivers around here provide excellent fishing and Omarama also has an established reputation for gliding due to the area's rising north-west thermal air currents. The air is cool and the skies exceptionally clear.

7 LAKE OHAU
From Omarama take SH 8, drive north 16 km to Clearburn, turn left and drive 17 km to Lake Ohau.

Lake Ohau marks the boundary between Canterbury and Otago, its affiliation keenly contested during the days of provincial government when both provinces laid claim to the Mackenzie Country. The lake is a popular fishing

location, surrounded by forests and impressive mountain ranges. There are numerous forest walks in the area and inviting places to picnic or relax, absorbing the serenity of the surroundings. Lake Ohau is not glacier-fed and is therefore a distinctive and beautiful deep green colour. The lake covers about 60 sq km and lies 519 m above sea level.

Return 17 km to SH 8, turn left and drive north 23 km via Twizel to Lake Pukaki. Turn left onto SH 80 and travel 55 km to Aoraki/

Lake Ohau abounds with plump trout and salmon.

55 ALPINE HEARTLAND

DRIVING TOUR ■ 241 KM ■ 1 DAY ■ AORAKI/MT COOK NATIONAL PARK

In the World Heritage Site that includes New Zealand's highest mountain and longest glacier, visitors can witness the powerful natural forces still at work carving out the majestic landscape of the Southern Alps.

Probably the most famous of the great parks on the main divide, the Aoraki/Mt Cook National Park has 27 of New Zealand's highest peaks concentrated within its boundaries. Over these reigns Aoraki/Mt Cook, a 3754 m monolith of rock, ice and snow. The early Maori named the mountain Aoraki, 'the cloud piercer', and made it the subject of a number of legends which describe its creation.

East of the park lies a vast tussock-covered area of austere beauty known as the Mackenzie Country, after a Scottish drover, James McKenzie, who is said to have discovered these highland plains. There are numerous stories about his exploits, many of them untrue, but it was recorded that he was caught near Burkes Pass one evening in 1855 with his dog Friday, driving a mob of 1000 sheep that had been stolen from a station in Timaru. McKenzie maintained he thought they were the sheep he had been hired to drive by an Otago farmer over a back-country route. McKenzie got away but was later caught at Lyttelton trying to find a ship to escape from Canterbury. Always protesting his innocence, McKenzie was sentenced to 5 years' imprisonment. He escaped from the Lyttelton prison three times in nine months before he was pardoned by the Governor of New Zealand.

Above the Hooker Valley Aoraki/Mt Cook towers in silent majesty.

◀1 HOOKER VALLEY

From Aoraki/Mt Cook village travel east 1 km on SH 80, turn left and drive 4 km on a rocky unsealed road to the DOC campground at White Horse Hill and the start of the Hooker Valley Track. Nearby is the site of the first Hermitage hotel which was built in 1884.

From the car park, walking for 30 minutes along the start of this track will give a taste of the power of the Hooker River and enable you to experience the majesty of the surrounding mountains. In spring the alpine meadows come alive with daisies and the famous Mt Cook lily. From the suspension bridges over the Hooker River on the first part of the walk you can see the giant schist boulders in the riverbed and if you stop and listen you are bound to hear the crack and thunder of rock and ice breaking from the huge peaks that surround the valley. The towering south-east face of Mt Sefton lies directly ahead, with its sheer ice faces, hanging glaciers and avalanche chutes. This is a spectacular landscape where you can witness the forces of nature at work carving the rock with wind, water and ice.

◀2 WAKEFIELD FALLS

Return to SH 80, turn left and travel 2 km, turn left onto Ball Hut Road and drive 3 km across the Hooker River Bridge to the

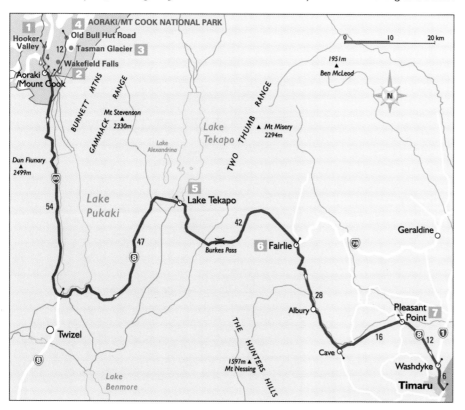

Mountain daisies.

An almost aerial bridge suspended among the mountains on the first part of the walk along the Hooker Valley Track.

Wakefield Falls Track signposted on the left.

The track follows the Blue Stream across an alluvial fan, climbing gradually to a viewpoint of the Wakefield Falls, nestled in a rocky defile. The walk takes 15 minutes.

3 TASMAN GLACIER

Continue 7 km along Ball Hut Road to the car park and the start of the track to the Blue Lakes and the Glacier Lookout.

From the car park follow the Glacier Lookout Track up to the Blue Lakes. It is an easy 10-minute climb from the road to reach this tranquil spot where visitors often stop for a swim in summer. It is another 10 minutes from the Blue Lakes to the top of the lateral moraine and a viewpoint out across the Tasman Glacier from where you can get an idea of how much rock is transported by a glacier. The entire valley floor, 70 m below, is carpeted in rocky mounds covering the

deep layer of ice. The ice is 200 m deep below the lookout and gets even deeper further up the valley. When Julius von Haast visited the area in 1862 the surface of the rock-covered glacier was higher than the lateral moraine, so you can see how much the glacier has shrunk with the warmer temperatures since then.

4 OLD BALL HUT ROAD

Continue 2 km to the end of Ball Hut Road.

The Old Ball Hut Road is blocked off beyond the car park area because it runs along the unstable lateral moraine on the southern edge of the Tasman Glacier. The road was originally built during the Depression years and is now gradually collapsing as the Tasman Glacier shrinks and the moraine wall subsides with the movement of the ice. The road is still used as a walking track and it is interesting to take a short walk along the route to see the effects of the subsidence, which has in places split the road in half. A 15-minute walk signposted from the road leads onto the lateral moraine and the Husky Flat lookout point. The ice below this lookout is 600 m deep compared with a depth of 200 m at the previous lookout point. You can see across the glacier into the Murchison Valley, with the clean ice of the Tasman Glacier in the distance.

5 LAKE TEKAPO

Return 12 km to SH 80, turn left and drive south 54 km along the shoreline of Lake Pukaki. Turn left onto SH 8 and travel 47 km to Lake Tekapo. From the road there are sweeping views across the turquoise waters

of the lake which gets its distinctive colour from the fine particles of powdered rock that are held in suspension in these glacial meltwaters. The Church of the Good Shepherd is signposted on the right.

The lake provides a picturesque, alp-framed setting for the Church of the Good Shepherd, making it one of the most photographed churches in the country. This lonely little church was built from stone and oak in 1935. A nearby statue of a collie dog is a tribute to the sheepdogs that helped develop the Mackenzie Country.

6 FAIRLIE

From Lake Tekapo continue east 42 km on SH 8 to Fairlie. Fairlie is known as the gateway to the Mackenzie Country and you will notice the marked difference in the scenery as you cross Burkes Pass on the main highway heading towards the coast.

Named after the birthplace of the town's first hotel owner in Ayrshire, Scotland, Fairlie features tree-lined avenues planted by the early settlers. The colonial Mabel Binney Cottage, the Vintage Machinery Museum and the historic limestone woolshed of the Three Springs Sheep Station are all located on the main highway west of the town.

7 PLEASANT POINT

Continue south 28 km on SH 8 to Cave, then 16 km north-east to Pleasant Point.

The railway museum at Pleasant Point is the resting place for the *Fairlie Flyer*, a 1922 vintage steam locomotive and carriages, one of which is a rare birdcage carriage dating to 1895, as well as the world's only Ford Model T railcar. A restored railway station filled with memorabilia from the era features an old manual telephone exchange, a vintage radio station and printing press as well as a reconstruction of a general store in the 1920s complete with authentic household items on sale during the period.

From Pleasant Point continue south-east on SH 8 for 12 km to Washdyke, take SH 1 and travel south 6 km to Timaru.

The height the Tasman Glacier reached in previous times is clearly marked on the valley walls. A carpet of rock protects the glacial ice.

SOUTH ISLAND

NORTH THROUGH CANTERBURY

56 THE CANTERBURY PLAINS

DRIVING TOUR ■ 222 KM ■ 1 DAY ■ PATCHWORK FARMS AND BRAIDED RIVERS

With a wall of mountains to the west and the Pacific to the east, Canterbury's plains are a seemingly endless stretch of flat, fertile farmland slashed by formidable rivers and prone to temperature extremes.

The vast expanse of the Canterbury Plains – more than 12,000 square kilometres – was once covered with forest, and coastal areas were inhabited by a sizeable Maori population. These early Maori ranged the plains hunting moa, using fire to flush the giant flightless birds from the forest. Over hundreds of years the trees as well as the birds were destroyed, leaving a barren, wind-blown waste. The first Europeans to arrive saw the plains as a desert, tussocky and gravelly and often lacking fresh water. They also saw the potential of the land and set to work to plough and plant and irrigate. Within a short time vast wheatfields began to replace tussock and the area became known as 'the granary of New Zealand'.

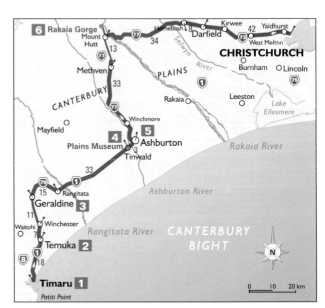

1 TIMARU

In 1837 Joseph Price set up a whaling station at Patiti Point, south of present-day Timaru. It was another 15 years before two brothers, Robert and William Rhodes, bought the land between the Opihi and Pareora rivers which they named the Levels, and later shrewdly began subdivision on the southern side of an area which the government had reserved for a town. When the first 120 settlers arrived in 1859 on the *Strathallan* from England, 60 houses had already been built on the far-sighted Rhodes' land. Today the centre of Timaru stands on part of the Levels.

The old Customs House on the corner of Strathallan Street and Cains Terrace is part of a historic precinct and dates back to 1902. Built in Oamaru stone in Corinthian style, this grand old building cost the provincial government about £2000 in its day and is now a restaurant. On George Street is the historic Landing Service Building, built between 1871 and 1875 and now the only one left in New Zealand. Timaru had no natural harbour at this time and cargo boats were used to ferry goods to and from vessels anchored offshore. They were hauled up slipways beside the Landing Service Building. Now restored, they house Timaru's information centre and a bar.

Most of the buildings in this lower part of the town are made from brick or bluestone. Fire was a major threat to the city in the early days, mainly because the principal water supply came from wells and rainwater held in tanks. In the summer of 1868 a furnishing warehouse on Stafford Street caught fire, the blaze sweeping up the road into George Street and destroying 29 buildings. The Gladstone Board of Works building (1874) on Stafford Street, the Edwardian-style Borough Council Offices (1912) and the Post Office (1880),

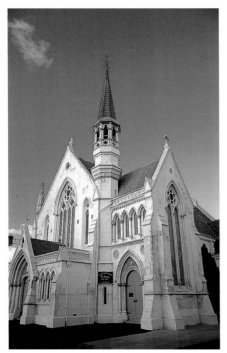

St Mary's Church, Timaru.

The Evans Atlas building in Timaru.

both on George Street, were built according to new regulations after the fire specifying brick or bluestone for all reconstruction work and new building.

Timaru's first permanent lighthouse was built in 1863 to replace the earlier method of setting a tar barrel alight to guide in ships at night. The two lanterns in the first lighthouse were not as effective as a burning tar barrel so in 1878 a 12 m tower was built with a fixed lantern. This was later replaced by a kerosene lamp, then a gas beacon and eventually an electronic beacon, during the 92 years the lighthouse operated as the main navigation light for the port. Today the lighthouse can be seen in Maori Park at the northern end of Caroline Bay.

2 TEMUKA

From Timaru take SH 1 and drive 18 km north to Temuka.

This small town has an Edwardian atmosphere, and its collection of delightful historic commercial buildings includes the brick Courthouse (1904) which is now a museum on Waiotahi Street, and the Post Office (1902) behind it just off the main road. Hope Cottage at 36 Alexandra Street and Mendelssohn House in Holly Terrace, as well as the huge redwood trees on King Street, date back to the pioneering days of the settlement.

Temuka is the country's leading manufacturing area for ceramic ware, an industry that began in the 1880s.

3 GERALDINE

From Temuka drive north 7 km on SH 1 to Winchester, turn left and travel 11 km north to Geraldine.

Pleasantly tucked into the folds of the surrounding hills, Geraldine dates back to 1854 when surveyor Samuel Hewlings built the first bark hut in Talbot Street. A number of the early settlers' cottages survive in this picturesque town which uses trees as

A restored traction engine at Tinwald.

RICHARD PEARSE, AVIATOR

A roadside memorial at Waitohi, 13 km west of Temuka, commemorates the achievements of New Zealand's pioneer aviator Richard Pearse.

Pearse was a Waitohi farmer and back-yard inventor and, although the date of his first controlled flight in March 1903, nine months ahead of the Wright brothers, has been disputed by historians, the fact remains that the aircraft he designed and built was far more technologically advanced.

The machine flown by the Wright brothers was basically a glider that had to be pushed down a slope to get airborne. The pilot lay prone on the wing and the aircraft landed on skids after a few metres of flight. Directional control in flight was achieved by warping the entire wing. Pearse had designed small hinged flaps, today known as ailerons, on the wings of his aircraft for lateral control. His aircraft had a variable pitch propeller and the pilot sat upright on a seat which slid on rails to enable the pilot to shift the centre of gravity. This incredible flying machine even had a tricycle under-carriage with a steerable nose wheel. A replica of Pearse's aircraft (right) is on display at the Museum of Transport and Technology in Western Springs, Auckland.

On his first flight, after a wheeled take-off run, Pearse became airborne for a few metres before crashing into a gorse hedge. Undaunted, he set about repairing the damage and soon learned to control the aircraft with yet more sophisticated features.

---

milestones. In the interesting Vintage Car and Machinery Museum on Lower Talbot Street are more than 30 cars dating back to 1905, a collection of tractors from as early as the 1920s and the world's last surviving 1929 Spartan biplane.

4 PLAINS PIONEER VILLAGE AND RAILWAY MUSEUM

Drive north out of Geraldine and follow SH 79 for 15 km, turn left onto SH 1 and travel north-east 33 km to Tinwald. Turn left onto the access road signposted to the Plains Pioneer Village and Railway Museum.

The museum at Tinwald features a fascinating range of fully restored and operational trains and traction engines brought back to life by dedicated enthusiasts. A restored K-88 Rogers locomotive, recovered from the Oreti River in Southland, hauled the first Christchurch–Dunedin express in 1878. A collection of some of the district's early buildings has been relocated in the 'village'.

5 ASHBURTON

Return to SH 1, turn left and drive 3 km north-east to Ashburton.

The first settlers arrived in this district bounded by the Rakaia and Rangitata Rivers in the 1850s and found it an inhospitable 'desert', without trees and buffeted by continual nor'westers that raised clouds of gritty dust. The determined pioneers began working the plains and within decades thousands of hectares were producing wheat and other crops. The open country suited livestock and vast flocks of sheep grazed the plains.

Today Ashburton features magnificent stands of trees and a number of impressive brick buildings, including the Catholic Church of the Holy Name and neighbouring presby-

tery, both built in 1907. These and the old houses in Havelock and Winter Streets make up part of an historic precinct.

From Ashburton travel 28 km north-east on SH 1 to the Rakaia River. The braided expanse of this river, once a formidable barrier to early settlers, is now spanned by the country's longest bridge (1.75 km). The salmon and trout fishing in the river draws anglers from all over the country. Continue north-east 47 km on SH 1 to Christchurch.

6 RAKAIA GORGE

Turn onto Walnut Avenue (next to the Ashburton Recreation Reserve) and head north 5 km, turn right onto SH 77, and continue north 28 km on SH 77 to Methven. Methven is popular as a summer and winter base for activities on nearby Mt Hutt. Continue 13 km north and turn right onto Inland Scenic Route 72 and continue north to the Rakaia Gorge.

The Rakaia Gorge is the point at which the Rakaia River leaves the foothills of the Southern Alps and begins to fan out as it traverses the Canterbury Plains to its mouth on the Canterbury Bight. On the north side of the gorge bridge is a carpark and a good walk that provides marvellous views of the gorge itself. It's also possible to look upriver and see old coalmine workings, and those with sharp eyes will be able to spot coal seams in the rock bluffs.

Return to Mt Hutt village and head east along the Inland Scenic Route 72 for 34 km to Homebush. Continue east on SH 77 to Darfield and follow SH 73 east 42 km to Christchurch. A faster route from Ashburton to Christchurch is to drive north-east 28 km on SH 1, crossing the Rakaia River on the country's longest bridge and continuing 47 km north-east to Christchurch.

57 CENTRAL CHRISTCHURCH

WALKING TOUR ■ 3 KM ■ 4 HOURS ■ ALONG THE AVON

From Cathedral Square in the very centre of the city many fine examples of Christchurch's famous Anglican Gothic architecture are within easy walking distance. Along the way, the peaceful Avon River meanders beneath overhanging trees and through glorious gardens.

Christchurch was founded as a well-ordered Church of England enterprise, intended to recreate a slice of England in the South Pacific. The Canterbury Association brought 3500 carefully selected settlers to Christchurch during the early years and the first 'pilgrims' arrived in four ships in 1850. Among these immigrants the gentry were well represented as well as tradesmen and agricultural workers. The best Canterbury land was acquired by those with social standing and money and in a short time huge sheep runs were producing even more wealth for their owners. Much of this capital went into Christchurch's civic buildings which were designed to be not only imposing but 'thoroughly English'.

The city's English heritage is evident today in the Gothic-style buildings, and the Avon River with its overhanging willows and small punts out on the water evokes images of a traditional English university town.

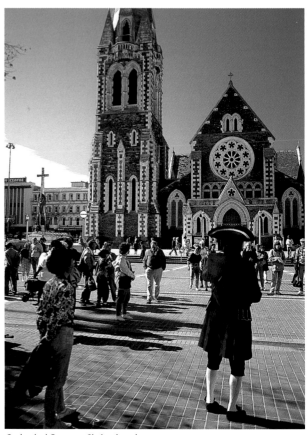

Cathedral Square, Christchurch.

1 CATHEDRAL SQUARE

At the heart of Christchurch is the Cathedral Church of Christ, the focal point of Cathedral Square. Plans were drawn up for the Cathedral shortly after the arrival of the 'first four ships' carrying immigrants to Christchurch. Work began in 1864 but came to a halt because of lack of funds and it was another 40 years before the Cathedral with its tall copper-sheathed spire was completed.

Nearby is the old Post Office and Four Ships Court where the names of the first pilgrims to arrive are engraved in the marble slabs on its walls.

2 ANTIGUA BOATSHEDS

From the Square, go west down Worcester Street to the brick Queen Anne-design Municipal Chambers. Nearby are statues of famous figures including Antarctic explorer Robert Falcon Scott and John Robert Godley, who led the first Canterbury Association settlers into an area that was largely an unwelcoming swampland at the time. Cross the old wrought-iron bridge over the Avon and turn left into Cambridge Terrace. On the right is the Canterbury Club, a long-established gentlemen's club built in 1873 with a hitching rail and original gas lantern on its street frontage. Follow Cambridge Terrace past the Bridge of Remembrance, a memorial to the New Zealand troops who died in the First World War. To the south across the river is the beautiful wooden church of St Michael and All Angels. The church was built in 1872 but the detached belfry dates back to 1860 and houses a bell from one of the first four ships. Continue along Cambridge Terrace, following the banks of the Avon to the Antigua Boatsheds.

The boatsheds were built in 1882 for the Christchurch Boating Club and are the only survivors of a number of similar boatsheds which once lined the Avon River. You can hire a vessel from the boatsheds to go exploring on the river or relax in a fully upholstered punt and enjoy the scenery while a boatman does all the work.

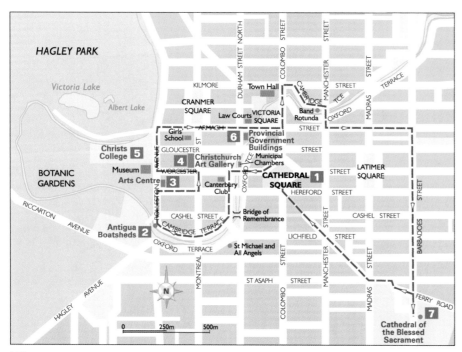

3 ARTS CENTRE

Continue along Cambridge Terrace heading north into Rolleston Avenue. The Arts Centre is on the right.

The Arts Centre, an impressive group of stone Gothic buildings, was formerly Canterbury University. The clock tower block was built in 1877 and the Great Hall in 1882. Construction continued well into the next century to complete the cluster of buildings which are grouped around two quadrangles. Adjoining the north quandrangle is Lord Rutherford's den, complete with some of the laboratory equipment he used. It was here that the famous scientist, who later split the atom, carried out experiments in the 1890s.

4 CHRISTCHURCH ART GALLERY

Head east to Hereford Street and north into Montreal Street. The Art Gallery is on the corner of Montreal Street and Worcester Boulevard.

Opened in 2003, the Christchurch Art Gallery is impressive with an expansive glass façade and extensive collection of New Zealand and international art.

5 CHRIST'S COLLEGE

Continue west on Worcester Boulevard. Ahead is the entrance to the 30 ha Botanic Gardens, enclosed within a loop of the Avon, with flower beds and conservatories set among the lawns and woods. A short distance further on the left is the Canterbury Museum (1870) which has excellent displays on moa and their hunters. Christ's College is the next complex of buildings on the left.

Grouped around a grass quadrangle are the beautiful stone structures that make up Christ's College. The Big School dates back to 1863 and is the oldest educational building still in use in the country.

6 PROVINCIAL GOVERNMENT BUILDINGS

Continue north on Rolleston Avenue to the junction with Armagh Street where an old

The Big School, Christ's College.

Landscaping and tree planting were under way in Hagley Park only 10 years after Christhurch's first European settlers arrived.

bridge crosses into Hagley Park. Landscaping and tree-planting was under way in the park just 10 years after the first settlers arrived in Christchurch. Turn right into Armagh Street heading east. Cranmer Square is on the left and the Gothic edifice of the old Christchurch Girls' School is on the right. Two blocks further on the right, on the banks of the Avon River, are the Provincial Government Buildings.

The Provincial Government Buildings are an excellent example of Gothic architecture combining stone and timber. Designed by Benjamin Mountfort, the city's most notable early architect, the wooden sections were built between 1858 and 1861. Redstone towers break up the lines of the vertical weatherboards and there is Gothic detailing on the wooden wings. The original council chamber features a stone-flagged corridor while the Provincial Council Chamber built in 1865 is a perfect example of High Victorian Gothic design with its intricate decoration and soaring roof.

7 CATHEDRAL OF THE BLESSED SACRAMENT

The Law Courts are on the opposite side of the road to the Provincial Government Buildings. Continue east on Armagh Street across a quaint old bridge to Victoria Square where statues of Queen Victoria (1903) and Captain Cook (1932) occupy a small open space that was once the commercial heart of the city. An old stone ramp nearby that leads down to the Avon was once used for watering horses. Turn left into Colombo Street and head north across a bridge to the Town Hall on the left with its impressive fountain. Turn right into Kilmore Street then right into Cambridge Terrace and head east along the Avon River to the Italianate

Edmunds Band Rotunda which dates back to 1929. Turn right onto Manchester Street and cross the Manchester bridge, take the second turn left and head east along Armagh Street then take the second turn on the right and head south 1 km down Barbadoes Street to the Roman Catholic Cathedral of the Blessed Sacrament on the left.

The impressive Roman Catholic Cathedral of the Blessed Sacrament is one of New Zealand's finest classical buildings and the most important twentieth-century church in Christchurch. Designed by F. W. Petrie, the building was opened in 1904.

Return north on Barbadoes Street, turn left onto Ferry Road and continue north-west onto High Street to get back to Cathedral Square.

The Cathedral of the Blessed Sacrament.

58 AROUND CHRISTCHURCH

DRIVING TOUR ■ 65 KM ■ 5 HOURS ■ ANTARCTIC ADVENTURE AND HILLTOP VIEWS

The Port Hills are the rim of an ancient volcano, encircling the drowned crater that is Lyttelton Harbour. The ridge road round the hills is a spectacularly scenic route with views of the sea, city, plains and mountains beyond.

When the four ships carrying Christchurch's first immigrants arrived at Lyttelton in 1850 the road over Evans Pass to Christchurch was not ready. A steeper bridle track had been cut across the Port Hills to Heathcote, so the early migrants made the trip on foot and dispersed across the plains, joined later by settlers from Australia to establish the vast sheep runs that were to become the economic base for the region.

Christchurch was established as a market town to supply the sheep stations and later the small farms that spread across the plains. While Christchurch soon boasted magnificent civic buildings and mansions that reflected the genteel aspirations and wealth of the Canterbury landowners, the hardworking port of Lyttelton retained a more modest character.

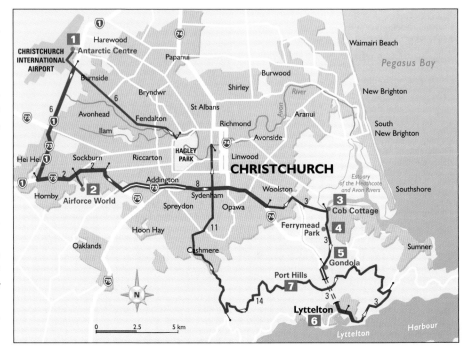

1 INTERNATIONAL ANTARCTIC CENTRE

From Hagley Park in central Christchurch drive west 2 km on Fendalton Road on the route signposted to the airport. Continue north-west 4 km on Memorial Avenue to the Christchurch International Airport which is straight ahead through the roundabout at the intersection with SH 1. Turn right at the next roundabout onto Orchard Road. The International Antarctic Centre is on the right.

A dramatically lit display at Airforce World.

For aviation buffs a visit to the Christchurch Airport will often provide views of the huge American C5 Galaxy transport aircraft that fly into Christchurch carrying supplies for Scott Base in the Antarctic. The award-winning International Antarctic Centre has outstanding displays including a walk-through ice cave, an Antarctic aquarium and a replica of the present Scott Base.

2 AIRFORCE WORLD
Return to SH 1, turn right and drive south 6 km. Turn left onto Main South Road (SH 73) and drive east 2 km then turn right onto Harvard Avenue. Airforce World is on the left.

The Royal New Zealand Airforce was established at Wigram in 1923. At the base, the world-class display area in the Airforce World museum features life-like figures enhancing displays of a collection of classic aircraft including the Spitfire, Grumman Avenger, Martin Canberra, Vampire and A4 Skyhawk.

3 COB COTTAGE
Return to SH 73, turn right and drive east 2 km onto Blenheim Road, then turn right onto Curletts Road. Follow SH 73 south-east 8 km onto the Christchurch Southern Motorway and Brougham Street which becomes SH 74, turn left at the roundabout into Garlands Road, drive east 1 km and turn left

onto Rutherford Street. Turn right at the next roundabout onto Ferry Road and drive east 2 km to Cob Cottage, located on the left across the Ferrymead Bridge.

This cottage was originally built in 1863 by one of the the early settlers. Restored in the 1940s, the small sod hut has been refurbished with authentic nineteenth-century furnishings and artefacts.

4 FERRYMEAD HISTORIC PARK
Return towards the Ferrymead Bridge and just before the bridge turn left onto Ferrymead Terrace. The Ferrymead Historic Park is on the right on the banks of the Heathcote River.

Based around a collection of some 60 nineteenth-century buildings, the park houses a huge array of relics and vintage transport. This is a 'working' museum that includes operating trams and steam trains. A ride by steam train along part of the original railway line linking Ferrymead with Christchurch takes you to a recreated 1910 township with a printing works and bakery in operation. You can ride an electric tram down the long main street which includes livery stables, a gaol and a blacksmith's forge.

5 CHRISTCHURCH GONDOLA
Continue south 3 km on Bridle Path Road to Tunnel Road and SH 74. The Christchurch Gondola is signposted on the left.

Christchurch's first settlers might well have gazed back at this view of Lyttelton Harbour, and the ships that were their last link with England, before they trudged on over the Port Hills.

The ornate Timeball Station above Lyttelton Harbour served a purely practical purpose.

The gondola climbs to the Mount Cavendish Complex, 500 m above sea level, providing extensive views north across Christchurch and south across Lyttelton and Banks Peninsula.

In the pioneering days the Bridle Path Road was part of the main route to Christchurch and the Canterbury plains. From Lyttelton Harbour the early settlers walked across the Port Hills on the old bridle path to Heathcote where a ferry crossed the Heathcote River. It was here in 1863 that New Zealand's first public railway was opened, linking Christchurch with the river port at Ferrymead using a steam locomotive operating on the 6.5 km section of line. Today the Lyttelton Tunnel enters the Port Hills at Heathcote. The first tunnel was built in 1867 to carry the railway, followed almost a century later by a road tunnel between Lyttelton and Heathcote.

6 LYTTELTON
Drive south-east 3 km through the Lyttelton Tunnel on SH 74 to Lyttelton.

The Lyttelton Museum on Gladstone Quay has a wealth of information on the port. During the early years of settlement, Lyttelton's growth exceeded that of Christchurch, which explains the large number of elegant nineteenth-century buildings that still survive in the area.

As well as numerous charming Victorian houses and cottages there are some notable historic churches. On Winchester Street are the Church of the Most Holy Trinity (1860), St John's (1864), and St Joseph's (1865). The town clock in Oxford Street was built as a memorial to Charles Upham, a notable doctor who practised in Lyttelton. Nearby on the site of the Canterbury Jail, which operated from 1851 to 1919, you can see the remains of the huge concrete prison walls and a few cells.

It is the eccentric style of the Timeball

Station (1876) on Reserve Terrace that most captures the imagination of visitors to Lyttelton. The position of a ball on a mast on top of the building was used to signal ships in the harbour, enabling them to set their chronometers. The building is one of only a few of its type in the world that remains in working order.

For steam enthusiasts, the restored steam tug *Lyttelton* takes visitors out on harbour trips during weekends over summer. Built in Glasgow, the *Lyttelton* arrived in New Zealand in 1907 and is the oldest tug in the country.

7 THE PORT HILLS
From Norwich Quay and SH 74 on the Lyttelton harbourside, drive east and turn left onto Oxford Street, then right onto Sumner Road. Drive north-east 3 km on Sumner Road, turn left onto Summit Road and drive 14 km west along the Port Hills.

A number of walks are signposted on this road. The Crater Rim Walkway leads through the Mount Cavendish Scenic Reserve. You can spend a few minutes on the track, or explore further into the reserve, from any one of a number of points along the road.

The Bridle Path Track, tracing the route the first immigrants took from Lyttelton, also starts from Summit Road. However, the scenic drive along the top of the Port Hills is still probably the best way to take in the views from this long ridgeline high above the city.

At the end of Summit Road turn right into Dyers Pass Road and drive north 7 km to the roundabout. Straight through the roundabout is Colombo Street, which will take you 4 km back to the city centre.

Summit Road winds its way along the Port Hills ridgeline, providing magnificent views in all directions and access to scenic reserves.

59 BANKS PENINSULA

DRIVING TOUR ■ 204 KM ■ 1 DAY ■ A RUFFLED COASTLINE AND A GALLIC TOUCH

If the French settlers who reached Akaroa in 1840 had arrived a few days earlier, the South Island may have become one of France's colonies. The French did not change New Zealand history, but they left their mark on Banks Peninsula.

Captain Cook mapped Banks Peninsula in 1770 when he circumnavigated New Zealand, but he recorded it as an island, an understandable mistake because the low-lying land bridge that connects the peninsula to the mainland is bordered to the south by Lake Ellesmere, a broad expanse of water that forms New Zealand's fifth-largest lake despite being only a few metres deep. The first Europeans to visit Banks Peninsula were flax traders, timber cutters, boat builders and whalers who sought shelter in the numerous bays and inlets around the almost circular peninsula.

A French whaling captain, Jean Langlois, bought a tract of land in 1838 and returned to France to establish the Nanto-Bordelaise Company and assemble a shipload of immigrants to colonise the peninsula. Within two years they set out. The French government sent a warship to accompany the 63 settlers but while they were on the high seas the Treaty of Waitangi was signed and they arrived to find that the British had got to Akaroa, hastily setting up a magistrate's court and hoisting the Union Jack, just five days earlier. Nevertheless, the French colonists settled at Akaroa and although the French land claim was sold to the New Zealand Company in 1849, they stayed on. Descendants of these colonists still live in Akaroa and many of the streets and houses have French names.

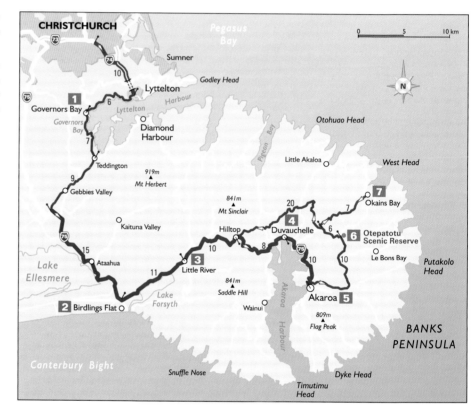

1 GOVERNORS BAY
From central Christchurch take SH 74 and head south-east 6 km, turn south onto Tunnel Road and continue 4 km on SH 74 to Lyttelton. Turn right onto Simeon Quay, then left onto Brittan Terrace. From this road there are views of the harbour and port facilities including the huge old Lyttelton Graving Dock built in 1883. After 1 km Brittan Terrace becomes Park Terrace which continues along the shoreline onto Governors Bay Road. Travel 6 km west to Governors Bay.

In 1850 Governor Sir George Grey arrived in HMS *Fly* and waited in this bay to welcome the first four ships bringing English migrants to Christchurch. St Cuthbert's Church dates back to 1862 and features thick rammed earth walls with a stone exterior.

2 BIRDLINGS FLAT
Continue south along the harbour for 7 km, turn right and drive 9 km south-west to reach SH 75. Turn left and travel 15 km south-east on SH 75. The access road to Birdlings Flat is on the right.

In 1840 the first team of bullocks used to plough the Canterbury Plains was landed here. In 1842 the area was named after W. M. Birdling who was the manager of a local estate. Today the flat, on the start of the long Kaitorete Spit that borders Lake Ellesmere, is a popular place for fishing and gemstone hunting.

3 LITTLE RIVER
Return to SH 75, turn right and drive 11 km north-east to Little River.

St Andrew's Church, built in 1879, stands on a site donated by W. Watson, who established on the Akaroa Peninsula a profitable cocksfoot seed industry. This grass was much in demand in the North Island for sowing in areas that had been cleared of forest. Near the Little River Domain stand two whaling pots, a reminder of early industry, while a statue beside the Maori Hall depicts Tangatahara, the chief responsible for killing the uncle of Te Rauparaha in a battle near Kaiapoi. In an act of revenge, Te Rauparaha

The Graving Dock at Lyttelton Harbour.

Akaroa Harbour, viewed from high on Summit Road.

destroyed Tangatahara's pa at Onawe and most of the defenders were killed and eaten.

4 DUVAUCHELLE

Continue east 10 km on SH 75 to Hilltop. Some of the best views of Akaroa Harbour can be obtained from Hilltop, especially from the grounds of the hotel that looks out across the water. Continue east 8 km on SH 75 to Duvauchelle.

This tiny settlement was named after Jules and Benjamin Duvauchelle, two brothers from the party of 63 French colonists, who were granted sections here. The hotel dates back to 1882.

5 AKAROA

Continue south-east 10 km on SH 75 to Akaroa.

With its eclectic mix of French and British architecture, Akaroa has retained the atmosphere of a Victorian seaside village. Located on an excellent harbour for boating and fishing, Akaroa was the site of a whaling station prior to the establishment of the town. The French missed their chance to establish sovereignty on the Akaroa Peninsula by as little as five days when the 63 French settlers brought out by the Nanto-Bordelaise Company arrived at Akaroa only to find the British flag already flying.

Many of the connections with France dating back to this period have survived and give a special flavour to the village. The Langlois-Eteveneaux cottage on Rue Lavaud, which now houses a museum, was prefabricated in France and erected on the site in 1845. It is interesting to visit the old French cemetery on L'Aube Hill, where headstones tell their own stories. The Customs House at Daly's Wharf was built from pitsawn totara in 1852 and three churches in the town were built in the 1860s. The wooden Akaroa lighthouse was first lit in 1880 on Akaroa North Head and stood there for a hundred years before it was moved to the township.

6 OTEPATOTU SCENIC RESERVE

Return north 2 km on SH 75 and turn right onto Summit Road around Akaroa Harbour. This scenic route provides good views out across the harbour and the surrounding countryside. Drive north 8 km to the Otepatotu Scenic Reserve signposted on the right.

Otepatotu means 'home of the fairies'. A 30-minute walk leads through an enchanting pocket of totara forest on the track to Lavericks Peak. Forest birds including the tui, kakariki, rifleman and tomtit abound in the trees along the path to the volcanic peak. From the top of the hill you can look out across Akaroa Harbour and the bays to the north and east on the coastline of Banks Peninsula.

7 OKAINS BAY

Continue north 6 km on Summit Road, turn right and drive 7 km north-east to Okains Bay.

This unspoilt bay is still populated with descendants of original settlers. The Maori and Colonial Museum at Okains Bay contains a fascinating collection of Maori artefacts including flax cloaks, war clubs, musical instruments and fishing gear. There is a rare 'god stick' over 500 years old and a number of 'kumara gods' which were placed in fields to ensure good crops. The museum has one of the few carved meeting houses in the South Island, a war canoe dating back to 1867 and a number of colonial buildings including a totara slab cottage that was originally built at the head of the Kaituna Valley in 1884. There is also cheese- and butter-making equipment on display from the old Okains Bay cheese factory and an outside bread oven which was originally built in 1878 at Lavericks Bay.

Return to Summit Road, turn right and drive west 20 km to Hilltop. Return 68 km to Christchurch via SH 75.

Langlois-Eteveneaux Cottage, Akaroa.

The Akaroa Lighthouse now sits near the town.

60 THE KAIKOURA COAST

DRIVING TOUR ■ 331 KM ■ 1 DAY ■ WHALES, SEALS AND MOUNTAINS OF SALT

From the gentle farmland north of Christchurch the transition to the Kaikoura coastline is dramatic. Grassy hills give way to rugged mountains that soar above the highway, and the ocean is a mighty presence.

The broad alluvial plains of Canterbury narrow as the highway heads north. The parallel mountain chains of the Inland and Seaward Kaikoura Ranges have been pressure-folded into an astonishing landscape where towering rock walls rise steeply from the sea.

The life of Kaikoura has always been linked to the sea. Centuries ago coastal settlements of Maori relished the crayfish that are still a rich harvest of these waters. A European whaling station established in the 1840s operated for 80 years. Whales still abound off the coast, but the boatloads who put to sea to seek these huge mammals are respectful tourists armed with cameras.

The Seaward Kaikoura Range swoops down to the rugged Kaikoura coastline.

1 KAIAPOI
From Christchurch take SH 1 and drive north 19 km to Kaiapoi. Turn right off the highway onto Ohaka Road then turn left into Williams Street which leads 1 km to the Kaiapoi River.

Kaiapoi was established in the 1850s, as a busy port on the Waimakariri River. The coastal trader *Tuhoe*, a two-masted schooner built in Auckland in 1919, has been beautifully restored and is moored on the river.

2 WAIPARA
Return to SH 1 and continue north 39 km to Waipara.

The large brick church of St Paul's in this small town was built as a memorial to George Henry Moore (1812–1905) by his daughter who inherited the fortune he had made through his vast Glenmark sheep station. Significant archaeological finds have been made in the Waipara area including the almost complete skeletons of 5 moa which were found in a swamp in 1939.

3 MAORI LEAP CAVE
Drive north-east 56 km on SH 1 to Cheviot through rolling farmland. As the journey continues north-east the landscape becomes more hilly, with stands of dense bush, and at Oaro the road meets the wild coast. It is 72 km from Cheviot to Maori Leap Cave, signposted on the left.

This 2-million-year-old limestone cave, formed by the sea, was not discovered until 1958. Inside the cave, where fossilised remains of sea mammals and birds have been found, are many colourful and fascinatingly formed stalagmites and stalactites.

4 KAIKOURA
Continue north-east 3 km on SH 1 to Kaikoura.

With its spectacular backdrop of the Seaward Kaikoura Range, the township follows the beachfront towards the peninsula and the sites of a number of Maori pa. The museum on Lustone Road has a range of artefacts and historical photographs as well as the old 1910 town gaol.

During the first weekend of October the town hosts Seafest, a celebration of the ocean that attracts thousands of visitors.

5 FYFFE HOUSE
Drive east 2 km along the Esplanade on the Kaikoura waterfront to the Fyffe homestead signposted on the right.

Robert Fyffe was the first European to settle in the Kaikoura area, establishing a whaling station in 1842. In 1857 Fyffe discovered an early moahunter burial site near his

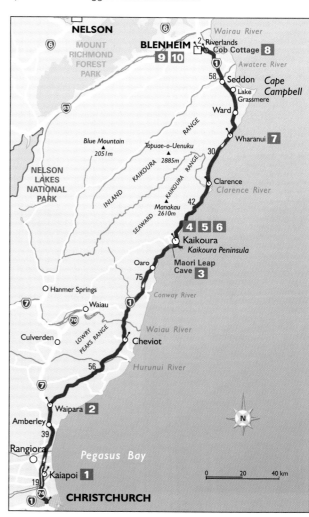

WHALE WATCH

In 1987 New Zealand's first commercial whale-watching trips began in Kaikoura and quickly gained an international reputation. The sperm whale, Hector's dolphin, dusky dolphin, bottlenose dolphin and New Zealand fur seal are the most frequently seen species, but pilot whales, killer whales, minke, humpback and southern right whales are sometimes also encountered on the trip. Sperm whales are more likely to be sighted from October to August while killer whales are usually seen from December to March.

The waters off the Kaikoura coast are often red with clouds of tiny krill, the food of the sperm whale. Warm and cold currents converging offshore create an upwelling effect, bringing nutrients up from the depths into the light zone along this section of coastline where the continental shelf slopes gradually to a depth of 90 m before plunging to over 800 m less than a kilometre from the shore. Spotter planes are used to locate the whales and the boats are equipped with hydrophones to pick up the sound of the whales under water.

house including an almost complete moa eggshell. Recent excavations near the Fyffe homestead have shown that the area was a moa-hunter settlement between 800 and 1000 years ago. The old cottage, which sits on its original piles partly made up of whale vertebrae, is open to visitors.

6 SEAL COLONY

Continue 1 km east past the Fyffe cottage to the end of Fyffe Quay Road and the eastern end of Kaikoura Peninsula.

From the peninsula there are outstanding views across the sea to the mountains. A walk around the rocks at the end of the peninsula will take you to one of New Zealand's most accessible seal colonies. The seals may look harmless while they are basking on the rocks in the sun, but these are wild animals in their natural habitat and you should be careful not to get between a seal and the sea.

7 WHARANUI

Return to SH 1 and continue north 42 km to Clarence and a further 30 km to Wharanui. This stretch of coastal highway is one of the most dramatic in New Zealand. Few signs of habitation appear along the lonely road that runs for 100 km between a wall of mountains and the pounding waves of the Pacific Ocean. The Kaikoura coast is famous for its crayfish (the name means 'to eat crayfish') and excellent for snorkelling, diving, fishing and surfing.

At Wharanui, the last coastal settlement before the highway turns inland to bypass Cape Campbell, is the picturesque stone church of St Oswald, built in 1927. From just past the church, looking north, the lighthouse on Cape Campbell is visible, marking the most easterly point on the South Island.

8 RIVERLANDS COB COTTAGE

Continue north from Wharanui 58 km on SH 1. The hill country around Ward, Seddon, and up the Awatere Valley was the area where large-scale pastoral farming began in the South Island. At Lake Grassmere you can

This pretty little cob cottage at Riverlands is completely furnished in late-1800s style.

see the huge piles of sea salt extracted by evaporation from a series of settling ponds in the area. At Riverlands the cob cottage is signposted on the left.

The cottage, built in 1860 for a local farmer, can be viewed complete with interior fittings, colonial furniture, clothing and household objects. These early houses were built using a mixture of puddled clay and straw which was either made into bricks or packed between forms.

9 BLENHEIM

Continue west 2 km to Blenheim.

Originally named Beavertown by a party of surveyors who identified with that animal when they were stranded in the area by floodwaters, the town was later renamed to commemorate the famous battle won by the Duke of Marlborough in 1704.

Known as the sunshine capital of New Zealand, Blenheim is located in the centre of Marlborough, New Zealand's famous wine-growing district (see box, page 94). Local art and crafts are displayed in many shops and galleries in the town. Seymour Square on Seymour Street features striking gardens as well as a clock tower and a multicoloured fountain on the site of the reclaimed swamp around which the early township was built in the 1850s.

10 BRAYSHAW MUSEUM PARK

1 km south-west of the town centre on New Renwick Road, off Maxwell Road.

At the 6 ha park you can see what Beavertown looked like in the early days. A colonial village has been recreated, with furnished cottages and authentically stocked shops. The park also features a huge display of early farming machinery and equipment.

Seals bask in the sun not far from the township on Kaikoura Peninsula.

61 PORT UNDERWOOD

DRIVING TOUR ■ 85 KM ■ 4 HOURS ■ BAYS FULL OF MEMORIES

The coast road along the eastern side of Queen Charlotte Sound is a route often overlooked by travellers, but those who make this winding scenic journey are rewarded with stunning views and glimpses back to an eventful past.

Much of the early European history of the South Island is linked to the eastern coastline of the Marlborough Sounds. At Ngakuta Bay the Rev. Samuel Ironside founded the Cloudy Bay Methodist Mission in 1840 after having taken part in the events leading up to the signing of the Treaty of Waitangi. Ironside had learned enough Maori to be able to preach a sermon within five months of arriving at Hokianga in Northland. He is said to have persuaded Tamati Waka Nene to make his famous speech which encouraged other chiefs to sign the treaty.

Converts from Ironside's mission station in the South Island travelled to most parts of the east coast, establishing 16 churches in the region. Whalers had preceded the missionaries along the coast and when Ironside arrived at Kakapo Bay he found 'half a hundred rude whalers, scum of every maritime nation and of the convict settlements of Australia' as well as 'cannibals and pagans of the Ngatitoa and Ngatiawa tribes' whom he described as more desirable neighbours than the whalers. It was from Ocean Bay on this part of the coast that Jerome Nugent Flood drove a flock of sheep south to Flaxbourne, the first of the great sheep runs that brought wealth and prosperity to the South Island.

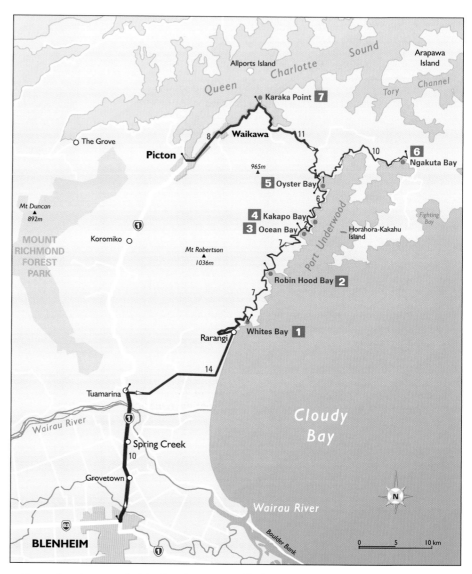

1 WHITES BAY
From Blenheim go north 10 km on SH 1 to Tuamarina, turn right and drive east 10 km towards Rarangi, a long exposed beach on the coast. Turn left inland and follow Port Underwood Road 4 km north to Whites Bay. The access road is signposted on the right.

In 1866 the first telegraph cable across Cook Strait came ashore at Whites Bay where you can visit a small telegraphic museum in the old cable station building. From the car park a 15-minute walking track leads through beautiful bush.

2 ROBIN HOOD BAY
Continue north on the unsealed Port Underwood Road 7 km to Robin Hood Bay.

The cob cottage at Robin Hood Bay is probably the oldest surviving dwelling in the South Island. It was built around 1850, originally as a whaler's home, but served as a schoolhouse from 1886 to 1917 with 18 pupils and boarders who stayed in the homestead. Although small, this was an exclusive primary school that catered for the children of the area's wealthy and enjoyed a national reputation, many of the pupils going on to Wanganui Collegiate and Christ's College.

3 OCEAN BAY
Continue north 7 km to Ocean Bay.

Ocean Bay, facing the Pacific near the entrance to Port Underwood, was named by

Old farm equipment near Tuamarina.

Robin Hood Bay, one of a succession of sheltered, secluded bays on the way to Port Underwood, was a lively settlement in the early nineteenth century.

early whalers. John Blenkinsopp (see box) had a whaling station here, but when the Sydney solicitor Unwin sent men and cattle to occupy the land Blenkinsopp had claimed to own and over which Unwin was mortgagee, the men were all killed in mysterious circumstances.

4 KAKAPO BAY
Continue north 2 km to Kakapo Bay.

Kakapo Bay is the location of the first onshore whaling station, established by John Guard whose grave lies in the tiny local cemetery. Guard set up the whaling station and possibly the first European settlement in the South Island, at Te Awaiti, an island in the Tory Channel, in 1828.

Guard's life was colourful and perilous. His schooner *Waterloo* was wrecked in 1833 and plundered by Maori, after which he abandoned Te Awaiti and began trading from his barque the *Harriet*. When this was wrecked off the Taranaki coast in 1834 his wife and children were held as hostages by local Maori and Guard was released to bring back a ransom of gunpowder. He returned with HMS *Alligator* whose crew rescued his family and attacked the Maori who had killed and eaten the crew of the *Harriet*.

Guard later settled his family at Kakapo Bay and became pilot on the HMS *Pelorus* and later the *Tory* on a series of surveys of the coast.

5 OYSTER BAY
Continue north 6 km to Oyster Bay.

This bay was visited by the HMS *Pelorus* in 1838 when she stopped for water and to make repairs. The *Pelorus* picked up John Guard and went on to explore the Marlborough Sounds, giving its name to Pelorus Sound. The small cottage at the northern end of Oyster Bay was built by John Guard's son. A whaling station operated in the bay from the 1840s to the 1880s.

6 NGAKUTA BAY
Continue north 1 km and turn right to reach Ngakuta Bay 10 km to the east.

The Rev. Samuel Ironside landed at Ngakuta Bay in 1840 to establish the second mission station in the South Island. It was Ironside who later warned Captain Arthur Wakefield, the leader of the Nelson settlement, not to proceed with his survey of the Wairau. After the Wairau massacre (see box), Ironside buried Wakefield and his mission broke up, as many of the local Maori returned to the North Island to avoid the anticipated reprisals. Ironside also moved to Wellington where for a number of years his extensive experience was put to use in the role of advisor on Maori affairs to successive governors.

7 KARAKA POINT
Return to Port Underwood Road, turn right and drive 4 km north to the highest point of Port Underwood Road with fine views of Horahora-Kakahu Island. On this island, British sovereignty was proclaimed over the South Island and the British flag raised in June 1840. Continue 7 km to Karaka Point.

A 15-minute walk leads across the site of Te Rae O Te Karaka, a Maori village and pa site that once featured defensive palisades and a number of dwellings. Today the traces remain of a defensive ditch cut across the headland and kumara pits are marked by shallow depressions. Deposits of burnt and broken shells indicate where the inhabitants feasted on large quantities of shellfish.
It is another 8 km west to Picton.

THE WAIRAU AFFRAY

John Blenkinsopp, an early whaler who operated out of Cloudy Bay near Benheim, was married to a relative of the Ngati Toa chief Te Rauparaha with whom he negotiated an agreement to take wood and water from Cloudy Bay in exchange for a cannon. The document the illiterate chiefs signed, however, gave Blenkinsopp title to a large area of land in the Wairau Valley. He took the deed to Sydney and mortgaged it to a solicitor, John Unwin, for £200. When Blenkinsopp drowned, his widow sold a copy of the deed to Col. William Wakefield of the New Zealand Company for £300. Te Rauparaha learned of the double dealing and tore up his copy of the deed, asking William Spain, the Land Commissioner, to resolve the dispute. Spain was too busy to intervene and Nelson settlers were already surveying the Wairau so Te Rauparaha and another Ngati Toa Chief, Te Rangihaeata, went with a group of followers to destroy the surveyors' property which they saw as products of Ngati Toa land. They pulled out survey pegs and burned raupo huts.

A group of Nelson settlers decided to arrest the chiefs for arson and set out in June 1843 with guns and ammunition although most of them had no experience with firearms. They found the chiefs with a group including women, children and old people camped at the Tuamarina Stream. An argument broke out when the magistrates informed Te Rauparaha that he was being arrested. One of the settlers fired a shot and in the exchange that followed some of the settlers fled, some surrendered and some were shot. About eight Maori were wounded and six killed including Te Rangihaeata's wife. The chief demanded revenge and the prisoners were tomahawked to death. In all, 27 of the settlers escaped and 22 died including Captain Arthur Wakefield, the brother of William Wakefield and the leader of the Nelson settlement.

INDEX

INDEX